SPECTRUM MULTIVIEW BOOKS

# CHRISTIAN

# ETHICS

FOUR VIEWS

EDITED BY STEVE WILKENS

CONTRIBUTIONS BY
Brad J. Kallenberg, Claire Brown Peterson,
John Hare, and Peter Goodwin Heltzel

IVP Academic
An imprint of InterVarsity Press
Downers Grove, Illinois

*InterVarsity Press*
*P.O. Box 1400, Downers Grove, IL 60515-1426*
*ivpress.com*
*email@ivpress.com*

*InterVarsity Press® is the book-publishing division of InterVarsity Christian Fellowship/USA®, a movement of
students and faculty active on campus at hundreds of universities, colleges, and schools of nursing in the United States
of America, and a member movement of the International Fellowship of Evangelical Students. For information about
local and regional activities, visit intervarsity.org.*

Slavers Throwing Overboard the Dead and Dying—Typhoon Coming On, *by J. M. W. Turner (1775–1851):
Museum of Fine Arts, Boston. Wikimedia Commons.*

*Cover design: David Fassett*
*Interior design: Jeanna Wiggins*
*Images: © Mina De La O/Getty Images*

*ISBN 978-0-8308-4023-6 (print)*
*ISBN 978-0-8308-9157-3 (digital)*

*Printed in the United States of America* ∞

 *As a member of the Green Press Initiative, InterVarsity Press is committed to protecting the
environment and to the responsible use of natural resources. To learn more, visit greenpressinitiative.org.*

**Library of Congress Cataloging-in-Publication Data**
*Names: Wilkens, Steve, 1955– editor.*
*Title: Christian ethics : four views / edited by Steve Wilkens ; with
 contributions by Brad J. Kallenberg, Claire Brown Peterson, John Hare, and
 Peter Heltzel.*
*Description: Downers Grove : InterVarsity Press, 2017. | Series: Spectrum
 Multiview Book Series (SPEC) | Includes index.*
*Identifiers: LCCN 2017005115 (print) | LCCN 2017008469 (ebook) | ISBN
 9780830840236 (pbk. : alk. paper) | ISBN 9780830891573 (eBook)*
*Subjects: LCSH: Christian ethics.*
*Classification: LCC BJ1251 .C496 2017 (print) | LCC BJ1251 (ebook) | DDC
 241--dc23*
*LC record available at https://lccn.loc.gov/2017005115*

**P** 29 28 27 26 25 24 23 22 21 20 19 18 17 16 15 14 13 12 11 10 9 8 7 6 5 4 3 2 1

**Y** 42 41 40 39 38 37 36 35 34 33 32 31 30 29 28 27 26 25 24 23 22 21 20 19 18 17

# Contents

# Acknowledgments

I deeply appreciate the commitment of InterVarsity Press to this project and their excellent support at each step of the process. Special thanks are in order for our editor, David Congdon.

The contributors to this volume have been a joy to work with, and I am thankful for their efforts in providing clear and forceful presentations of their ethical theories and offering insightful and charitable responses to each other.

The Center for Research in Ethics and Values at Azusa Pacific University provided funds for release time. I am sincerely grateful for this gift of time and their encouragement of faculty research at our institution.

My university colleagues are indeed colleagues in every meaningful sense of the word. My thanks go out to them for their patience and expertise during all the times I used them as sounding boards. You know who you are.

Finally, I want to acknowledge the support of my wife, Debra, and children, Zoe and Zack, who tolerate my frequent disappearances to engage in research, editing, and writing.

# Introduction to Four Theories of Christian Ethics

*STEVE WILKENS*

**As far as we can tell,** humans alone are endowed with a conceptual category inhabited by words like *duty, evil, justice, rights, law, mercy,* and *virtue.* In fact, we seem incapable of thinking about our world apart from the vocabulary of *fairness, goodness, crime, love, guilt,* and *blame*—terms loaded with moral meaning. Moreover, ethical terms and the concepts behind them perform a unique task. They do not simply describe a state of affairs; they go beyond the declarative world of "is" and speak in the language of *should* and *ought.* A particular action may be accurately described as theft or a murder, but these labels are more than just the observation of fact. *Theft* and *murder* are prescriptive words; they refer to that which *ought not* be and take us into the universe of standards, responsibility, and obligation.

Another notable observation about our moral impulse is that we often prefer to act contrary to its direction. We believe that we ought to think and behave in a certain manner and simultaneously desire to do something quite different. This battle between moral beliefs and actual inclinations is the dark side of the ethical mystery, and it is never too far from the surface throughout our discussion. However, embedded in the tension between our desire and our sense of duty is a related puzzle. What is the source of this moral sense? Since ethical beliefs impose demands on us that often run contrary to our desire and behaviors, these obligations seem to originate in some external authority. But what is this authority?

The quest to discover the origin of moral authority launches us into an on-going conversation that offers a broad array of options. Some have concluded that the conflict between our inclinations and our sense of duty can be explained in purely psychological or sociological terms. Thus, Thrasymachus declares that the pull of justice is nothing more than "the interest of the stronger party," a linguistic lever by which the powerful control the weak.[1] Nietzsche reverses the order and argues that moral prohibition is the means by which the weak mitigate the power of the master class.[2] Evolutionary psychology believes that the moral tug is a genetic development from our prehuman past. Prosocial attributes such as sharing, mutual defense, and individual sacrifice increase the prospects of group survival and are thus traits "selected" by the evolutionary process.[3]

While these theories reduce the moral impulse to purely psychological, social, or biological origins, this should not obscure the reality that most thinkers throughout history have concluded that our sense of moral duty cannot be explained apart from an external and transcendent reality. In the ancient world the metaphysical foundation was known by names like the Good, Logos, the Decrees of Heaven, Pure Being, or the One. Christian intellectuals often borrowed heavily from these ancient sources in framing their own ethical ideas. However, Christianity's concept of a good and personal God who becomes flesh in Jesus Christ is very different from an impersonal Form of the Good or the Greek Logos. Likewise, while classical Greek thought generally doesn't have a concept of creation *ex nihilo* (from nothing), this Christian doctrine tends to cement the connection between God and goodness. If God creates *all* things, this also seems to include the moral status of all things. Thus, belief in God as a personal and moral being who is responsible for and involved in creation seems to eliminate the possibility of separating God and goodness.

## CHRISTIANITY AND ETHICS

Despite broad agreement within Christianity that moral goodness is a divine attribute and is revealed in God's work within history, particularly in the person and work of Jesus Christ, Christians are often divided on moral

---

[1] Plato, *The Republic*, trans. Desmond Lee, 2nd ed. (New York: Penguin Books, 1987), 338c.

[2] "Slave morality from the outset says 'No' to what is 'outside,' what is 'different,' what is 'not itself,' and *this* No is its creative deed." Friedrich Nietzsche, *On the Genealogy of Morals*, trans. Walter Kaufmann and R. J. Hollingdale (New York: Vintage Books, 1989), 1.10.

[3] See Edward O. Wilson, *Consilience: The Unity of Knowledge* (New York: Vintage, 1998), 282.

theory. Several reasons exist for these divisions. First, we are shaped by different theological traditions that place different accents on, or offer contrasting interpretations of, the divine attributes. Thus, the texture and direction of our moral considerations will be influenced by whether we begin from divine justice, reason, goodness, or sovereignty, and they will be further shaped by specific notions of what is entailed by these attributes.

Second, Christians differ about how God communicates moral knowledge. Is it mediated solely via Scripture, through the ongoing story of God's formation of a people, through experience and reason, or by some combination of these elements? These factors will also inform the extent that Christian ethicists look to sources beyond Scripture and theology for guidance. To what degree is it permissible to allow philosophy, science, social theory, and other disciplines to inform our moral conclusions?

Variations in Christian ethical approaches also arise from differing anthropological conclusions. How is human reason related to our volitional capacities? To what extent does sin dull our God-given capacities, and does grace enable us to respond to God's moral and spiritual demands prior to or after justification? Is sin and evil to be viewed primarily as an individual issue, or is it manifest most distinctly in the disruption and perversion of social structures and relations? Should we expect the moral Christian individual or community to exhibit continuity with general moral expectations, or is Christian ethics characterized by contrast and discontinuity with conventional morality?

Finally, while ethical discussion often focuses on the individual's decisions about moral questions, Christian ethics encompasses social life as well. Thus, we will encounter divergences about the place and role of the body of Christ in ethical formation and how the believer is properly related to communities and institutions outside of faith's sphere. Does faith call Christian communities to stand apart as a contrast model to fallen systems? Do ethical demands drive us into conversation and grassroots engagement with the social problems of one's culture? Is it legitimate to form coalitions with those who do not share our Christian faith to combat social ills, or is the Christian worldview so distinct that partnerships with nonbelievers ultimately dilute or denature Christian motivations and modes of social action and witness? All these factors influence how Christians move from doctrine to formulate a Christian approach to ethical matters.

## ETHICAL SYSTEMS

When ideas are designated as "systems," "paradigms," or some other synonym, we inevitably create distortions. Thus, we admit to a certain degree of necessary misrepresentation in the categorizations within this book. First, this process will often join under one heading thinkers who will differ sharply at important junctures. Second, just as reality is often too messy to keep everything in its designated compartments, ideas from one system often overlap in significant ways with others. Thus, for example, various commentators designate Aquinas as an exemplar of divine command theory, virtue ethics, or natural law theory, and do so with some justification. As a result, we admit that those familiar with the field will be justified in questioning whether specific groups and individuals have been properly identified.

Three of our systems—divine command theory, virtue ethics, and natural law—have been and remain viable options within Christian ethics for centuries. Excluding any of them would be almost unthinkable. However, because each ethical tradition has a long history and multiple ongoing intramural disagreements, some familiar with these debates may disagree that our advocates represent the most robust or viable variation within the theory. This is unavoidable, and we will attempt to mitigate this by acknowledging some of the different strains and emphases of each theory in this chapter. Finally, what we have called prophetic ethics is not, unlike the other three, a conventional or easily identifiable label. Indeed, it includes groups not necessarily thought to be natural bedfellows. Nevertheless, we find it a necessary addition to the book since it represents an ethical perspective that clearly does not fit within the other three models and exhibits enough family resemblance to justify a single heading encompassing the diverse groups represented within it. In short, labels are blunt instruments that often do violence to the nuances and particularities of any system. Since the text is directed toward a general audience, our aim is that the benefit of using broad categories, characteristics, and theological associations will offset the potential damage in the specifics that are glossed over or remain unmentioned.

Finally, by focusing attention on Christian ethics, we have omitted paradigms commonly found in surveys of ethical theory. For example, utilitarianism is a major force in contemporary ethics but lacks a large following among Christian ethicists.[4] While Kantian ethics influences many Christian thinkers, his attempt to ground the ethical enterprise on purely rational basis is viewed as problematic by many. Emotivist/positivist approaches encounter a double complication in pronouncing both ethical and religious language as nonsensical. Moral relativism in its various forms does not fit easily into Christian systems that look to the divine nature as the foundation of moral goodness. In short, by limiting our scope to Christian ethics, we will ignore many ethical models that have a significant number of advocates today.

The remainder of this chapter will focus on three main tasks for each of the ethical theories. First, a brief overview will provide some of the salient characteristics of each theory. This will be followed by a glimpse at historical developments in each ethical paradigm, with examples of variations within each model. Finally, since attention will be focused on Christian iterations of these theories, each section will end with scriptural passages that are commonly cited as supportive of each ethical approach. Although elements of each of these theories can be found in Scripture and from the earliest days of the church, they are presented here and in the body of the book in the order they first receive extended systematic treatment within Christian scholarship.

## VIRTUE ETHICS

The premise of this book is that ethical theories differ in significant ways, but this often obscures another observation that is equally true: competing theories often lead to similar actions. Decisions about whether we should lie about trivial matters or engage in unprovoked physical assault rarely hang on whether we embrace a particular ethical theory. Conversely, individuals who share the same moral theory often arrive at different responses to specific situations. These observations help explain why virtue theorists argue that, while the outcomes of our choices are not inconsequential, the more

---

[4]William Paley's *Principles of Moral and Political Philosophy* (1785) is not only the classical statement of Christian utilitarianism, but he could also lay rightful claim to being the father of utilitarianism. Bentham is generally viewed as the first utilitarian thinker, but Paley's book was published before Bentham's *Introduction to Principles of Morals and Legislation* (1789) and enjoyed broader readership for decades. A more recent form of Christian utilitarianism is Joseph Fletcher, *Situation Ethics: The New Morality*, 2nd ed. (Louisville, KY: Westminster John Knox, 1997).

significant moral activity occurs at the motivational level. In other words, the main goal of ethics is not to get the right actions but to mold people who possess the right character qualities or virtues.

*Virtue* comes from the Greek *aretē*, often translated as "excellence." Thus, virtue ethics is concerned primarily with developing our various capacities toward their ideal. This teleological orientation signals that anthropological questions will quickly surface; we cannot move to ethics until we give an account of the sorts of beings we are, the potentials we possess, and the internal and external hindrances that inhibit progress toward excellence. While it does not discount reason, virtue ethics places a more intense gaze on human dispositions, motivations, emotions, relationships, and affections. Because of this, virtue ethics often emphasizes imitation and enculturation into habits and durable dispositions as the primary means of moral growth. Thus, this process assumes a community responsible for moral development.

Virtue ethics is deeply indebted to the ancient philosophers, especially Plato (c. 427–347 BCE) and Aristotle (384–322 BCE). Plato argued that moral ideals such as justice and courage are Forms, the eternal and unchanging archetypes of all specific and imperfect acts of justice and courage. The highest Form is the Form of the Good, which stands at the apex of a hierarchy of Forms. This location indicates that ethics is not simply one facet of reality alongside others. Instead, all reality is derived from and conditioned by goodness. Second, Plato believed that the Forms are known by reason. However, as we ascend toward the Good its exalted status makes direct knowledge difficult, and we are forced to resort to analogies. Plato's preferred analogy is to compare the Good to the sun. As with the sun, we cannot "look at" the Good directly for more than a fleeting moment, but its light enables us to "see" (i.e., know) all other things.[5] Thus, true knowledge transcends the mere accumulation of facts and skills. Knowing, rightly defined, always has a moral/spiritual component, an idea that Christian virtue ethics later finds attractive.

While the Forms provide an otherworldly foundation for Plato's ethics, he is also interested in virtue's this-worldly benefits. The *Republic* envisions a society composed of various functions: artisans, soldiers, and rulers. Each

---

[5]See, for example, Plato, *Republic* 505a–509c.

group functions best (i.e., excellently) when governed by its corresponding virtue. Thus, the artisans should possess the virtue of moderation, the auxiliary/soldier class should exhibit courage, and the philosopher-kings must acquire wisdom.[6] When all classes function harmoniously and in the proper order, society manifests justice. This collection of virtues—moderation, courage, prudence, and justice—is known collectively as the "cardinal [fundamental] virtues" and exerts great influence on later ethics.[7]

The teleological component of Plato's ethics becomes more pronounced in Aristotle. Humans, like plants, have a nutritive capacity and, like animals, are capable of physical movement and sensation. However, reason, which includes both the capacity for intellect and volition, is unique to human beings and our most exalted capacity.[8] Thus, to become a *good* human (i.e., to achieve our *telos*), we must develop both intellectual and moral virtues.[9]

The virtues are acquired by a process that begins with obedience to rules and authorities until certain behaviors become habitual. As we mature, we recognize that intellectual rigor and moral moderation are qualities that allow individuals to flourish, and thus seek to internalize them through discipline and repeated practice. However, the apex of moral development is when we do not simply will ourselves to act in accordance with virtue but when we intellectually grasp the importance of virtue for ourselves, the city, and the universe since "not only is reason the best thing in us, but the objects of reason are the best of knowable objects."[10]

Virtue ethics was the dominant approach in Christianity through the early medieval period, but it underwent modification to make it more compatible to the new context. The church, not the *polis*, becomes the new setting for moral development. Moreover, acquisition of and growth in the virtues was not envisioned as an intellectual pursuit but as one that

---

[6]Just as Plato views social classes hierarchically, the virtues also exhibit this pattern. A good artisan lives moderately but will not necessarily be advanced in courage or wisdom. However, for a soldier to possess courage, moderation must first be developed. Likewise, rulers can attain wisdom only once temperance and courage have been acquired. See *Republic* 426-35.

[7]The cardinal virtues are also taken up by other ancients such as Cicero, who states that virtue has "four divisions: prudence, justice, fortitude, and temperance." See *Treatise on Rhetorical Invention*, in *The Orations of Marcus Tullius Cicero*, trans. C. D. Yonge, vol. 4 (London: George Bell, 1888), II, liii.

[8]Aristotle, *Nichomachaen Ethics*, in *The Basic Works of Aristotle*, ed. Richard McKeon (New York: Random House, 1941), 1097b-1098a.

[9]Ibid., 1103a.

[10]Ibid., 1177a.

results from the imitation of Christ. In view of these new goals, while Christianity readily adopted Plato's four cardinal virtues, it also adds the three theological virtues of faith, hope, and love. The latter orient us in our relationship to God, while the cardinal (or human) virtues facilitate peaceful and just human relationships. However, while they are distinct in this way, "the human virtues are rooted in the theological virtues" and are dependent on them.[11]

One strand of early Christian virtue ethics found a home within the monastic tradition and took on a pastoral emphasis. Here, the seven virtues (four cardinal virtues and three theological virtues) were often juxtaposed to lists of vices or "deadly sins."[12] An early list of eight sins comes from Evagrius (346–399) and was modified by Gregory I (c. 540–604), who reduces the number to seven and identifies pride as "the queen of sins,"[13] which, after taking possession of a "conquered heart, surrenders it immediately to seven principal sins, as if to some of her generals, to lay it waste."[14] In this pastoral context, virtues and the practices by which they are gained are viewed as antidotes to the deadly sins.

Virtue ethics also found more intellectual expressions in medieval Christianity.[15] Augustine (354–430), for example, refers to the seven virtues throughout his massive writings, and builds his *Enchiridion* around an exposition of the three theological virtues. While each virtue allows us to bring different dimensions of our being into accord with God's will, they are ultimately all unified in love, "For when there is a question as to whether a man is good, one does not ask what he believes [faith], or what he hopes for, but what he loves."[16] The unity of all virtue in love is so foundational

[11]Catechism of the Catholic Church 1804, Vatican.va, accessed October 21, 2016, www.vatican.va /archive/ENG0015/__P65.HTM.

[12]A popular early variation on the usual virtue list is found in the allegorical poem *Psychomachia* (c. 410) in which seven vices attempt unsuccessfully to defeat their corresponding virtues. In this list, humility, kindness, abstinence, chastity, patience, generosity, and diligence are listed as the antidotes for (respectively) pride, envy, gluttony, lust, wrath, greed, and sloth. See Prudentius, *Psychomachia*, ed. T. E. Page, trans. H. G. Thomson (Cambridge, MA: Harvard University Press, 1949).

[13]For the evolution of the sin lists see Rebecca Konyndyk DeYoung, *Glittering Vices: A New Look at the Seven Deadly Sins and Their Remedies* (Grand Rapids: Brazos Press, 2009), 25-31.

[14]Gregory I, *Morals on the Book of Job*, 3 vols. (London: J. Rivington, 1844), 31.45.87.

[15]For a discussion of the two streams of virtue ethics in medieval theology, see Jean Porter, "Virtue Ethics in the Medieval Period," *Cambridge Companion to Virtue Ethics*, ed. Daniel C. Russell (New York: Cambridge University Press, 2013), 70-91.

[16]Augustine, *Enchiridion on Faith, Hope, and Love* (Washington, DC: Regnery, 1996), 135.

for Augustine that no matter how much our dispositions conform to virtuous ideals, these dispositions "are rather vices than virtues so long as there is no reference to God in the matter . . . [because] they are inflated with pride."[17] Thus, the question of true virtue is, for Augustine, inescapably linked with salvation.

Although Aquinas (1225–1274) is often linked to natural law, he also makes a major contribution to virtue ethics. Drawing on Aristotle's teleological approach, Aquinas argues that a virtue is the proper use of the power of a capacity.[18] Aristotle's influence is also seen in Aquinas's reference to the intellectual virtues (understanding, science, and wisdom) alongside the moral and theological virtues. Although the intellectual virtues allow reason to contemplate the divine and the perfect, the moral virtues are superior since they make us good and are not susceptible to evil uses.[19] The moral virtues are the means by which we discipline our appetitive powers. Of the cardinal virtues, Aquinas assigns a unique role to prudence because "moral virtue cannot be without prudence, because prudence is the habit of choosing, i.e., making us choose well."[20] Aquinas argues that the moral virtues may be acquired by habituation, but they may also be divinely infused. The latter prepare us not for the imperfect forms of happiness in this life but for the perfect beatitude of heaven. Of the theological virtues, love is the highest because it brings us nearer to God than all others.[21]

Virtue ethics remained popular in the modern period but assumed new forms. Numerous Renaissance scholars, especially in the Italian Renaissance, reacted to the corruption of the medieval church by returning to the classical philosophers to advance secular (though not necessarily non-Christian) rulers whose governance is shaped by intellectual prowess and moral character.[22] A related turn, or perhaps a detour, appears in Machiavelli's

---

[17]Augustine, *The City of God*, trans. Marcus Dods (New York: Modern Library, 1993), 19.25.

[18]Aquinas, *Summa Theologica*, trans. Fathers of the English Dominican Province, I-II.55.1, New Advent, accessed October 21, 2016, www.newadvent.org/summa/index.html.

[19]Ibid., I-II.56.3.

[20]Ibid., I-II.58.4.

[21]Ibid., I-II, q. 66, a. 1. ad. 6.

[22]To see how both Platonic and Aristotelian traditions influenced this phase of virtue ethics, see Luca Bianchi's "Continuity and Change in the Aristotelian Tradition," and Christopher S. Celenza's "The Revival of Platonic Philosophy," chapters 4 and 5 respectively in James Hankins, ed., *The Cambridge Companion to Renaissance Philosophy* (New York: Cambridge University Press, 2007).

(1469–1527) philosophy. He maintains the focus on preparing secular rulers for governance, but virtue morphs into *virtù*, the skills and dispositions of the warrior. Whereas virtue ethics strives for the human ideal, *virtù* aspires to the pragmatic strategies necessary for gaining and maintaining political power.[23]

Virtue and statecraft are linked also in Thomas Hobbes (1588–1679), who takes the additional step of combining empirical science's methods to moral and political thought. He views the state of nature as war "of all men against all men," which renders life "solitary, poor, nasty, brutish, and short."[24] In this state, good and evil were not natural characteristics but refer instead to one's capacity for survival.[25] This transforms virtue from a means of emulating transcendent ideals to a tool of preservation. As a result, Hobbes argues that "the sum of virtue is to be sociable with them that will be sociable, and formidable to them that will not."[26]

Lord Shaftesbury (1671–1713) maintains classical virtue theory's emphasis on teleology and the notion that all properly functioning (i.e., virtuous) entities contribute to a greater good. However, he argues that it is "by affection merely that a creature is esteemed good or ill, natural or unnatural."[27] Thus, Shaftesbury is usually viewed as the originator of the moral sense approach (or sentimentalism), in which sentiment arising from concrete experience, rather than discursive reason, is the foundation of moral judgment. The moral sense approach is adopted by David Hume (1711–1776), who argued that we commit the "naturalistic fallacy" if we attempt to move from a factual state of affairs (Jane shot Ralph without provocation) to a moral claim (murder is evil). Thus, "morality is determined by sentiment. It defines virtue to be *whatever mental action or*

---

[23]Machiavelli contrasts *virtù* with fortune, the uncontrollable twists of fate. Both shape a ruler's life, but the virtuous ruler will develop the character qualities under one's control because "he who relies less upon Fortune has maintained his position best." Niccolò Machiavelli, *The Prince*, ed. and trans. Peter Bondanelli (New York: Oxford University Press, 2005), 21.

[24]Thomas Hobbes, *Leviathan* (Charlottesville, VA: InteLex, 1995), 5.3, 13.9.

[25]"And therefore he that foreseeth the whole way to his preservation (which is the end that every one by nature aimeth at) must also call it good, and the contrary evil." Thomas Hobbes, *The English Works of Thomas Hobbes: The Elements of Law* (Charlottesville, VA: InteLex, 1995), 17.14, electronic ed.

[26]Ibid., 17.15.

[27]Lord Shaftesbury, *Characteristics of Men, Manners, Opinions, Times*, ed. Lawrence E. Klein (New York: Cambridge University Press, 2004), 170.

*quality gives to a spectator the pleasing sentiment of approbation*; and vice the contrary."[28] By connecting pleasure and sentiment, Hume nudges virtue ethics toward utilitarianism, which reserves a place for the virtue but usually defines it either as a means to or form of pleasure.[29]

The Enlightenment sought a more scientific ethical approach and granted ultimate intellectual authority to the rational autonomous individual, which undermined the communities and traditions that were central to virtue ethics. However, recent years have seen renewed interest in our social and historical contexts and have cast doubt on whether reason, as understood by the Enlightenment, was capable of discerning moral truth. Many trace the revival of virtue ethics to Elizabeth Anscombe's 1958 article "Modern Moral Philosophy." She argued that the dominance of Christian thought after the classical period nudged thinkers toward "a *law* conception of ethics" in which moral standards are determined by divine mandate.[30] When scholars later abandoned transcendent foundations for law, deontological ethical systems became indefensible.[31] Anscombe concluded that a return to the Aristotelian tradition offered the only defensible position for ethics.

Alasdair MacIntyre echoes much of Anscombe's criticism of the Enlightenment project, arguing that the ultimate outcome of autonomous moral rationality was emotivism, the notion that "all moral judgments are *nothing but* expressions of preference . . . attitude or feeling."[32] He also agrees that Aristotle's teleological orientation should be recovered. What he adds is the idea that teleology assumes a communal narrative that provides a shared definition of virtue and prescribes the practices necessary to pursue it. Thus, for MacIntyre, "A virtue is an acquired human

---

[28]David Hume, *An Enquiry Concerning the Principles of Morals* (LaSalle, IL: Open Court, 1953), appendix 1, ¶10.

[29]For example, Mill says, "Those who desire virtue for its own sake, desire it either because of the consciousness of it is a pleasure, or because the consciousness of being without it is a pain." John Stuart Mill, *Utilitarianism* (London: Electric Book, 2001), 4.9.

[30]G. E. M. Anscombe, "Modern Moral Philosophy," *Philosophy* 33, no. 124 (January 1958): 16.

[31]Ibid., 14-15.

[32]Alasdair MacIntyre, *After Virtue*, 2nd ed. (Notre Dame, IN: Notre Dame University Press, 1984), 11. MacIntyre says that the success of earlier versions of Enlightenment ethics was due to the lingering fragments of previous traditions. However, Enlightenment ethics eventually became unstable because those traditional fragments existed alongside, not within, its formulations.

quality the possession and the exercise of which tends to enable us to achieve those goods which are internal to practices and the lack of which effectively prevents us from achieving any such goods."[33]

Stanley Hauerwas picks up the narrative element by pointing out that the church is constituted by the story of God's work among his people. This narrative should not be viewed as an ethical to-do list that summarizes our duties. Instead, "ethics is first a way of *seeing* before it is a matter of *doing*. The ethical task is not to tell you what is right or wrong but rather to train you to see."[34] Because the Christian narrative is countercultural, the community in which we hone our moral skills is the worshiping church, which teaches us what it means to be a humble, patient, and hopeful people, virtues one fails to find in ethical systems informed by different narratives.

Finally, Linda Zagzebski offers a version of virtue ethics that is distinct from divine command theory and natural law by arguing that "God is essential to morality, not because it comes from either his intellect or his will, but because it comes from his motives.[35] Grounding goodness in divine motivation rather than sovereignty avoids the charge that ethical values are arbitrary commands. Because goodness originates from God's character, "All valuable properties of states of persons get their value for their similarity to the properties of states of God."[36] This situates the incarnation at the center of the moral task because in Jesus Christ we see more clearly the divine motives as well as the "central paradigmatic good person."[37]

While one rarely finds the word *virtue* in translations of Hebrew Scripture, *ḥokmâ*, usually rendered "wisdom," provides numerous parallels with virtue ethics. For example, we are informed that the Proverbs are

> For learning about wisdom [*ḥokmâ*] and instruction,
> > for understanding words of insight,
> > for gaining instruction in wise dealing,
> > > righteousness, justice, and equity;

---

[33]Ibid., 191.
[34]Stanley Hauerwas and William H. Willimon, *Resident Aliens: A Provocative Christian Assessment of Culture and Ministry for People Who Know That Something Is Wrong* (Nashville: Abingdon Press, 1989), 95.
[35]Linda Zagzebski, *Divine Motivation Theory* (New York: Cambridge University Press, 2004), 185.
[36]Ibid., 341.
[37]Ibid., 232.

> to teach shrewdness to the simple,
>> knowledge and prudence to the young. (Prov 1:2-4 NRSV)

Embedded in this is the view that the virtuous life encompasses our intellectual, moral, and spiritual capacities, that it has a teleological orientation, and that it is a communal process that passes on values to the young. A more narrative intersection with virtue ethics is found in the story of Daniel, whose wisdom (virtue) allowed for success in secular affairs and sustained him in faithfulness to God. Virtue theorists also note that diaspora Judaism is strongly influenced by Greek virtue tradition. Particularly striking are passages in Wisdom of Solomon and 4 Maccabees that explicitly refer to the four cardinal virtues.[38]

When virtue theorists look to the New Testament, advocates often direct our attention to Philippians 4:8: "Finally, beloved, whatever is true, whatever is honorable, whatever is just, whatever is pure, whatever is pleasing, whatever is commendable, if there is any excellence and if anything worthy of praise, think about these things" (cf. Lk 6:43-45). In the same book, the "kenosis hymn" of Philippians 2:5-11 stresses the humility of Christ, with the admonition to "let the same mind be in you that was in Christ Jesus." Also central to virtue ethics is the "fruit of the Spirit" (Gal 5:22-23), which parallel virtues critical to a healthy Christian life.

## NATURAL LAW

Natural law theory believes that moral precepts exist independently of our judgments, are binding on all people, and are knowable by reason. Indeed, natural law's Christian proponents say that moral law exists and is accessible, though not perfectly known, even prior to God's revelation of it through Scripture. Otherwise, why would moral precepts like truth-telling, respect for others, or the right to self-defense be found in every culture? Moreover, empirical evidence reveals that violations of natural law bring harm while living according to it yields flourishing. Thus, advocates argue that it is odd

---

[38]"And if anyone loves righteousness, / her labors are virtues; / for she teaches self-control and prudence, justice and courage; / nothing in life is more profitable for mortals than these" (Wis 8:7 NRSV). "Now the kinds of wisdom are rational judgment, justice, courage, and self-control" (4 Macc 1:18 NRSV). An additional parallel with Greek sensibilities occurs in the next verse, which gives precedence to our rational capacities, especially in their task of taming the passions.

to conclude that God's moral will is beyond our mind's mental capacity.[39] While these rational moral precepts are also embedded in Scripture, they would reflect God's will and carry divine authority even if absent from Scripture. Therefore, these laws are not simply obligatory for Christians. Since all are subject to God and have knowledge of these laws, natural law is obligatory for all.

A second critical element is the belief that human beings have a nature. In this definition, *nature* is a teleological term that refers to our proper end or goal. To function "naturally," then, means to obey rational principles that allow attainment of our moral ideal, both individually and collectively. In other words, the moral principles of the natural law are not simply guide-lines for individual conduct but are the standards against which we should judge the validity of all civil and international law. Thus, just as natural law argues that there is objectivity in the moral laws governing individual action, social structures such as nations, communities, and marriage are not simply arbitrary entities conjured up by human beings but are ordained by God and possess a divinely given purpose.

Natural law has its origins in classical philosophy. Aristotle speaks of a "law of nature" and says that "every one to some extent divines a natural justice and injustice that is binding on all men, even on those who have no association or covenant with each other."[40] While Aristotle's references to natural law are sparse, a robust version of this theory arose in Stoicism. The Stoics believed that the entire universe is a single interconnected organism, one that could be called either Nature or God, governed by Logos (or reason). This resulted in a deterministic metaphysics in which every event was necessitated by the logic that permeated the universe. Because all that occurs manifests the perfect reason governing the cosmos, each thing happens as it should and is good.[41] Although all events are predetermined,

---

[39]As C. S. Lewis puts it, our natural ethical knowledge indicates that "what is behind the universe is more like a mind than it is like anything we know." See C. S. Lewis, *The Abolition of Man* (New York: HarperOne, 2015), 31-32.

[40]Aristotle, *Rhetoric* 1373b, in *The Basic Works of Aristotle*, ed. Richard McKeon (New York: Random House, 1941). See also *Nicomachean Ethics* 1134b, in which Aristotle speaks of a natural justice that "everywhere has the same force and does not exist by people's thinking this or that."

[41]Cicero quotes Chrysippus as teaching "that divine power resides in reason, and in the soul and mind of the universe; he calls the world itself a god, and also the all-pervading world-soul, and . . . the common and all-embracing nature of things, and also the power of Fate, and the Necessity

our moral task is to attune our mind, which is a "spark" of the rational Logos, to rational principles, strive for an emotional detachment (*apatheia*) from events that appear to be evil, and learn self-control.[42]

Stoicism's influence on early Christianity manifested itself more in its emphasis on self-control, while its natural law foundation receded into the background. Moreover, even though numerous early Christians referred to natural law, it plays a different role than for natural lawyers. Augustine, for example, refers to "a law in the reason of a human being who already uses free choice, a law naturally written in his heart, by which he is warned that he should not do anything to anyone else that he himself does not want to suffer, all are transgressors according to this law, even those who have not received the law given through Moses."[43] The last part reveals a significant departure from natural law ethics since he, like most early Christian thinkers, viewed natural law as convicting us of wrongdoing but insufficient to move us toward salvation.

The rediscovery of Aristotle's philosophy by medieval Christianity led to a natural law revival, which receives its classic articulation in Thomas Aquinas. For Aristotle, the highest good was happiness, a *telos* achievable only when a person lives according to one's nature. Aquinas adapts this idea to Christian doctrine by arguing that God draws us to goodness and salvation (the ultimate form of happiness) via laws that govern the various dimensions of human life.[44]

Law must originate from a proper authority if it is to be legitimate. God, as the creator and governor of all that is, has rightful authority to be the lawgiver over every dimension of creation. In addition, the function of law

---

that governs future events." Cicero, *De Natura Deorum*, trans. H. Rackham (Cambridge, MA: Harvard University Press, 1967), 1.39.

[42]"Remember that it is not he who reviles you or strikes you who insults you, but it is your opinion about these things as being insulting. When, then, a man irritates you, you must know that it is your own opinion which has irritated you." Epictetus, *Enchiridion*, trans. George Long (Mineola, NY: Dover Publications, 2004), 20.

[43]Augustine, "Letter 157," in *The Works of Saint Augustine: A Translation for the 21st Century: Letters 156–210*, ed. Boniface Ramsey, trans. Rowland Teske, vol. II/3 (Hyde Park, NY: New City Press, 1990), 3.15. See also Augustine, *The Free Choice of the Will* 1.6.15, in *Fathers of the Church: Saint Augustine: The Teacher, The Free Choice of the Will, Grace and Free Will*, ed. Roy Joseph Deferrari, trans. Robert P. Russell (Washington, DC: Catholic University Press, 1968).

[44]While natural law's reliance on laws parallels divine command theory, natural law argues that laws are not susceptible to change. In contrast, many advocates of divine command believe that God can suspend or change divine imperatives.

is to "command or forbid," and since reason's proper function is to command, "law is something pertaining to reason."[45] Thus, God's laws are products of the divine logic and are comprehensible to human reason. Finally, since happiness is what rational activity strives for when used properly, legitimate laws serve the common good.[46]

Because humans are multidimensional beings, God's laws pertain to different aspects of our existence. Eternal law refers to God's governance of the entire universe, both rational and nonrational. The nonrational world participates in eternal law from necessity. Thus, eternal law governs and describes the physical universe's regularities. Natural law is the participation of rational beings in eternal law, which provides humanity with our "inclination toward [our] proper act and end."[47] Rational beings alone know our end and are free to resist the laws that facilitate its attainment. Thus, natural law ushers us into the realm of moral activity since it prescribes what we *ought* to do. Human (or positive) law is derived from natural law and governs our social and political affairs. It should be congruent with natural law, but how it is expressed will be determined by local factors. Good human law prepares individuals for the higher moral demands of natural law and is intended to restrain evil within society so that those who want to live ethically can do so. These three forms of law are accessible to reason and are known by general revelation. Finally, divine law is given to us to achieve the ultimate happiness of salvation. Because salvation is a supernatural end, the means by which we attain knowledge of it are beyond (but not contrary to) the reason's natural scope.[48] Thus, divine law is known by special revelation.

Concerning natural law specifically, since God has endowed all humans with reason, the primary precepts of moral laws are universally known, are binding on all, and contribute to the community's benefit. The four foundational precepts of natural law are that we should pursue good and avoid evil, preserve life and combat that which threatens it, reproduce and care for our offspring, and seek knowledge and live together with others.[49] Secondary precepts follow logically from the moral first principles. Some, such as "do

---

[45]Aquinas, *Summa Theologica* I-II.90.1.
[46]Ibid., I-II.90.2.
[47]Ibid., I-II.91.2.
[48]Ibid., I-II, q. 91, a. 4, ad 1.
[49]Ibid., I-II, q. 94, a. 2.

not take innocent life," are known by all and are always binding. Other precepts, such as "do not steal," are not known by all but are nonetheless obligatory for all.[50] Finally, some secondary precepts may not be known to all and allow for exceptions. For example, Aquinas argues that, as a general principle, property ought to be restored to its rightful owner. However, when returning property may result in a greater harm, such as when restoration of a weapon may result in one fighting against one's own country, preservation of innocent life takes priority.[51] Aquinas emphasizes that natural law itself is insufficient for salvation, but it prepares us for the salvific knowledge available in divine law. In this way, nature is perfected by grace.

While Aquinas raised the profile of natural law in the late medieval period, the early modern period moved it in new directions. For example, Francisco Suárez (1548–1617) argues that natural law originates in God's will rather than in divine reason.[52] While Aquinas draws a closer connection between God's will and reason, Suárez says that reason's proper role is cognition while it is God's will that makes law obligatory. Nevertheless, reason allows us to discern moral law and to guide our will toward obedience.

A second notable modification to natural law during this period was the movement toward political theory and international law. In large part, application of natural law, viewed as a source of universal and rational truth, was proposed to resolve the doctrinal and political differences that followed the Reformation. Hugo Grotius (1583–1645), for example, bypasses theological or biblical justifications for natural law and focuses on common human sociability as a foundation. Evidence for natural law thus relies only on "shewing the necessary Fitness or Unfitness of any Thing, with a reasonable and sociable Nature."[53] Since all humans manifest reason

---

[50]Aquinas argues that taking others' property in extreme need is not theft since it is necessary for the preservation of life. See ibid., II-II, q. 66, a. 7, ad. 2.

[51]Ibid., I-II, q. 94, a. 4.

[52]"All the things that the natural law dictates as bad are prohibited by God through a special precept and act of will by which he wills to bind and obligate us by the force of his authority to obey those dictates." Francisco Suárez, *De Legibus* 2.6.8, trans. Alfred J. Freddoso, University of Notre Dame, accessed October 21, 2016, www3.nd.edu/~afreddos/courses/301/suarezdelegii6.htm.

[53]Hugo Grotius, *The Rights of War and Peace*, ed. Richard Tuck (Indianapolis: Liberty Fund, 2005), I.1.12.1. Samuel von Pufendorf likewise grounds natural law in our social nature: The "Precepts of the Law Natural may primarily and directly be derived from . . . Sociality." Samuel von Pufendorf, *The Whole Duty of Man According to the Law of Nature*, ed. Ian Hunter and David Saunders, trans. Andrew Tooke (Indianapolis, Liberty Fund, 2003), 1.3.13.

and are social beings, Grotius argues, international law grounded in natural law should take precedence in authority over local rules and customs in matters of war.

John Locke (1632–1704) also provides a ready illustration of natural law's influence on political philosophy. He argues that prior to the institution of government, "the state of nature has a law of nature to govern it, which obliges everyone: And reason, which is that law, teaches all mankind . . . that all being equal and independent, no one ought to harm another in his life, health, liberty, or possessions."[54] These natural rights, which Locke views as the logical extension of natural law, shape the Declaration of Independence's assertion that "life, liberty, and the pursuit of happiness" are "inalienable rights" granted by our Creator and "self-evident" to rational beings.[55]

While many contemporary scholars continue to advocate natural law along Thomistic lines, a more recent development is the "new natural law." This approach sidesteps potential problems of constructing ethics on a theoretical foundation, particularly the idea that all things have a "nature." Instead, it focuses on practical reason and thus begins the moral inquiry from the logic embedded in human practices. Germain Grisez, usually designated as new natural law's founder, says that "the first practical principle [do good and avoid evil] is like a basic tool which is inseparable from the job in which the tool is used; it is the implement for making all the other tools to be used on the job, but none of them is equivalent to it, and so the basic tool permeates all the work done in that job."[56] John Finnis expands this by arguing that life's good-making features—beauty, the pursuit of knowledge, friendship, and religion—are obvious from the patterns of human life and that the primary moral principle is that rationality "ought to choose and otherwise will those and only those possibilities whose willing is compatible with integral human fulfilment."[57]

---

[54]John Locke, *Second Treatise of Government*, ed. Richard Howard Cox (Wheeling, IL: Harlan Davidson, 1982), 2.6.

[55]In addition, given Aquinas's definition of the primary precepts, natural law bubbles just below the surface in contemporary debates about abortion, marriage, end-of-life issues, and the nature and purpose of human institutions.

[56]Germain Grisez, "The First Principle of Practical Reason: A Commentary on the Summa Theologiae, 1-2 Question 94, Article 2," *Natural Law Forum* 10 (1965): 198.

[57]John Finnis, *Natural Law and Natural Rights* (New York: Oxford University Press, 1980), 283.

The go-to biblical passage for natural lawyers is Romans 2:14-15:

> When Gentiles, who do not possess the law, do instinctively what the law requires, these, though not having the law, are a law to themselves. They show that what the law requires is written on their hearts, to which their own conscience also bears witness; and their conflicting thoughts will accuse or perhaps excuse them. (NRSV)

Numerous Old Testament passages assume that non-Jews know their moral duty and are justifiably punished for violations of it (e.g., Amos 1:2–2:3). Finally, Psalm 19:1 views the created order as evidence of God's activity—"The heavens are telling the glory of God; / and the firmament proclaims his handiwork"—and moves seamlessly to language about God's laws.

> The law of the LORD is perfect,
>    reviving the soul;
> the decrees of the LORD are sure,
>    making wise the simple;
> the precepts of the LORD are right,
>    rejoicing the heart;
> the commandment of the LORD is clear,
>    enlightening the eyes;
> the fear of the LORD is pure,
>    enduring forever;
> the ordinances of the LORD are true
>    and righteous altogether. (Ps 19:7-9 NRSV)

## DIVINE COMMAND THEORY

Janine Marie Idziak defines a divine command moralist as "one who maintains that the content of morality (i.e., what is right and wrong, good and evil, just and unjust, and the like) is directly and solely dependent on the commands and prohibitions of God."[58] This definition rests on three critical pillars. First, divine command theory starts from volition rather than reason (natural law) or affection (virtue ethics). God's commands are a product of the divine will, and correspondingly the proper human response

---

[58]Janine Marie Idziak, *Divine Command Morality: Historical and Contemporary Readings* (New York: Edwin Mellon, 1979), 1.

is obedience (i.e., adjustment of the will) to these requirements. Second, since these directives originate in God's will, they may be opaque to reason and thus are known, or at least most clearly known, by revelation. Advocates argue that these two elements fit nicely with Scripture's emphasis on faith as the condition for favor with God and the fact that human nature has been denatured in the fall, and reason along with it, rendering our cognitive capacities unreliable moral or theological guides.[59] Finally, since God is a sovereign being, no external standards determine what God will or must command. Otherwise, such a standard imposes a limitation on God's freedom or power.[60]

Once we digest the implications of these three elements, we might anticipate that divine command theory will draw fire from critics, especially nontheists. After all, both natural law and virtue theory have a more positive view of general revelation and thus find more common ground with secular counterparts. And while prophetic ethics, like divine command theory, relies more heavily on special revelation, it frequently builds broad alliances with secular counterparts to work toward healing social wounds. Thus, the particularity of divine command theory almost immediately brings questions from outsiders.

At the center of these criticisms is the Euthyphro dilemma. In his dialogue with Euthyphro, Socrates asks, "Is the holy approved by the gods because it's holy, or is it holy because it's approved [by the gods]?"[61] A Christianized version that replaces "the gods" with God, asks, Does God command the good because it is good, or does something become good because God commands it? The first option says that God's commands point toward the good, which implies that some moral standard exists independently of God, a view in tension with divine command theory. The second option says that good things are good because God makes them so. This seems to make it possible for God to have made anything (torturing children seems to be the favorite example) morally honorable (the "arbitrariness problem") and to drain the word *good* of meaning (the "vacuity

---

[59]For this reason, divine command theory is often connected with a commitment to *sola Scriptura*.
[60]Richard Swinburne, *The Coherence of Theism* (New York: Oxford University Press, 1977), 205-9.
[61]Plato, *Euthyphro* 10a, in *The Last Days of Socrates*, trans. Hugh Tredennick and Harold Tarrant (New York: Penguin, 2003).

problem") since good simply means "God-commanded." Other questions follow quickly: Doesn't divine command imply that only theists can be moral? Since different religions have different gods who issue often-contradictory commands, how do we determine which mandates are authoritative?[62] Doesn't a moral approach that advocates obedience to rules infantilize us, reducing us to passive responders rather than encouraging moral autonomy?

Responses to these challenges usually take us to metaethics, which studies ultimate ethical foundations. Divine command theorists note that common ethical ideas and activities become incoherent if we discover that they lack a trustworthy foundation. For example, most individuals, theists and non-theists, agree that keeping promises is a basic moral rule and that this and other ethical principles are objective and obligatory rather than culturally dependent, optional, or invented. Advocates of divine command theory argue that without some transcendent foundation[63] it is difficult to envision an adequate and objective ground for the binding nature of these rules.[64] In contrast, Christianity's God, a sovereign, personal, and moral being, provides explanatory power for our sense of the universality of, and obligation to, moral rules.[65]

The previous sentence is pivotal because divine command theory does not simply say that God gives commands. Instead, it argues that the divine attributes provide the necessary authority and cause those commands to be characterized as both good and binding. However, while divine command theorists generally agree which characteristics apply to God, different understandings of these attributes account for nuanced versions of this theory. Two examples are found in the later medieval period, where divine command theory finds its earliest systematic expressions.

---

[62]See Wilfrid J. Waluchow, *The Dimensions of Ethics: An Introduction to Ethical Theory* (Peterborough, ON: Broadview Press, 2003), 101.

[63]Plato, for example, offers a transcendent but nontheistic metaethical alternative by grounding ethics in the Form of the Good. See his *Republic* 508e.

[64]In this way, divine command theory turns Euthyphro's Dilemma against critics by asking them to identify a source other than God as the standard of goodness.

[65]One need not be a theist to embrace this conclusion. J. L. Mackie, an atheist, agrees that God would offer normativity to our moral statements. However, the absence of God leads him to embrace moral skepticism. J. L. Mackie, *Ethics: Inventing Right and Wrong* (New York: Penguin, 1991), 47-49.

Duns Scotus's (1266–1308) view of goodness's origin is clear: "Everything other than God is good because it is willed by God and not vice versa."[66] However, he does say that the Decalogue's first four commandments are natural law; they are "first practical principles known from their terms or as conclusions necessarily entailed by them."[67] Thus, duties to God are necessary instantiations of the divine logic that cannot be otherwise. However, the "second table" of the Decalogue, which regulates human interaction, can be changed by God since these commandments "contain no goodness such as is necessarily prescribed for attaining the goodness of the ultimate end."[68] Since there is no necessity with regard to the created order and its contingent ends, God can freely determine the moral rules governing human-to-human relationships and has the liberty to include any commandment desired, even one that would make stealing or lying a moral good. By contrast, William of Occam (c. 1285–1347) allows greater latitude for divine freedom by stating that God's sovereignty entails that even the "first table" of the Ten Commandments is subject to God's will alone. "There is no act which God is obligated to bring about; therefore He can bring about any act as such without any wrongdoing, as well as its contrary . . . [thus God can] totally cause the act of hating God without any moral evil."[69]

In places, Martin Luther (1483–1546) can sound like an ardent advocate of natural law. In discussing how secular authorities should adjudicate disputes, he states, "But it is love and natural law, with which all reason is filled, that confer . . . good judgment."[70] However, sin's influence has distorted our original nature and made virtue impossible apart from faith. Thus, Luther's

---

[66]Duns Scotus, *Ordinatio* 3, suppl. dist. 37, n. 6, quoted in Duns Scotus, *Duns Scotus on the Will and Morality*, ed. William A. Frank, trans. Alan B. Wolter (Washington, DC: Catholic University of America Press, 1997), 16. Scotus goes so far as to say that God's freedom means that he could create humans such that our natural inclinations, even prior to the fall, would be contrary to God's moral will. *Duns Scotus on the Will and Morality*, 178.

[67]Ibid., 202.

[68]Ibid.

[69]William of Occam, *On the Four Books of the Sentences* (2, 19), quoted in Idziak, *Divine Command Morality*, 57.

[70]Martin Luther, *Secular Authority*, quoted in John Calvin and Martin Luther, *Luther and Calvin on Secular Authority*, ed. Harro Höpfl (New York: Cambridge University Press, 1991), 42. Barth strikes a similar tone when he states that the ethical event occurs when "something [within the realms of our spheres of activity or relationships] is commanded or forbidden, and is therefore good or bad." Karl Barth, *Church Dogmatics* III/4, eds. G. W. Bromiley and T. F. Torrance (Edinburgh: T&T Clark, 1961), 31.

opening words of his *Treatise on Good Works* state, "We ought first to know that there are no good works except those which God has commanded, and there is no sin except that which God has forbidden. Therefore, whoever wishes to know and to do good works needs nothing else than to know God's commandments."[71]

Many contemporary philosophers have offered variations that are responsive to criticisms previously noted. One response comes from Richard Mouw, who shifts from the question of whether the divine imperatives are "right-making" and emphasizes instead that God's commands are "right-indicating"; they provide the means by which we *know* the good. Thus, while he leaves open the possibility that divine commands are also right-making, "we can confidently accept God's commands as reliable moral guidelines."[72] In this way, he sidesteps the metaethical question while defending the Reformed notion that only special revelation provides a reliable ethical guide.

Robert Adams, on the other hand, is committed to the view that God's commands are "right-making," but his "modified divine command theory" argues that ethics is not grounded in God's commands per se but in the divine character and God's gracious actions toward us.[73] In this manner, Adams avoids the criticism that God's commands are arbitrary. A loving God would not command us to act cruelly. And since moral law is the natural implication of an eternally loving God, we avoid the criticism that an external standard of goodness limits God's freedom. Moral goodness is God's nature, not something external to God. Thus, God's sovereignty remains intact, but its definition focuses more on love than freedom or coercive power.

In the Genesis 2 creation account, the first words God addresses to the humans is a command: "You may freely eat of any tree in the garden; but of the tree of the knowledge of good and evil you shall not eat, for in the day that you eat of it you shall die" (Gen 2:16-17 NRSV). Scripture supplies a plethora of commands that originate from God, and it is obvious that these

---

[71]Martin Luther, *Treatise on Good Works* (Auckland, NZ: Floating Press, 2009), 28, ProQuest ebrary.
[72]Richard J. Mouw, *The God Who Commands* (Notre Dame, IN: Notre Dame University Press, 2004), 30.
[73]Robert H. Adams, "A Modified Divine Command Theory of Ethical Wrongness," in *Philosophy of Religion: An Anthology*, ed. Charles Taliaferro and Paul J. Griffiths (Hoboken, NJ: Wiley-Blackwell, 2003), 472-73. Adams admits that his version of divine command requires prior commitment to a Judeo-Christian understanding of the divine attributes and character.

directives are authoritative. Moreover, numerous passages in Scripture emphasize God's ability and authority to do all things (e.g., Gen 18:14; Phil 3:21), even to the extent that we see God commanding individuals to do things that are typically viewed as immoral, such as the directive to Abraham to sacrifice Isaac. Divine command advocates also note that Scripture stresses obedience (e.g., Deut 4:37-40; Lev 18:4; Mt 28:20), even without any guarantee that reason can grasp why God imposes particular obligations. Finally, divine command theorists point out that most Christians, when asked to identify the essence of Christian ethics, go directly to the Ten Commandments, all couched in imperatives. Thus, the moral mandate of God's people may be summarized in the words "Be careful to obey all these words that I command you today, so that it may go well with you and with your children after you forever, because you will be doing what is good and right in the sight of the LORD your God" (Deut 12:28 NRSV).

## PROPHETIC ETHICS

Of the ethical paradigms in this volume, prophetic ethics may have the broadest range of expressions. However, several shared characteristics set it apart. First, prophetic ethics finds its foundation in ecclesiology and mission rather than the divine attributes (divine command theory) or a vision of human flourishing (natural law and virtue ethics). This ecclesial model means that, while the other models find their primary expression in individual ethics (although all are certainly adaptable to a social ethic), the starting point for prophetic ethics is social justice, which is understood to be the visible reflection of the values of God's kingdom.

Because the church has a unique character and calling, Christian ethics cannot simply supplement or fine-tune secular models in order to devise a moral paradigm. James William McClendon likens the latter to offering a Kantian defense of utilitarianism which, if valid, would refute the very argument one intends to justify.[74] Instead, prophetic ethics directly challenges and critiques all other theories, presenting Christian ethics as "off the spectrum" of conventional moral theories rather than occupying some point on a continuum alongside other paradigms. Thus, prophetic ethics is usually

---

[74]James William McClendon, *Systematic Theology*, vol. 1, *Ethics* (Nashville: Abingdon Press, 1986), 331.

critical of Christian virtue ethics and natural law for adopting preexisting moral systems and attempting to sanctify them.

The particularistic nature of this approach generates its prophetic element. An ethics grounded in kingdom ideals provides an alternative vision of a society built on love rather than dependence on military, political, or economic power. However, this prophetic witness is not just outward to the world but stands as a reminder to the church that is has often been seduced by worldly levers of power. As Walter Rauschenbusch puts it, "The Church, which was founded on brotherhood and democracy, had, in its higher levels, become an organization controlled by its upper classes for parasitic ends, a religious duplicate of the coercive State, and a chief check on the advance of brotherhood and democracy."[75] Thus, prophetic ethics often has restorationist tendencies. It seeks to go behind a history of church-state alliances to recover more primitive models of Christian community that avoided complex ecclesiastical hierarchies, expected persecution, shared a common life of simplicity, and served the oppressed.

An additional characteristic of prophetic ethics is its emphasis on the corporate dimension of sin. Forms of Christian ethics that focus attention on individual behaviors and decisions fail to recognize the "principalities and powers," organized systems established by the powerful who are the primary beneficiaries. As a result, those outside the circles of social and economic power are excluded and unheard. The prophetic model argues that Christian ethics must name and combat the systems that perpetuate enslavement and oppression if it is to get at the root of sin.

A final general characteristic of prophetic ethics is criticism of approaches that fix attention on theory and doctrine while failing to engage the world on behalf of the silenced and the poor. Instead of grounding ethics on theoretical foundations, some segments of prophetic ethics emphasize praxis, the activity of the community in constant conversation with the narrative that sustains the community.[76] The language of praxis recognizes that social

---

[75] Walter Rauschenbusch, *Theology of the Social Gospel* (New York: Macmillan, 1917), 73.

[76] As Clodovis Boff defines it, "I mean 'praxis' in the sense of the *complexus of practices* orientated to the transformation of society, the making of history. Praxis then has a fundamentally political connotation for me inasmuch as it is through the intermediary of the political that one can bring an influence to bear on social structures." Clodovis Boff, *Theology and Praxis: Epistemological Foundations*, trans. Robert Barr (Maryknoll, NY: Orbis, 1987), 6.

structures and traditions embed ways of life that transcend rational analysis and even determine what is considered rational. Thus, we are called to immerse ourselves in the world through engagement, not distanced analysis.

The Anabaptist movement is an early corporate manifestation of the prophetic model.[77] Its origins are in the Radical Reformation, which argued that the Magisterial Reformation wrongly diagnosed the church's root problem as theological rather than structural and ethical. As a result, the emergent Protestant groups failed to erase Christianity's entanglements with political structures, which inevitably led to the latter co-opting Christianity for its own ends. The Anabaptists saw the church as distinct from any other type of human association, a "contrast model" with alternative notions of power and security. Thus, they eschewed military might and adopted pacifism, proclaiming confidence in the power of peace and love. Likewise, they opted for the Believer's Church model in which baptism stood as the public witness of affirming adults who consciously embraced the way of Christ and renounced all other allegiances. As a visible witness to an alternative community, they sought consensus in church and life decisions; stressed simplicity of life, dress, and speech; and often lived communally.

In more recent forms of prophetic ethics, two new characteristics emerge. While Anabaptism originated among dispossessed and persecuted people, later advocates of prophetic ethics often come from positions of power and privilege, especially within the universities. Second, while early Anabaptists (and some current groups) had isolationist tendencies due to concerns about the corrupting influences of culture, more recent manifestations of prophetic ethics emphasize cultural engagement.

The Social Gospel movement of the early twentieth century vividly illustrates these shifts. Finding its impetus in the Second Great Awakening, which combined its call for personal repentance with a rejection of slavery, care for the poor, and confrontation of the rampant alcohol abuse, the Social Gospel of the early twentieth century ministered to those in the growing urban areas of the United States and Canada.

At the heart of the Social Gospel is an emphasis on the corporate dimension of sin. As Rauschenbusch expresses it, "The individualistic gospel . . .

---

[77]The groups most closely identified with the Anabaptists include Mennonites, Amish, and Hutterites. However, similar tendencies were also found in many of the early Baptist groups.

has not given us an adequate understanding of the sinfulness of the social order and its share in the sins of all individuals within it."[78] For many in this movement, postmillennialism, which anticipated the establishment of God's kingdom on earth, created the overarching vision for bringing this world's social structures into conformity with kingdom ideals. For this to occur, Washington Gladden says, we must recognize that "the law of love governs the whole of life; that it defines our relations to men not only in the home or in the church, but in industry and commerce and politics."[79] Thus, the Social Gospel moved from the church to the streets, often aligning itself with labor movements in seeking the right to organize, better wages, and humane working conditions. It adopted populist political agendas, and many advocated Christian socialism as a necessary step toward economic justice. The YMCA became a vehicle for helping rootless young men transition to urban centers. Schools were founded to allow the poor to escape illiteracy, and transition centers helped new immigrants adapt to their new country. The best-known popular expression of the Social Gospel is Charles Sheldon's novel *In His Steps*, which frames its signature question, "What would Jesus do?," against the background of this age's social ills.

Liberation theology retains the Social Gospel's concern for the poor and engagement with the social dimension of sin, but spreads in new directions. While the Social Gospel was a Protestant phenomenon, Liberationist thought originates in the Catholic context and only later finds a Protestant audience. Second, liberationist thought transcends the Social Gospel's North American context to encompass Latin American, feminist, African, Asian, and black theologies, just to mention a few of its various forms.

Liberation theology argues, as the name signals, that the gospel message is one of liberation. As Gustavo Gutiérrez puts it, "The theological meaning of liberation is . . . a question *about the very meaning of Christianity and about the mission of the Church.*"[80] However, he argues that the theme of deliverance has been perverted by the financially comfortable and empowered, who "spiritualize" liberation. Thus, liberationists are critical of those who read the

---

[78]Rauschenbusch, *Theology of the Social Gospel*, 5.
[79]Washington Gladden, *Social Salvation* (New York: Houghton Mifflin, 1902), 10.
[80]Gustavo Gutiérrez, *A Theology of Liberation: History, Politics, and Salvation*, trans. and ed. Caridad Inda and John Eagleson (Maryknoll, NY: Orbis, 1973), xi.

Exodus story, for example, as deliverance from bad habits and individual sins while ignoring the physical, financial, and political enslavement experienced by the majority in the world yet today.

Because today's poor and oppressed are in the same circumstances as those to whom Scripture was originally addressed, liberation thought seeks a "theology from below," an understanding of God's narrative as viewed through the eyes of the marginalized. Indeed, their status puts them in a better position to hear the gospel clearly than the empowered. Thus, liberation theology speaks frequently of the "preferential option for the poor," in which we are exhorted to interpret Christianity through the experience of those impoverished and to hear Scripture's message as a mandate to overturn the unjust systems that perpetuate poverty, normalize racism and sexism, and render the majority invisible.[81]

Postcolonial thought shares many of the concerns of liberation theology with a couple of exceptions. First, its wariness about the influences of colonizing metanarratives cast suspicion on doing theology from below. As Edward Said notes in his pioneering book on colonization and the Orient, Orientalism was not a fact but a constructed reality based on power, in which the powerful shape the images for both themselves and those who are dominated.[82] Thus, it is not simply the oppressor who falls prey to distorted views of Scripture's message but also those under the sway of the colonizer's metanarrative.

Christianity itself frequently comes in for severe criticism by postcolonial scholars because of alliances made with colonizers. As Aimé Césaire says, the primary culprit in distorting the view of those colonized "is Christian pedantry, which laid down the dishonest equations *Christianity = civilization, paganism = savagery*."[83] Thus, Christian advocates of postcolonial theology argue that we need to apply a rigorous "hermeneutics of suspicion" that reveals how cultural, racial, and gender stereotypes have been used to

---

[81]Originally, the preferential option for the poor was framed as a critique of the institutional church's role in siding with oppressive governments rather than the marginalized. However, in 1991, Pope John Paul II used the phrase to describe the church's social responsibility in his comments on the centennial of Pope Leo XIII's papal statement on capital and labor (*Rerum Novarum*). See John Paul II, "Centesimus Annus," art. 11, New Advent, May 1, 1991, www.newadvent.org/library /docs_jp02ca.htm.

[82]Edward W. Said, *Orientalism* (New York: Vintage Books, 1978), 5-6.

[83]Aimé Césaire, *Discourse on Colonialism*, trans. Joan Pinkham (New York: Monthly Review, 1972), 11.

subjugate others and continue to shape postcolonial consciousness. Particularly critical in this process is a thorough reexamination of biblical interpretation since "the Bible was used in the colonial past not only to save but also to 'civilize' native peoples and thus to legitimate the claims made by the colonizers that their dominance over the colonized was justified."[84]

Prophetic ethics frequently refers to Jubilee as a pivotal ethical passage in the Old Testament. The command that slaves are to be freed and all property returned to its original owner or heirs on the fiftieth year (Lev 25:10) is viewed as a model for erasing structural economic inequities within the community.[85] The practice of leaving the edges or corners of the field for the benefit of the orphaned and widowed (e.g., Lev 19:9-10; 23:22; Deut 24:19) is also used as a template for the church's duties to provide for the poor. Amos 5:21-24 and Micah 6:8 are paradigmatic passages for condemning religious practices that neglect justice.

In the New Testament, the words and activities of Jesus take center stage in prophetic ethics. In Matthew 25:31-46, Jesus states that the standard by which we will be judged is determined by our response to those in need. At the beginning of his ministry, Jesus closely ties his messianic identity to the prophetic message of justice, liberation, and healing for the poor, captive, blind, and oppressed (Is 61:1-2). Perhaps more than any other scriptural passage, however, prophetic ethics cites the Beatitudes (Mt 5:3-12; cf. Lk 6:20-22) and its message of hope and blessing for the persecuted and dispossessed.

---

[84]Kay Higuera Smith, Jayachitra Lalitha, and L. Daniel Hawk, eds., *Evangelical Postcolonial Conversations: Global Awakenings in Theology and Praxis* (Downers Grove, IL: IVP Academic, 2014), 25.

[85]Closely related is the "sabbath year," in which slaves are to be set free on the seventh year (Ex 21:2; Deut 15:12; Jer 34:14).

# 1

# Virtue Ethics

*BRAD J. KALLENBERG*

**If a burglar is breaking into the house,** *it is too late to begin lifting weights.* Underneath the humor, there is a truism: you are always becoming the person you are. This truism is the basis for a model of ethics.[1]

## WHAT IS VIRTUE ETHICS?

It is sometimes helpful to think about moral situations as having three logical moments: *agent(s)* perform *action(s)* that result in *outcome(s)*. One brand of ethics treats outcomes as the most important consideration in determining right and wrong (e.g., utilitarianism). Another brand of ethics claims that some actions are right or wrong regardless of outcomes. What makes for rightness or wrongness in their eyes is the *kind* of deed an action is (e.g., Kantianism). And of course, every kind of ethicist will insist that *both* action and outcomes are germane to serious ethical analysis. But virtue ethics takes special note of the agents doing the deed. In the first place, virtue ethics considers the deed in relation to "human excellence" or to the question, what is human life *for*? In addition to consideration of the human *telos* (where the Greek word *telos* names the "end" or "intended purpose" of a being or artifact), in the second place, virtue ethics also seeks thick descriptions rather than thin ones.[2] Since just about any act can be made to align

---

[1]As always, I am grateful to terrific colleagues Mac Sandlin, Aaron James, and Ethan Smith who have made insightful and clarifying suggestions to earlier drafts of this essay.
[2]The term *thick description* was coined by the Gilbert Ryle and was later made famous in cultural studies by Clifford Geertz. Gilbert Ryle, "The Thinking of Thoughts: What Is 'Le Penseur' Doing?," in *Collected Papers* (New York: Barnes & Noble, 1971), chap. 37, http://lucy.ukc.ac.uk/csacsia/vol14/papers/ryle_1.html.

with some principle or other provided the deed is described thinly enough, virtue ethics works hard to attend to all the particulars related to agents, actions, and outcomes.[3] Consider the following example. Francis of Assisi is championed as the paradigm of charity. Refusing to take over his father's prosperous enterprise, Francis disavowed his family wealth by stripping naked and swapping his rich man's tunic for the flea-ridden rough shirt of a local beggar. Thereafter becoming the most famous of the mendicant preachers, Francis's self-induced poverty is taken by some to be a morally supererogatory habit. If, however, I model my own life after St. Francis and give away my fortune (ha!), I would not be acting in imitation of St. Francis. Why? Because his life and mine are similar only under "thin" descriptions: "religiously minded males intent on growth in personal holiness." If the descriptions are made slightly more "thick" so as to include marital status (Francis never married; Kallenberg is married and father of three children), then the voluntary poverty that is heroic in Francis's case may prove to be downright immoral in my own![4]

With respect to human excellence Aristotle has famously said,

> It is no easy task to be good. For in everything it is no easy task to find the middle. . . . Any one can get angry or to give or spend money—that is easy— but to do this to the right person, to the right extent, at the right time, with the right aim, and in the right way, that is not for every one nor is it easy; that is why goodness is both rare and praiseworthy and noble.[5]

While agreeing with Aristotle, I hasten to add that not only is the noble deed difficult to execute, it is almost as difficult rightly to describe! Part of what makes thick description tricky relates to the acuity (or lack thereof) of moral eyesight. Even a highly detailed description may fail to make the point to an audience that is morally myopic. Outcomes and action classes are both included in thick description. But thick description does not end

---

[3]See chap. 1 of Charles Pinches, *Theology and Action: After Theory in Christian Ethics* (Grand Rapids: Eerdmans, 2002). For an example of the difference detail description makes see Brad J. Kallenberg, "The Descriptive Problem of Evil," in *Physics and Cosmology: Scientific Perspectives on the Problem of Natural Evil*, ed. Nancey Murphy, Robert John Russell, and William R. Stoeger (Vatican City State: Vatican Observatory Press, 2007), 297-322.
[4]This illustration is reproduced from Kallenberg, "Descriptive Problem of Evil," 301.
[5]Aristotle, *Nicomachean Ethics*, in *The Complete Works of Aristotle* (Bollingen Series 71:2), ed. Jonathan Barnes (Princeton, NJ: Princeton University Press, 1984), 2.9.

with answering "What *kind* of deed was done?" and "What happened next?" Nor is it sufficient to detail the action's object, extent, timing, intention, and manner as Aristotle suggests. In addition, an adequate description must be made of the identity of the agent. The agent's character is made clear by a triple-level analysis.

When I was a college student, my friend Matt and I stood one night outside his rental house in the grungy part of the city when a large sedan with six passengers drove slowly past us. We were joking and laughing—as Christians are wont to do! Suddenly the car slammed on its brakes about twenty feet beyond where we stood. A muscular guy leaped from the car and stormed toward us wielding a tire iron, furious because he thought we were laughing at him.

At that moment I had a variety of options I might have taken. I could run. (Since Matt and I were running partners, I knew that I was faster than Matt!) I could close the distance and preemptively land the first punch. I could interpose myself between Matt and the attacker, shielding my friend from harm, come what may. Then again, I could act crazy, say by drooling or singing "Feeling Groovy" at the top of my lungs. Whatever I chose to do, there are three levels to describe "doing right."

The first level of analysis considers whether what I do is the "right thing" or the "wrong thing." Let's suppose, for sake of argument, that under these conditions fleeing the scene is the "wrong thing" to do and that shielding Matt from harm is the "right thing" to do. The second level considers why I did it. I might do the right thing for ignoble reasons. Perhaps I wanted to impress female onlookers peeking through shuttered windows or alternatively to get a psychological hold over Matt by placing him in my debt. Such reasons would certainly cheapen the moral value of my deed even if I did the "right thing." But let's suppose further, again for sake of argument, that I shield Matt for a good reason, for love of my friend. There is a third level to consider—namely, the character I embody. For in the weeks to come the chatter in our circles might go one of two ways. "Kallenberg did *what*? Really? Are you certain? Surely not . . . not Brad J. Kallenberg! I don't believe it!" Or the banter might have the opposite flavor: "What a great guy! That is just the sort of thing Kallenberg would do! Why, I remember last month when he . . ."

Whether or not my friends are surprised is a crucial index of the sort of character I embody. This threefold description is how a virtue ethicist describes the *telos* or goal of human living: doing the right thing for the right reason and having your friends never be surprised.[6] Implicit in this triple-level account is that the encounter with the tire iron, odd though it may be, was yet one more action that serves to constitute my character and to extend that character into the future—assuming my survival!

From the vantage of *Christian* virtue ethics, the point is never simply to extend my personal story. Rather, as a Christian I am implicitly committed to extending Jesus' story. And this can happen on two levels, both on the individual level and on the corporate level. The first level can be seen in the first chapter of Philippians.

I've often been bothered by the fact that Paul seems so unconcerned that the gospel was being preached in the wrong manner—out of jealousy, strife, selfish ambition, and even with an eye to injuring Paul (Phil 1:15-17)! But Paul shrugs, "What then? Only that in every way, whether in pretense or in truth, Christ is proclaimed; and in this I rejoice" (v. 18 NASB). While it is surely right for Christians to worry about the confusion that may ensue when the gospel message is parroted by fakers, Paul sees a deeper good in play. What the fakers cannot do to Paul is prevent the extension of the *real* story line. In verse 20, Paul uses the Greek term *megalynō* to connote that he wins in either case: "According to my earnest expectation and hope, that I will not be put to shame in anything, but that with all boldness, Christ will even now, as always, be magnified (*megalynō*) in my body, whether by life or by death." The term *megalynō* is generally translated as "exalt" or "magnify." But such a rendering leaves unspecified the question, With respect to *what* will Christ be magnified? Will Christ be greater in terms of *glory, time, wealth, extension, education, job security*, or what? I suggest a *narratival* magnification fits this context best. The character and plot line of Paul's life physically *extends* (a legitimate meaning of *megalynō*) the story of Christ in time and space. Paul's biography recapitulates Christ's story. On the one hand, some hearers may genuinely convert to follow Jesus *despite* the ill will of the fake preachers. On the other hand, even if there are

---

[6]Ralph McInerny, *Ethica Thomistica*, rev. ed. (Washington, DC: Catholic University of America Press, 1997), 90-99.

no converts, the message still comes through loud and clear. Why? Because Christ's self-emptying (kenotic) character is made well known by Paul's imitation of Christ, namely, the unjust suffering that he willingly and joyfully endured ("for the joy set before Him" [Heb 12:2 NASB]).[7]

So *Christian* virtue ethics analyzes moral situations relative to the *fit* of its action as measured against the character of Christ revealed in the Gospel narratives. For virtue ethics the metric is not so much effectiveness as faithfulness to the gospel. On the first level, faithfulness to the story has been considered on the individual level.

The second level on which the story of Jesus can be extended resembles the first, but exceeds it in important ways. Individual agents may approach similarity to aspects of Christ's character, as we saw in Paul (and which Paul may have learned by witnessing Stephen's prayer of extravagant forgiveness— in *imitatio Christi*—while being stoned). In addition, a community *as a whole* can be shaped in the pattern of Christ (i.e., Christomorphic). Later in the same chapter, Paul urges, "Only conduct yourselves [*politeuomai*] in a manner worthy of the gospel of Christ" (Phil 1:27 NASB). Hiding behind the English translation is a unique verb. The term *politeuomai* is not about behaving ourselves as much as it is about forming the right kind and manner of *polis* (community). This command is fulfilled at the individual level by individual faithfulness to Christlikeness. Yet the character of the whole community is not simply the summing up of the individual parts, for the community has its own order of reality and character. That character exercises top-down influence on the parts.[8] It is this level of consideration—the level of "form of life" or "communal character" that can resemble Christ in ways that no individual can. It is together that we achieve "mature man [*andra teleiōn*], to the measure of the stature which belongs to the fullness of Christ" (Eph 4:13 NASB). It is together that we physically extend (*megalynō*) the incarnation in the world. It is together that we constitute the "body of Christ" with Christ as our only head. To the extent that churches in the West are stripped down to nothing more than microcosms of (un)civil society, this corporate *telos* is obscured.

---

[7]Unless otherwise noted, Scripture translations are my own.

[8]For an accessible account of top-down causation see Nancey Murphy, *Beyond Liberalism and Fundamentalism* (Philadelphia: Trinity Press International, 1996), chap. 6.

In short, virtue ethics revolves around the question, what kind of people/persons ought we be? In order to see how we might begin to respond to this kind of question in concrete situations, we must get clear on two terms: (1) Who is the "we"? and (2) What is meant by "ought"?

## WHO IS THE "WE"?

Theologically speaking, human beings are created animals who do our living in a material world by means of finite material bodies. To be human is to be enfleshed, embodied, incarnate. In this section I will investigate what it means to be a "human moral agent" by attending to the nature of our bodiliness. Although we each, as members of the species *homo sapiens*, presume to have insider knowledge about human agency, I will begin with reminders of what Jesus' incarnation shows us about being human.

In the first place, bodies matter. The incarnation was a great deal of trouble to undergo if, in the end, bodies don't really matter. I mean, why didn't God simply send a philosophical treatise instead of *embodying* the kingdom in a living, breathing, suffering, bleeding, dying human person?[9] Apparently the kingdom could not be embodied without a body. As fourth-century theologian Gregory of Nazianzus famously put it, "That which [Christ] has not assumed He has not healed."[10] Christ rescued us *entirely*—heart and mind, emotions and will, soul and *body*—by taking on our humanity in every aspect. Bodies matter because Christ took on a human body. Moreover, if human bodies were of no import, why bother with resurrection? For not only do we worship a risen Savior who is eternally incarnate, we too are promised eternal life with a body—resurrected, to be sure, but a body nonetheless.

The bodiliness of Jesus' human existence is pretty plain to see. He got hungry, thirsty, and tired. He walked from place to place and had to sit down from time to time. He wept when his friend died and bled when stabbed with a spear and bruised when pummeled with fists. Of particular interest for us is the fact that Jesus, whose body is fully human, shared with

---

[9]The plural pronoun of Luke 17:21 indicates this translation: "The kingdom of God is among y'all." Jesus himself stood in their midst as the embodiment of the coming/now-here reign of God.

[10]Gregory of Nazianzus, "To Cledonius the Priest Against Apollinarius (Ep. 101)," ed. Philip Schaff and Henry Wace, A Select Library of Nicene and Post-Nicene Fathers, series 2, vol. 7 (1890), www.ccel.org/print/schaff/npnf207/iv.ii.iii.

human beings these bodily traits: some of his knowledge was incomplete (his human brain, like ours, only weighed a couple of pounds). He wasn't born an adult but as a helpless baby who slowly grew up physically, socially, and mentally (Lk 2:52). Along the way Jesus formed dispositions and habits.[11] And one of the things he had to learn was obedience. Importantly, the way he learned obedience was through *bodily suffering*.[12] Don't misunderstand me: Jesus never failed to obey. But he *learned* obedience as a process over time, like we do. He wasn't ready to go to the cross at age twelve, because at age twelve he was successfully obeying twelve-year-old-sized commands. Not until adulthood was he ready for the ultimate obedience. Until that moment he was still in process; he was still learning. (The author of Hebrews uses the verb for learning that in the noun form means "disciple.") Perhaps Jesus' greatest temptation was to resist temptation using divine resources. But he did not take the divine shortcut. He obeyed perfectly while doing so *humanly*. Jesus opted to learn how to obey by taking the same route we must: by starting with easy tasks and tackling more and more difficult ones as he grew. In this way his body, and our bodies, *learn* obedience. That is part of what incarnation means. It is the *bodily* aspect of the human condition that will help bring virtue ethics into focus. I'll explain the irreducibly bodily nature of virtue ethics by stating and defending four claims.

*The quality of any human person's knowledge is a function of the quality of that person's habits.* This claim is obvious enough in technical fields: a person who hasn't practiced (i.e., formed habits) at integration has poor knowledge of calculus. But the claim has implications for the moral life as well. When Luke described Jesus' custom of praying in the Mount of Olives (Lk 22:39), he uses the word *ethos*, the standard Greek word for "habit." When the first vowel is lengthened, the cognate *ēthos* connotes "character." These two are the etymological sources for the English "ethics." For the Greeks, one's character was public. One's *ēthos* was simply the constellation of all of one's habits. Moreover, one's character was also thought to be stable. Although the young could not display firm and

---

[11]"As was his custom" Jesus arose early to pray in a lonely place, went to the synagogue, taught the crowds, and so on (e.g., Lk 4:16; 22:39).

[12]"Although he was a Son, he learned obedience through what he suffered" (Heb 5:8 NRSV).

unchangeable character, through the tending of one's habits over a long time, one's character eventually becomes "steady" (*hexis*) or second nature. The Greeks were pretty optimistic on this point and perhaps unjustifiably so. Nevertheless, it seems uncontroversial to claim that there is an ordinary connection between habits and character: the person who acts in a generous manner time and time again is counted on to act with similar generosity the next time too. We call such a character "generous" and thereby know, basically, what to expect from such a person.

The shaping of character takes time. The series of intentional acts that goes into the formation of habits (and eventually character) involves increasing attunement to one's surroundings. If a repeated action is the beginning of a habit, what is habituated is one's disposition to take his or her surroundings in a particular way. The world is a vast blooming, buzzing confusion. What causes us to notice one aspect rather than another is due, in large part, to previous bodily action. Theologian G. Simon Harak relates a poignant story.

> When I was younger, I studied karate for a few years, going three times a week for practice. One day, two fellow students of theology and I decided to go to a movie. Fran was a former Marine sergeant. John was a bright and articulate student. After we had bought our tickets individually, we regrouped in the lobby. "Did you see that guy on the other side of the ticket booth?" Fran asked me. "Yeah," I replied. "He sure was cruisin' for a bruisin', wasn't he?" "You know," Fran said, "the look on his face . . . I was just waiting for him to try something," and he put his right fist into his left palm. I started to say, "If he made a move on me, I would've . . ." but John interrupted us by saying, "What guy?"
>
> The facts are these: Fran and I saw this young man, and we were ready even to fight with him. John, a bright and alert person, didn't even perceive him. Why? The key lies in our respective backgrounds. In our history, Fran and I shared a training in violence. It was, significantly, a physical training which disposed us to "take things in a certain way." Specifically, we were "looking for trouble." And we found it. John, with no such training, didn't even perceive the "belligerent" young man.[13]

---

[13]G. Simon Harak, *Virtuous Passions: The Formation of Christian Character* (Mahwah, NJ: Paulist Press, 1993), 34.

To the extent that the previous bodily actions are repeated frequently over a long enough span of time, the training of one's "eyesight"—what he or she is disposed to see—becomes a part of his or her character.

The connection of habits and "moral eyesight" can make sense out of otherwise puzzling biblical texts. The psalmist insists that

> With the loyal you [Yнwн] show yourself loyal;
>> with the blameless you show yourself blameless;
> with the pure you show yourself pure;
>> and *with the crooked you show yourself perverse.* (Ps 18:25-26 NRSV)[14]

Translators sometimes shy away from translating the Hebrew *patal* as "perverse" or "twisted." But the psalmist is not knocking God but speaking the truth about the inability of the twisted person to see all things, even God, as anything but twisted. A second puzzling passage comes from the eighth chapter of Mark's Gospel.

As a young Christian I was always a bit sheepish about the healing of the blind man in Mark 8:22-26. After all, I reasoned, the Christ I worshiped was fully God as well as fully man, so why couldn't Jesus heal the blind man on the first try? Why did it take the Son of God a do-over to get it right? And why did Mark's Jesus seem entirely unconcerned by the initial flop? As I matured I was taught about the crucial importance of reading each pericope in *context.* As I read more widely I discovered that this man wasn't the only person in Mark who couldn't see clearly.

Mark's Gospel has a "breathless" quality that comes from the presence of the word "and" (*kai*) at the beginning of nearly every paragraph. So regular is the use of *and* that when it is missing, it signals a sectional break. (Remember, chapter and verse numbers were later additions to Scripture.) Mark 8:1 lacks an *and*, as does Mark 9:38. This means that Mark 8:1–9:38 is thematically connected as a single section. What is the theme? Blindness! If we move paragraph by paragraph we can notice a recurring pattern.

---

[14]To cite another example, Paul remarks to Titus, "To the pure, all things are pure; but to those who are defiled and unbelieving, nothing is pure, but both their mind and their conscience are defiled" (Tit 1:15 NASB).

Mark 8:14-17: After cleaning up from feeding the four thousand (Mk 8:1-10) and arguing briefly with the Pharisees (Mk 8:11-13), the disciples are in the boat, having forgotten to take bread along. Jesus begins teaching about the "leaven of the Pharisees," and the disciples misunderstand. Jesus asks, "Do you not yet see or understand?" (v. 17).

Mark 8:15-21: Jesus continues to interrogate the disciples about the previous miracle, ending with *"Do you not yet understand [see]?"*

Mark 8:27-33: Jesus and the disciples are walking throughout Caesarea Philippi. The moment after Peter makes his public confession of Jesus as the Messiah, he sticks his foot in his mouth, *not seeing* the possibility of crucifixion. Jesus rebukes him: "Get behind me, Satan! For you are setting-your-mind (*phroneō*) not on divine things but on human things" (v. 33).

Mark 9:9-13: The disciples are arguing privately because *they couldn't see* what "rising from the dead" could possibly mean.

Mark 9:14-29, 30-32: after another miraculous healing, Jesus returns to the topic of his impending death and resurrection. *"But they did not understand [see] what he was saying and were afraid to ask him"* (v. 32).

The healing of the blind man (Mk 8:22-26) sits in the middle of five other stories of blindness.

Mark's juxtaposition of the disciples' obtuseness with the healing of the blind man makes it clear: *the repair of human moral vision may be a process that takes time.* The timely changing of how we are disposed to take the world is what I'm calling habit and character formation.

Does the relation between the quality of our character and the quality of our knowledge mean that God is prevented from coming to us unbeckoned, from breaking into darkness with divine revelation? Of course not. When God breaks in we call it grace. But the fact that God can break in, and sometimes opts to do so, is poor grounds for ignoring the way that insight and understanding ordinarily develop according to growth in the quality of the knower's habits and character. In fact, the close connection between repeated actions in the body may help explain why the author of 2 Peter describes the path to fruitful knowledge in stepwise fashion:

Now for this very reason also, applying all diligence,

in your faith supply virtue [*aretē*],

and in *your* virtue [*aretē*], knowledge,

and in *your* knowledge, self-control,

and in *your* self-control, perseverance,

and in *your* perseverance, godliness,

and in *your* godliness, brotherly kindness,

and in *your* brotherly kindness, love.

For if these *qualities* are yours and are increasing, they render you neither useless nor unfruitful in the true knowledge of our Lord Jesus Christ. (2 Pet 1:5-8 NASB, modified)

What begins with saving faith is followed not by "knowledge" but by "virtue." The term *virtue* simply means good habits. (Bad habits were called vices.) Although the New Testament avoids general appeal to the concept *aretē*, that it uses the term here sends a clear message: what is born of faith grows first by virtuous habit (guided, of course, by tutelage of mature others—more on that later). The young disciple's subsequent growth in knowledge and other desirable traits from this list is dependent on the formation of good habits.

***Forming habits is biological.*** God invented habits. Biology students can tell us that even the lowly flatworm can "learn" to turn right at the end of a T-shaped petri dish if it encounters a saline solution in the left well frequently enough! Habit is simply how animal bodies learn. I emphasize *bodies* here because even for the human animal an enormous percentage of learning happens below the level of the neocortex. Throwing a Frisbee, tying a necktie, riding a bicycle, recognizing the sound of a clarinet, walking upright, dreading the dentist, tying shoes in the dark, knowing that coffee is brewing, and so on—these are all bits of knowing *stored in the body*.

Humans share this kind of learning with animals. The difference between us and the animals is that animals form habits under someone else's direction (or by happenstance), while human beings can form habits intentionally, as an aid toward long-range self-governance. Having a neocortex does not enable human beings to bypass the painful process of bodily learning. Not at all.

Think of how difficult it is to learn to ride a bicycle. Destin Sandlin recently demonstrated how difficult it is to master riding. The experiment posed to him was whether he, an avid biker, could ride a bicycle with oppositely geared handlebars (turn right to go left, and turn left to go right). It sounds simple, but it is not. His neocortex, the part of the brain that reasons abstractly, issued instructions on which way to turn. But his body kept overruling him. In fact, he practiced every day for *eight months* until it "clicked." (Of course, once it did "click," he could no longer ride an ordinary bicycle.) Meanwhile his six-year-old son mastered the alternative bike in just two-weeks.[15]

Steering a bike is *not* controlled by discursive reasoning processes (also called "theoretical reasoning") but by bodily know-how.[16] Bodily know-how is a crucial component in ethical reasoning or, more broadly speaking, "practical reasoning." By means of practical reasoning we order our ways aright (Ps 50:23 NASB) en route to godliness becoming "second nature," fragile though this acquired nature be.

***Humans form habits intentionally.*** Ordinary people do not give public addresses to large crowds or run marathons in under four hours or willingly slay other humans in battle. But ordinary persons can be trained to do such things. (Whether any of these skills are wise to acquire is another matter.)

The notion of intentional habit formation has a long presence in Christian history. The Hebrew Bible begins with the Torah having set for us to follow a trajectory or right path.[17] Our role, in response, is to "walk" in this path or way. Walking in the "way of wisdom"[18] is not a task that is easily checked off but one requiring of us hourly, daily, weekly, seasonally, and yearly attunement. The Psalms in particular are chock full of admonitions to "walk in the way." In fact, from the vantage of the Psalter, the *blessed* life is equated with the *walking* life.[19]

---

[15]See "The Backwards Brain Bicycle—Smarter Everyday 133," *YouTube*, accessed October 23, 2016, www.youtube.com/user/destinws2?app=desktop. See also http://viewpure.com/MFzDaBzBlL0 ?ref=bkmk.

[16]For an introduction to this topic see Gilbert Ryle, "Knowing How and Knowing That: The Presidential Address," *Proceedings of the Aristotelian Society, New Series* 46 (1945): 1-16.

[17]The Hebrew noun *torah* is related to the verb *yarah*, meaning to "throw a stone" or "shoot an arrow." The flight path of the projectile is said to have a "direction" or *torah*. Consequently, *torah* can have both the prescriptive sense of "law" and descriptive connotation of a social more or custom.

[18]Hebrew *derek ḥokmâ* (Prov 4:11).

[19]Psalm 1:1 uses the verb "Blessed is the one . . ." When *'šr* is in the Piel it means "to bless" (Mal 3:12). When the same root is in Qal, it means "to walk" (Prov 9:6).

The conceptual era that followed the Hebrew Bible was that of ancient Greece. Greek culture was dominated by four schools of thinking: Plato, Aristotle, the Stoics, and the Cynics. Where "walking in the way" in the Hebrew Bible was conveyed as a communal activity, some of the Greek thinkers viewed the moral life as more of an individual affair, as an individual quest for truthfulness.[20]

For example, Stoic philosophers practiced regular examination of conscience by reporting to friends any discrepancy between what they should have done and what they actually did.[21] The aim of this practice of examination was self-mastery. Stoic asceticism (*askēsis*) was characterized by two actions working in tandem. Since these terms get picked up by New Testament writers (also writing in Greek), it serves us well to consider them closely.

The first action is *meletaō*. This Greek word sometimes gets translated as "meditation," but that doesn't quite express the significance of *meletaō* or its Hebrew counterpart, *hagah* (e.g., Ps 1:2). The English word *meditation* connotes ruminating about something pleasant (such as a string quartet by Dvořák or the sun setting over a lake) or something timelessly true (say, the conservation of momentum or Fibonacci's sequence). But the Greeks would

---

[20]To repeat the above reference to Psalm 1, verse 5 conveys the idea that the righteous wind up together in assembly, but the sinners have been scattered by the wind and their path is not well worn enough to be called "a way." In fact, the "trail" the sinner treads itself cannot be seen, but the righteous travel a "highway" (Ps 84:5). While Plato (Socrates) conceived the *polis* as isomorphic with the human soul, the moral life was still heroically individualistic, as Socrates's own life demonstrated. Aristotle's view was more communal, his account being more obviously dependent on the practice of friendship as constitutive of the moral life. Yet for Aristotle, the perfect friend (= the perfectly virtuous person) seems liable to forget about contingency, the moral luck involved in his or her achievements, and thus to forget the indebtedness to others' role in his or her progress and rather to assess perfection in terms of "self-sufficiency." One way to take "self-sufficiency" is to conclude that perfect friendship forged between perfectly virtuous persons has the curious end result that neither person really needed the other. Consequently, the self-sufficient person seems to make for a poor friend and threatens the fabric of community. See Jennifer A. Herdt, *Putting on Virtue: The Legacy of the Splendid Vices* (Chicago: University of Chicago Press, 2008), 41-43. For an account by authors who take "self-sufficiency" as communally located but still find Aristotle's friendship falling short of Christian friendship, see Stanley Hauerwas, with Charles Pinches, *Christians Among the Virtues: Theological Conversations with Ancient and Modern Ethics* (Notre Dame, IN: University of Notre Dame Press, 1997), chap. 3, esp. 38-43.

[21]I stumbled on this surprising and insightful history while researching technological ethics. Michel Foucault, "Technologies of the Self," in *Technologies of the Self: A Seminar with Michel Foucault*, ed. Luther H. Martin, Huck Gutman, and Patrick H. Hutton (Amherst: University of Massachusetts Press, 1988), 16-49.

have called these examples "contemplation," which in the case of math and logic belongs strictly to "theoretical reasoning." Theoretical reasoning deals with universal and necessary truths, which is to say, truths that can't be otherwise.[22] By stark contrast, the messy world of living systems and interpersonal relationships is not treated so much by theoretical reasoning as by "practical reasoning."

The last sentence is an extremely important one. Insofar as ethics involves human beings, ethics exclusively calls for an exercise of *practical* reasoning, a kind of practical savvy that takes note of contingencies and is never completely sure of results. We can see the predominance of practical reasoning for early Christians simply by surveying New Testament vocabulary. The New Testament *never* uses *theōria* in the abstract sense (the Greek term for theoretical reasoning). And the kind of knowing associated with theoretical reasoning, *epistēmē*, in which one is certain of having the correct answer (as in the certainty of knowing 2 + 2 = 4) is likewise absent from the New Testament.[23] In sharp contrast, practical reasoning and the attending concepts show up regularly. The most distinctive of these concepts is the name for the skill acquired when one becomes practically wise: *phronēsis*. This term for practical wisdom goes beyond simple "savvy," emphasizing the thought processes that go into mulling over a plan, always with an eye to taking action. The wise man (*phronimos*) builds his house on a rock; Christ-followers are called to be wise (*phronimos*) as serpents, though harmless as doves; the companions to the five female morons (*mōrai*) were five wise young women (*phronimoi*); Peter is rebuked for failing to consider (*phroneō*) God's priorities; Christians can plan to act (*phroneō*) regarding either things of the Spirit or things of the flesh; we are adjured to exercise the mind (*phroneō*) of Christ, and so on.[24]

Practical reasoning is the kind of reasoning needed when there cannot be one clear, right answer "in the back of the book." It is the mode of reasoning

---

[22]If it is raining outside, we can intelligibly say, "It might not have been raining." But we cannot intelligibly say, "It might *not* have been the case that 2 + 2 = 4."

[23]The exception to these absences is the word used to describe the skill, or virtue, of this kind of reasoning; the Greeks called it *sophia*. But biblical authors used *sophia* to distinguish the kind of wisdom that originated from God and that which the worldly philosophers deemed as wise. The New Testament does not use *sophia* to describe a human trait except by gifting of the Spirit.

[24]In order: Mt 7:24; 10:16; 25:2; 16:23; Rom 8:5-7; Phil 2:2, 5.

needed for coping with the messy, contingent, highly unpredictable world in which even the most reliable, brand-new machines can bend, break, or melt rather than work as they "should,"[25] the kind of world in which relationships will cool, sour, and wither without constant care. But I'm getting ahead of myself.

Back to the Stoic form of asceticism that involves two steps. Step one is *meletaō*. For the Stoics, *meletaō* belongs to practical reasoning. It involves thinking about the real world with an eye to acting. For the Stoics, *meletaō*

> is composed of memorizing responses and reactivating those memories by placing oneself in a situation where one can imagine how one would react. One judges the reasoning one should use in an imaginary exercise ("Let us suppose . . .") in order to test an action or event (for example, "How would I react?").[26]

In short, *meletaō* is a kind of imaginative training exercise. One improves one's future responses by anticipating in advance real situations through mental role-play.[27] It involves both memorizing a treasury of set responses and then going further by envisioning how one might embellish on a set response to adapt to a never-before-encountered situation.[28] Perhaps the ultra-shy person, before venturing out, will rehearse the steps needed for taking the city bus. Since people will likely be encountered, the shy person might arm himself or herself with adequate quips for responding to uninvited interactions, all the more likely if the bus is very late or very crowded.

The apostle Paul refers to this culturally familiar notion in his first letter to Timothy (1 Tim 4:13-16). He reminds Timothy to attend to the "readings," "exhortations," and "teachings." We can imagine that such things contain the stock scripts Timothy needs to rehearse (such as "rejoice always" and "pray constantly"). Timothy is told to *"practice [meletaō]* and *inhabit*—live into, 'be in'—these things." The result? His progress would be evident to everyone (v. 15). This result should not be a surprise. Virtue ethics expects moral progress to be possible. And insofar as character is public, one's progress (or lack

---

[25] See Brad J. Kallenberg, *By Design: Theology, Ethics and the Practice of Engineering* (Eugene, OR: Cascade Books, 2013), chap. 2.

[26] Foucault, "Technologies of the Self," 17.

[27] Athletes do this sort of mental prep work before competing.

[28] Even the most brilliantly witty improv actors spend *hours* memorizing one-liners, humorous character voices, gestures, and so forth. See Samuel Wells, "Drama as Improvisation," in *Improvisation: The Drama of Christian Ethics* (Grand Rapids: Baker, 2004), 59-70.

thereof)[29] will be on display for anyone to observe. The link between moral progress and the stock treasury of behavioral scripts is *meletaō*. The present tense imperative mood of both verbs (i.e., both *meletaō* and *inhabit* or *be in*) indicates a continuous or repeated action. Timothy is to live into Christian teaching by means of the ongoing practice of mental rehearsal called *meletaō*.

The second action word that New Testament writers borrow from Greek culture is *gymnazō*, from which we get the English *gymnastics*. Some prominent Greek voices, such as Aristotle, tended to use *meletaō* as the generic term for training.[30] But others, like the Stoics, were more explicit in reminding us that training is *bodily*. As important as mental preparation is, training is incomplete unless bodies are exercised. This exercise included regularized activities like rehearsing dance moves or gymnastic routines. And it also involved more open-ended exercises, such as scrimmages and improv role playing.

The physical side of spiritual-moral training was quickly picked up by the earliest Christians. Recall that Christianity was illegal in the empire until the fourth century.[31] For some three hundred years there were unpredictable waves of persecution, some of which were very severe. During this era we read reports of the most eccentric forms of Christianity.[32] They practiced sleep deprivation, light deprivation, intentionally poor diet (mixing ashes with their food), semi-starvation (fasts of 2, 3, even 40 days), self-induced isolation, and self-inflicted pain (e.g., binding up limbs with leather thongs until the limb went numb; when the straps were released the returning blood supply to the limb was excruciatingly painful). These are certainly strange tales. Most Christians today are embarrassed by these oddballs who claimed to follow Jesus. Today we would quickly refer them for psychiatric treatment and hospitalize them for their own safety. But wait a minute! What if there was method in their madness? What if, given their justifiable expectation of imminent torture at the hands of pagan rulers, these oddballs were *training themselves to endure*?[33] The Romans had gotten quite creative

---

[29]Think of Hymenaeus, Alexander, and Philetus (1 Tim 1:20; 2 Tim 2:17).

[30]See Aristotle, *Nicomachean Ethics* 3.5; 7.10.

[31]Christianity became legal around 313 and mandatory around 387.

[32]Eusebius, *The Church History*, ed. Paul L. Maier (Grand Rapids: Kregel Academic, 1999).

[33]Maureen A. Tilley, "The Ascetic Body and the (Un)Making of the World of the Martyr," *Journal of the American Academy of Religion* 59, no. 3 (1991): 467-79.

in their methods of torture.[34] What if the so-called whacko Christians were not so whacko after all, but Christians of the utmost seriousness and practical wisdom? Fourth-century church historian Eusebius recounts the tale of one Christian woman who could not be broken.

> Blandina was filled with such power that those who tortured her from morning to night grew exhausted and admitted that they were beaten, for they had nothing left to do to her. They were astounded that she was still alive, since her whole body was smashed and lacerated, and they claimed that any one of the tortures was enough to end life, let alone a succession of them augmented. But the blessed woman, like a noble athlete, gained in strength while confessing the faith and found comfort in her sufferings by saying, "I am a Christian and nothing wicked happens among us."[35]

It was cases like these that turned the tables on paganism. Rather than the torturer breaking the will of the Christian, *the practiced resilience of the Christian broke the will of the would-be torturers.*

Returning to New Testament ethics, we find *gymnazō* applied in Hebrews 5:14, "But solid food is for the mature [*teleiōn*], for those whose faculties [*aisthētrion*] have been fully trained [*hexis*] by bodily exercise [*gymnasia*] to skillfully discern [*diakrisis*] good from evil." Two terms indicate that, according to the author of Hebrews, bodily exercise *completes* the formation process. The word *teleiōn* connotes "mature" in the sense that such ones have achieved their purpose or *telos*. In addition, the author uses the word *hexis*, which in Greek culture meant "second nature" or a steady, stable character. The upshot of the training was improved discernment.

We don't need convincing that good and evil are not always easy to tell apart. Although sometimes they can be. The answer to the question "Shall I murder my neighbor?" can be looked up in any number of ethical tables. But we quickly run into difficulty with the murkier cases. Then perhaps we need something more like a "reliable nose." Today we use terms like *reliable nose, good ear, delicate touch,* and *skilled eye* to refer to highly trained surgeons,

---

[34]Thieleman van Braght, ed., *The Bloody Theater or Martyrs Mirror of the Defenseless Christians Who Baptized Only upon Confession of Faith, and Who Died for the Testimony of Jesus, Their Savior, from the Time of Christ to the Year A.D. 1660 Compiled from Various Authentic Chronicles, Memorials, and Testimonies*, 14th ed. (Scottdale, PA: Herald Press, 1985).
[35]Eusebius, "Martyrs in Gaul," in Maier, *Church History*, 172.

engineers, musicians, and so on—practitioners who have spent long years honing their skillful habits through physical practice (typically under the tutelage of a master). Likewise, in Hebrews 5:14, the word for "perceptive faculties" (*aisthētria*) refers not to perceptiveness available to anyone but perception by those who have been fully trained. The doctor reading an X-ray, the musician listening to a performance, the engineer observing a faulty mechanism—these practitioners each perceive things *obvious* to them but lost on the rest of us. Let's face it, even when the physician tries to show us what the X-ray "clearly shows," we can't see anything remarkable at all. But that is because we are unexercised.

We may live in a democracy, but virtue ethics is not democratic. Virtue ethics is a varsity sport. Those who work hardest and respond well to coaching make the most progress and therefore get the most playing time.

It is no surprise that the first Christians valued skilled judgment and discernment. What may be surprising is the notion that "a good nose" for telling good from evil is not something one is born with. It is not something that one can simply turn on like a light switch. Rather, skilled judgment is developed slowly by bodily training. But why should Christians find that so surprising? The incarnation of the Son together with the repeated promises of our bodily resurrection seem to constitute a pretty strong hint that whatever else the Christian life is, it cannot be anything but bodily. Despite the temptation to think of the mind as the complete controller of the body (a view inherited from Plato), we know that repeated bodily activity has been shown to change the physical structures in the brain.[36] This recent finding underscores the importance of virtue ethics. The way of wisdom in ethics need not begin with a speculative theory. Rather, it may begin by bodily training.

This section began with the claim that "humans form habits intentionally." But now I must clarify *whose* intention is at work. On the one hand, according to virtue ethics, every intentional act is inherently a moral act. There may be *nonintentional* actions, such as when I absent-mindedly scratch my chin. (This class of actions I share with my dog, who also scratches her chin.) But insofar as an act is done intentionally—insofar as I *have* a reason for

---

[36]Jeffrey M. Schwartz, "Neuroanatomical Aspects of Cognitive-Behavioral Therapy Response in Obsessive-Compulsive Disorder," *British Journal of Psychiatry* 173, suppl. 35 (1998): 38-44.

acting—my action is value laden.[37] ("Having a reason" is not something I can say of my dog; although she can act *for* a reason, only humans *have* reasons in acting.) But that is not to say that *mine* is the sole intention embodied in the action I carry out. For example, a carpenter's apprentice may be intending to cut one hundred dovetail pins to practice her carpentry skills, but a master carpenter to whom she is apprenticed may have earlier noticed her shoddy dovetails and assigned her the hundred cuts as a training regimen. Her cutting of the hundred pins embodies her intentions but also the intention of the master who trains her.

The possibility of multiple intentions being realized in a given human act turns ethics into a team sport. But before we can examine the sociality of ethics, I must examine one final, oft-overlooked aspect of the condition in which we find ourselves constrained to live out our ethics.

***Habit formation is opposed by entropy.*** Habits have staying power, but only up to a point. Their failure is attributed to a stubborn feature of the fallen world. As members of the physical world, human lives are subject to the same conditions that the material world is subject. Chief among these is *entropy*.

Not all energy in a closed system can be harnessed. Some of it will be wasted. The energy that cannot be harnessed is called "free energy." The rule of physics is this: "Free energy always increases." The increase of free energy is why your coffee grows cool, why engines overheat, why a clean room gets messy, why the guitar goes out of tune, why the windup toy winds down and stops. Entropy is the name given to explain why mechanisms may bind, break off, or melt; why cars rust; why living things sicken and die. Entropy is the tendency of things to become more random and disordered.

We live in an entropic world. To a large extent, human living is matter of coping with entropy around us. We clean the room, we repair the machine, we rewind the toy, we lubricate the engine, we tune the guitar, and we reheat our cold coffee. In each instance we are adding energy to the system to lessen or postpone the effects of entropy. In our entropy-coping existence

---

[37]Charles Pinches, "Human Acts Are Moral Acts," in *Theology and Action: After Theory in Christian Ethics* (Grand Rapids: Eerdmans, 2002), 87-110. Pinches is commenting on Thomas Aquinas, *Summa Theologica*, trans. Fathers of the English Dominican Province (New York: Christian Classics, 1981), I-II.1.1.

we have an ally in the fact that systems are nested. I stand outside the mini-system of the windup toy and can add energy to that system by winding up the toy. The earth as a whole is a macrosystem that receives a constant injection of energy from outside itself, from our sun. Without the sun everything on earth would have run down long, long ago. Between the extremes of the mini- and macrosystems is where we do most of our living. At every level of system, we are busy adding energy to combat entropy.

In addition to the gift of sunshine that makes the crops grow without the farmer knowing how (Mk 4:26-27), entropy is a slow enemy and can be delayed by another phenomenon of creation. Newton tells us that something in motion tends to stay in motion. A moving object "wants to," and would, stay in motion were it not for the slowdown drag of entropy. Physicists call this tendency "momentum." One of the ways engineers are trying to store energy in the twenty-first century is by using giant flywheels. These heavy wheels are very heavy and very difficult to put into motion. But once they get up to speed, they tend to keep spinning. They won't spin forever (there is no such thing as perpetual motion), because entropy in the form of friction will eventually win the battle and the flywheel will stop. But imagine: if the tiny motors that get the flywheel up to speed were, say, solar powered, then in the nighttime the flywheel might return the favor by turning turbines to generate electricity until morning.[38]

Since human beings belong to the material world, it is not surprising to learn that there are human analogs to momentum as well as entropy. We know it is ridiculous to say that "I fell out of love while brushing my teeth!" One might *realize* that love had died during a toothbrushing. But love is like a flywheel; it takes time to get it up to full speed and then has a tendency to continue spinning. This is why breakups are so painful; the official relationship may be over, but the love flywheel continues to spin, perhaps for a long time while love winds down. And that slow grinding and winding down hurts.

What we are calling "habits" are on the side of momentum. The fact that we can form habits is an enormous gift from our Creator. We could have all

---

[38]Beacon Energy in Stephentown, NY, is currently building a 20-megawatt flywheel for energy storage. See "World's Largest Flywheel Energy Storage System," *Energy Digital*, June 1, 2011, www.energydigital.com/greentech/1775/Worlds-Largest-Flywheel-Energy-Storage-System.

been born stupid, flightless birds, like the emu![39] Thank God, *we* can *learn*! Both our bodies and our minds can retain each learned lesson (at least for a while). But not forever.

Entropy in the human world shows itself in the difficulties we face retaining our learning and keeping skills from going rusty. Entropy also affects our relationships. A close friendship that is left untended for weeks on end will slowly cease to be a close friendship. In short, "entropy" names the susceptibility of any given friendship to fall into disrepair. And therefore we must *work* at communicating, for *mis*communication is an ever-present danger.

In addition to causing friction between friends, entropy also hinders human virtue formation. Obviously, it is far easier to *fall* into a bad habit than it is to *form* a good one. That we use different terms, *fall* versus *form*, indicates that the playing field is tipped against character development. If character is to improve, it will take a regular, repeated, or even constant injection of energy. And although growth of habit means one will be slightly more disposed to see and act in the habituated way, there are no guarantees. Even the most trenchant habits have a failure rate. In fact, a habit in one set of conditions may not hold firmly if one simply changes context.[40] As a theologian I might prefer to use the term *sin* to *entropy*. The point is the same whatever the term. Entropy opposes any and every attempt we undertake to do good. But we are assisted by a long list of gifts. Taken together, we call these gifts "God's grace." It is grace that we can learn and form habits; it is grace that we are raised by others we learn to call family; it is grace that we received adequate nutrition while our newborn brains were developing; it is grace that we were educated by teachers with sound learning.

## WHAT IS MEANT BY "OUGHT"

No one is born an expert at anything. We each enter human existence as complete and utter novices. Human existence has been going on for millennia, and we, as the tiniest of players, enter the game three years before we

---

[39]A bird trainer once said that the emu was the only bird he had never been able to train. Apparently, the emu's memory lasts only about fifteen minutes. So most of the daily training time is wasted by the emu getting to know the "new" trainer—who had been coming every day for weeks on end!

[40]Alex Spiegel, "What Vietnam Taught Us About Breaking Bad Habits," *National Public Radio*, January 2, 2012, www.npr.org/sections/health-shots/2012/01/02/144431794/what-vietnam-taught-us-about-breaking-bad-habits.

are potty trained. So how do the tiny, untutored players learn what *ought* means? Well, they begin in the way they learn all spoken words, by hearing a term over and over within a particular context, the word's "home," so to speak.[41] We learn what *chair* means by hearing it spoken while we are sitting on, climbing onto, sliding off of, stubbing toes on, and losing crayons into chairs. Later we will count, fetch, and stack chairs. We may even reupholster chairs or play musical ones. We learn what *God* means by hearing and saying the word in a host of contexts: praying, thanking, singing, evangelizing, confessing, and so on. Likewise the rudimentary sense of the word *ought* (as well as *should*, *must*, and the like) is picked up by its association with ordinary daily activities:

> Sally, you *shouldn't* hit your brother.

> (*children singing*) "Everybody *ought* to go to Sunday school, Sunday school, Sunday school."

> Johnny, make your bed! You *have to* make your bed before you go out to play. You *must* make your bed this instant. You *ought to* make your bed every day.

In simplest terms, words like *should* and *ought* slowly become associated with the form of life in which we are trained to act against (some) passions and desires. A child is both malleable and conflicted. At one level it wants to pull the cat's tail, but at another level it learns that this will have painful consequences or disappoint Mom. With repetition, the child somehow transfers the desire to avoid consequences to the desire to no longer do the bad thing.[42] As the child grows, he or she encounters more nuanced occasions for hearing *should* and *ought*: "You should keep your knee over the soccer ball when kicking" and "You'd better clamp that before drilling!" Coaching tips are perceived as weightier when the (young) adult, who has sampled many practices in childhood, settles on a small handful of practices to focus on for a lifetime (say, engineering and carpentry, or piano and gardening). The "oughts" learned in the context of skill-based practices are simultaneously bound up with notion of excellence in the respective practice. The mentor assigns the "oughts" to lead the apprentice to excellence.

---

[41]Ludwig Wittgenstein, *Philosophical Investigations*, ed. G. E. M. Anscombe and Rush Rhees, trans. G. E. M. Anscombe (New York: Macmillan, 1953), §116.

[42]This transfer comes much easier to children than to adults. See chap. 1 of Herdt, *Putting on Virtue*.

So far so good. We understand that a novice who is incapable of seeing what an expert practitioner sees must be coached by means of heuristics or tips that she or he *can* understand, albeit imperfectly for now but will come to understand fully in time.[43] The novice's devotion to the ongoing task of implementing tips and training regimens is a function both of their love for the practice itself and their trust in the coach.

Once, while out walking my dog past the local tennis courts, I tried an experiment: I offered a sound coaching tip to a perfect stranger who was practicing his serve.[44] His response? "I'm just messing around; I don't want to get any better." Which translated meant, "Mind your own business!" Fair enough! He did not trust me (why should he?) and perhaps really didn't care about improving. As a result, there was nothing more for me to say. But let's suppose that instead of a hack tennis player, we encounter someone who is living badly. And when we offer tips for improvement, the hack at living says, "I'm just messing around; I don't want to live better!" Are we left tongue-tied? Or are we not rather tempted to say, "But you *ought* to want to live better!" Here the word *ought* transcends any locally chosen goals and locally administered tips. One may freely choose to pursue excellence in tennis, or not. If excellence in tennis is the goal, then what the player ought to do is obey tips issued by a qualified coach. But in the case of human living, the purpose or *telos* (i.e., that which human life is *for*) is given, not chosen. (On this theological point all four authors agree.)

We may imagine that we are free to choose a different *telos*, but we'd be mistaken to think so. The human *telos* is not ours for the choosing any more than horses can choose to fly. Sadly, the fact that the human *telos* (i.e., what human life is *for*) is not optional does not make discernment of it any easier. Nevertheless, the connection between *telos* and obligation is still fundamental even when we have only a novice's grasp of the *telos*.

Take Wilt Chamberlain for example. The former basketball star reportedly claimed, by his own reckoning, to have slept with over twenty thousand different women. I have sometimes asked one half of an ethics class to defend

[43]Billy Vaughn Koen, *Discussion of the Method: Conducting the Engineer's Approach to Problem Solving* (New York: Oxford University Press, 2003), 26-58.
[44]My shameless interruption was inspired by Wittgenstein's illustration in Rush Rhees, "Some Developments in Wittgenstein's View of Ethics," in *Discussions of Wittgenstein* (Bristol, UK: Thoemmes Press, 1996), 97.

the claim "twenty thousand is good" and the other half to defend the claim "twenty thousand is bad." After a lot of embarrassed chuckling, the reasons start to trickle in on both sides. Sooner or later someone in the class thinks to do the math: his claim equates to more than 2.3 women per day. Suddenly the penny drops: Chamberlain's sexual feat entirely displaced the possibility of his maintaining a single long-term intimate relationship. Chamberlain may have chosen this *telos* freely. But even secular students are apt to feel sorry for Chamberlain because he was mistaken. Why? Because dying without an intimate life partner is *not* what human life is for. So, one aspect of the human *telos* appears to be intimate friendship. Human life is for making and keeping friends, especially a life partner. That much specificity about the human *telos* is pretty undisputed (even if Christians sometimes disagree about what "intimate life partner" entails).

Virtue ethicists claim that if we had a clear grasp of the *telos*, moral obligation would be straightforward. We know clearly what wristwatches are *for* and therefore, we are crystal clear about how a wristwatch *ought* to perform.[45] But the human *telos* is not so straightforward. In fact, people have been arguing about what is "the Good" or "excellence" for as long as they've been able to speak. And note, since we each enter the debate as untutored novices, any single individual's grasp on the *telos* is going to be affected by the quality of our coaches and our respective moral progress to date. Left to our own devices, serving as one's own moral coach may well end disastrously. The trouble in the book of Judges—"All the people did what was right in their own eyes" (Judg 17:6; 21:25 NRSV)—does not indicate the pervasiveness of moral relativism but the poor quality of each person's moral "eyes." The untutored human being, when presented with the human *telos*, cannot see it any more clearly than his or her character allows. Fortunately, the Savior was crucified and raised again to rescue us from, among other things, our poor moral eyesight. The plan of salvation is to save us from the condition described in Psalm 18, "To the crooked, You appear as twisted."[46]

***The "oughts" of practices.*** As a first step in naming the human *telos*, virtue ethicists, including Christian virtue ethicists, examine arenas in which the

---

[45] Alasdair MacIntyre, *After Virtue: A Study in Moral Theory*, 2nd ed. (Notre Dame, IN: University of Notre Dame Press, 1984), 58.

[46] Hopefully it is obvious that humans need much more repair than simple clearing of our moral eyesight!

*telos* rises close to the surface (as we saw earlier with friendship).[47] One such arena is practice.[48] (By *practice* I mean any social enterprise through which novices are progressively trained by experts to acquire skills by means of which they can both excel and grow to appreciate the goods that all insiders recognize.) Examples of formative practices include medicine, engineering, carpentry, music, and so on. Many practices are the means by which human beings have come to cope with the contingent, entropic world.[49] Such practices are valued by the rest of us for their usefulness to society. But practitioners themselves also value the practice for goods that only an insider can appreciate. (Why else would someone play triple-A baseball, take a degree in theater, or become a theologian? Not for the wages!)

Taken together all the practices constitute the warp and weft of life in community. We cannot all be doctors, but some of us had better be doctors. We cannot all be musicians, but some of us had better be or we as a community will fall short of achieving the human Good. So goes Aristotle's argument in book one of *Nicomachean Ethics*. And the *telos* he thinks we're questing for? Aristotle is a bit vague, but at the level of community life he describes the *telos* as *eudaimonia*, a Greek term that literally means "good spirit" (perhaps as in, "There's a sweet, sweet spirit in this place") or, as it is more commonly translated, "well being." At the level of the individual, the human *telos* with respect to practice is simply to excel at the practice(s). That description remains equally vague since, as we know, understanding of the standards of excellence within a practice can be only as deep as the novice has progressed in the respective training regimen.

*The "oughts" of tradition.* A second arena in which *telos* comes close to the surface is tradition.[50] By "tradition" I mean to borrow Alasdair MacIntyre's

---

[47]Brad J. Kallenberg, "The Master Argument of MacIntyre's *After Virtue*," in *Virtues and Practices in the Christian Tradition: Christian Ethics After MacIntyre*, ed. Nancey Murphy, Brad J. Kallenberg, and Mark Thiessen Nation (Notre Dame, IN: University of Notre Dame Press, 1997), 7-29.

[48]See Alasdair MacIntyre, *After Virtue: A Study in Moral Theory*, 3rd ed. (Notre Dame, IN: University of Notre Dame Press, 2007), 187. See also Nancey Murphy, Brad J. Kallenberg, and Mark Thiessen Nation, *Virtues and Practices in the Christian Tradition: Christian Ethics After MacIntyre* (1997; repr., Notre Dame, IN: University of Notre Dame Press, 2003).

[49]The twelfth-century theologian Hugh of St. Victor is the first to see engineering, *ars mechanicus*, as part of the gracious, redemptive plan of God. For an account of Hugh's *Didiacalicon* see Kallenberg, *By Design*, chap. 10.

[50]MacIntyre, *After Virtue*, 222. MacIntyre expands this definition beginning on page 12 of the second volume in his trilogy, *Whose Justice? Which Rationality?* (Notre Dame, IN: University of Notre Dame Press, 1988).

notion of a group of people who exist across time and are identified by their ongoing (sometimes explicit, sometimes implicit) discussion about what the Good is. When the argument breaks the surface into explicit discussion, it is necessarily carried on in a particular conceptual language.[51] For example: "What is the chief *telos* of being human?" "To glorify God and enjoy Him forever" says the Westminster Confession (1646). The conceptual language all Christians share is a product both of our adherence to narratives and our engagement in practices that are distinctive to living out the gospel together. Our Christian tradition had its inception at Pentecost, when a group of people were animated by God's Spirit to rally around authoritative voices and texts (Peter's sermon, Paul's letters, the Evangelists' Gospels, the Hebrew Bible, etc.). These voices and texts launched a conversation in a peculiar Christian dialect.[52] To say the same thing differently, we as Christians cope with our environment in distinctive ways, both in our manner of speaking and by our manner of doing. We might say that the Christian tradition (in MacIntyre's sense) is about a particular pattern of communal living, one dominated by the practices of witness, worship, works of mercy, discipleship, and (Spirit-directed) discernment[53] as well as distinctive manner in executing all practices (for example, *charity* hospitals).[54] Of course, what the phrase "distinctive manner" actually means when applied to this or that practice is something we as novices must suffer to learn progressively, as we are coached by those who've been in the game longer than we.[55] Perhaps the most we can say is that our life together, the confluence of all these practices, ought to be shaped like Jesus. (More on this

---

[51]For the clearest explanation I can muster concerning the relation of tradition to ethics, see Brad J. Kallenberg, "Tradition-Based Rationality," *Colossians Forum* (blog), July 25, 2012, www.colossian forum.org/2012/07/24/glossary-tradition-based-rationality.

[52]It is a common phenomenon that any group that exercises practical reasoning together will quickly develop their own conceptual language. For an account of this among design engineers, see Louis L. Bucciarelli, "Designing, Like Language, Is a Social Process," in *Engineering Philosophy* (Delft, Netherlands: Delft University Press Satellite, 2003), 9-22. For an account of the linguistic character of Christianity, see Herbert McCabe, *Law, Love and Language* (New York: Continuum, 2004).

[53]Nancey Murphy, "Using MacIntyre's Method in Christian Ethics," in Murphy, Kallenberg, and Thiessen Nation, *Virtues and Practices*, 30-44.

[54]Andrew T. Crislip, *From Monastery to Hospital: Christian Monasticism and the Transformation of Health Care in Late Antiquity* (Ann Arbor: University of Michigan Press, 2005).

[55]And of course sometimes coaching goes awry and the practice becomes deformed. Such is the fragile nature of both the world and our virtues.

later.) Rephrased in terms of "tradition" the *telos* of human life is faithfully to extend the ongoing discussion about the Good by becoming conversant in the language called Christian and by means of assiduous participation in identity-constituting practices.

*The "oughts" of narrative.* The third arena, just as nuanced and involved as practice and tradition, is "narrative." Parents use narrative, or story, to raise their children (think of "Honest Abe," "The good Samaritan," and so on) because human beings live story-shaped lives, and it is only by means of stories that children learn how to tell what fits and what doesn't fit. This claim is a mouthful. I mean to say that ethics can't do without stories. Truth be told, even the nothing-but-the-facts scientist cannot get along without stories! Consider: the formula $F = m \cdot a$ is *not* obvious as a standalone expression. A novice might conclude that the force of love is found by multiplying the mass of an elephant by the acceleration of the economy. These misapplications are "obvious" only to those who have been trained to understand which force, which mass, and which acceleration are relevant. How was this highly specific skill of similarity recognition cultivated? Story problems, *tons* of story problems. As in physics, so too in theology. Stories are how we learn theology. For example, the divinely revealed name YHWH Yireh (roughly, "the Lord provides") is but a law sketch that calls to mind the much longer tale of Abraham that culminates in the episode of Genesis 22.

The stories or narratives Christians cling to are not all of equal weight. We learn to consider some texts "canonical" insofar as these are the yardsticks we live by. The *telos* of human living according to the narrative slice of virtue ethics, then, is *to live faithfully to the right stories*. But again, which stories trump which others for priority, and what manner of following makes for faithfulness and is something novices must be trained into?

To recap: virtue ethics is inconceivable apart from close attention to the human condition. We each begin life naked and untutored and inarticulate. To become fully human requires much training. Since we cannot train ourselves, we are—especially initially—at the mercy of those who surround us and who give us tips for going on in the right way. If all goes well, we get a jump start into the habit-formation process. Whether we form the "right" habits—aka virtues—is uncertain since our entire community is battered by a world that is entropic on both the material and social level. And rather than conclude that each must "do what he or she *can*," as the saying goes, virtue ethicists must say rather that each is constrained to "do as he or she is *inclined*," for each will do what he or she sees as fitting insofar as his or her inclinations have been previously formed by involvement as practitioners in practices, as voices in our tradition, and as living characters in canonical narratives.

Everything in the former paragraph holds also for *Christian* virtue ethics, except for the parts that are entirely different! Aristotle recognized humility as a habit, but disdained it as a *nasty* habit (i.e., vice). For followers of Jesus, humility is not a vice but a virtue of the highest order. What parts are the same and which ones differ is a matter for training. For those who are in Christ, "it is a whole new world."[56] And we can act—virtuously or viciously—only in the world we can see.[57]

## APPLICATION

For virtue ethics there is no such thing as an ethical problem "in general." Even recognizing relevant similarities between a new problem and one previously dealt with can be tricky, despite being armed with the thickest of descriptions. No, every ethical problem is unique, because each one is situated in a particular, never-to-be-repeated context. Consequently, I'm tempted to stop writing now. But I hope one final illustration will make clear the primary lens through which virtue ethicists view every ethical problem in particular. Before we can ask, What ought so-and-so do? we must first ask, What sort of people ought we be?[58]

---

[56]This is a more literal rendering of 2 Corinthians 5:17 and was a favorite emphasis of my own first and best ethics teacher, James William McClendon.

[57]Duke ethicist Stanley Hauerwas frequently repeated this dictum of Iris Murdoch's after first referring to it in Stanley Hauerwas, "The Significance of Vision: Toward an Aesthetic Ethic," in *Vision and Virtue* (1974; repr., Notre Dame, IN: University of Notre Dame Press, 1981), 30-47. Original citation from Iris Murdoch, *The Sovereignty of Good* (London: Routledge & Kegan Paul, 1970), 35-36. Other Hauerwas uses are Stanley Hauerwas, "The Demands of a Truthful Story: Ethics and the Pastoral Task," *Chicago Studies* 21, no. 1 (1982): 65-66; Stanley Hauerwas and William Willimon, *Where Resident Aliens Live: Exercises for Christian Practice* (Nashville: Abingdon, 1996), 59; and see Stanley Hauerwas, with James Fodor, "Murdochian Muddles: Can We Get Through Them If God Does Not Exist?," in *Wilderness Wanderings: Probing Twentieth-Century Theology and Philosophy* (Boulder, CO: Westview Press, 1997), 155-70.

[58]When analyzing the issue of abortion, Hauerwas proclaims that the parable of Matthew 25 requires Christians to be on the side of both the unborn child and on the side of the single, unwed

I worry about technology. I worry about the ways technology alters our form of life. And I worry that this alteration warps the kind of community Christians ought to be. The 1789 version of the Book of Common Prayer contains a morning prayer that thanks God "especially for having delivered us from the dangers of the past night."[59] The words strike us as odd. Why does the prayer sound a bit childish to us? Think about it: *we* do not give thanks with such intensity because we did not fall asleep terrified of the darkness. Why not? Because *we have electric lights*. Has the electric light forever altered the fervor of prayer? Quite possibly. We may never know that former fervor, because those who lived prior to electrification (c. 1860s) are no longer around to tell us what it was like.

Electricity has become deeply embedded in our contemporary form of life. *Embeddedness* is one mark that qualifies a technology as *politically* successful. Historian of technology John Staudenmaier observes that some technologies count as successful simply because they work well. Glide dental floss is one such product. Yet if all the dental floss in the land popped out of existence tonight at midnight, no one would notice! That is because dental floss, as well as it works, has not become successful in the sense that it fundamentally shapes our community, our *polis*. By contrast, consider asphalt. Asphalt works reasonably well, although it is ever in need of repair. But if all the asphalt in the land popped out of existence at midnight, life would screech to a halt—the loss of truckways, parking lots, suburban roads, airport tarmacs, and so on would shut down shipment of food, medical supplies, mail, building supplies, ad infinitum. Asphalt is "politically" successful because it has become deeply embedded in our corporate life.[60] We could not live for long without it. So too for electricity, the automobile, and indoor plumbing. And so too for the smartphone.

---

mother-to-be, because both the child and the mother are "the least of these." Hauerwas then proceeds to ask, What kind of community must we be to become capable of supporting both unborn children and outcast mothers? Stanley Hauerwas, "Abortion Theologically Understood," in Murphy, Kallenberg, and Thiessen Nation, *Virtue and Practices*, 221-38. See also Stanley Hauerwas, *A Community of Character* (Notre Dame, IN: University of Notre Dame Press, 1981).

[59]"Morning Prayer," in The Book of Common Prayer, Episcopal Church (London: reprinted for J. Debrett, opposite Burlington House, Piccadilly, 1789).

[60]John M. Staudenmaier, "The Politics of Successful Technologies," in *In Context: History and the History of Technology; Essays in Honor of Melvin Kranzberg*, ed. Stephen H. Sutcliffe and Robert C. Post (Bethlehem, PA: Leigh University Press, 1989), 150-71.

That the smartphone is ethically troubling can be seen from any number of angles. There is systemic injustice at the level of the device: the technology is completely dependent on "conflict minerals," such as tantalum. In the Congo, tantalum is being mined under great duress and sold to developed nations, the proceeds of which fund treacherous civil wars and genocide campaigns.[61] The devices are assembled by economic slaves, typically somewhere in Asia, whose working conditions are so poor that managers at one plant had safety nets installed outside worker dormitories to prevent suicidal workers from succeeding in jumping to their deaths.[62] Social media such as Facebook is kept attractive by relentless "content moderation." A team of over 100,000 work around the clock *in real time* preventing offensive posts (like footage of actual beheadings).[63] The two billion smartphones in operation today depend on massive data storage infrastructure, euphemistically called "the Cloud." Actually the Cloud is an enormous fleet of warehouses in remote locations, each burning as much energy as a small town.[64]

These facts are startling enough to give ethicists of any stripe grounds for objecting to the use of smartphones as morally tainted. But as a virtue ethicist I am also deeply worried about the change to our corporate form of life that social media is precipitating as the smartphone becomes "politically" successful in Staudenmaier's sense. For example, studies are beginning to show that our attention span related to words is shrinking. (This news can't help but be troubling for "people of the Book.") Young adults can easily absorb a four-hour film without any flagging of energy. But those same persons cannot read printed text for four hours, much less listen with comprehension to four hours of audio lecture. Of course, who would be dumb enough to attempt to deliver a four-hour *audio* lecture! Umm, his name was Abe Lincoln. When Stephen A. Douglas debated Lincoln in Peoria, Illinois, neither was

---

[61]See, e.g., Jessica Benko, "Making and Unmaking the Digital World," *New York Times*, June 5, 2015, www.nytimes.com/2015/06/07/magazine/making-and-unmaking-the-digital-world.html?src=xps.

[62]See, e.g., Charles Duhigg, David Barboza, with Gu Huin, "The iEconomy; In China, the Human Costs That Are Built into an iPad," *New York Times*, January 26, 2012, http://query.nytimes.com/gst/fullpage.html?res=9C02E2D71438F935A15752C0A9649D8B63.

[63]See, e.g., Adrian Chen, "The Laborers Who Keep Dick Pics and Beheadings Out of Your Facebook Feed," *Wired*, October 23, 2014, www.wired.com/2014/10/content-moderation.

[64]See, e.g., James Glanz, "Power, Pollution and the Internet," *New York Times*, September 22, 2012, www.nytimes.com/2012/09/23/technology/data-centers-waste-vast-amounts-of-energy-belying-industry-image.html?pagewanted=all&_r=0.

a candidate for major office like US Senate or president. They were both ordinary citizens debating ordinary issues on an ordinary stage. Douglas spoke
uninterrupted for *three hours*. Lincoln's reply—amicably postponed until after
dinner—was *four hours* long. No pictures, no sloganeering, just seven hours of
highly nuanced debate that presumed the listeners not only had familiarity
with historical precedents but also could handle "irony, paradox, elaborate
metaphors, fine distinctions, and the exposure of contradiction."[65] The
audience who could listen with comprehension comprised *ordinary* folk—
bankers, housewives, farmers, and delivery boys. But that was 1854.

I'm unsure whether the dropping attention spans of (some? most? all?)
individuals counts as a distortion of our form of life. So let me try to make
the case from a different vantage point. I claim that social media has become
embedded in the same manner the automobile has—namely, by making us
a covetous people.

It is common knowledge that Henry Ford's assembly line revolutionized
manufacturing. Before Ford, manufacturing was done on a small scale by
craftsmen and their guild. Since Ford, it is all assembly line all the time:
relatively unskilled laborers work like mad to join together pieces previously
machined to spec.[66] What is less commonly known is that a second revolution was precipitated a decade later by Ford's competitor at General
Motors: Alfred Sloan. Ford may have changed the process, but Sloan
changed the *telos* of manufacturing. Previously the purpose of making cars
was the car itself. But for Sloan, the "primary object" was "not just to make
cars" but "to make money."[67] Ford changed industry, but Sloan succeeded
in changing our whole culture. Instead of purchasing an artifact out of
need—as my grandparents did—my parents' generation learned to purchase
out of sheer desire. Historian Emma Rothschild explains:

> Sloan's idea for upgrading consumer preferences was that automobiles should
> change each year, and should each year become more expensive (at least relative

---

[65]Neil Postman, *Amusing Ourselves to Death: Public Discourse in the Age of Show Business* (New York:
Penguin Books, 1985), 47.
[66]Merritt Roe Smith, "Army Ordnance and the 'American System' of Manufacturing, 1815–1861,"
in *Military Enterprise and Technological Change: Perspectives on the American Experience*, ed. Merritt
Roe Smith (Cambridge, MA: MIT Press, 1985), 39-86.
[67]Emma Rothschild, *Paradise Lost: The Decline of the Auto-Industrial Age* (New York: Random
House, 1973), 38.

to the cost of production). The rate at which people trade in their old cars would grow. Each year, the new-model cars would have more improvements added on, different engines, different styling, different comfort features. Cars of the same shape and size, made from the same basic metal parts, could be sold with different equipment, at different prices. . . . Sloan wrote that "It is perfectly possible, from the engineering and manufacturing standpoint, to make two cars at not a great difference in price and weight, but considerably different in appearance."[68]

Sloan's strategy became known as "turnover buying," and the entirety of Western culture embraced it. You'll have to forgive my jaundiced eye: my grandma taught my mother how to darn socks so that they'd last forever! Yet when my socks seem even a touch saggy, the nice man in the brown truck delivers a bag from Amazon to my front door! How long are socks *supposed* to last? How long do cars last? How long do smartphones last? The turnover time of the smartphone is now *less than three years.*

Every three years we are suckered into desiring a new version of a device that pretty much does what the last one did, only costs more.[69] Seems like Sloan won that ideological battle. But our coveting isn't bounded by lust for the device itself, whether it is the iPhone 6 or the iPhone 643. Free apps like Facebook profitably sell advertising that pops up constantly on smartphone displays. While some users pat themselves on the back for resisting the lure of pop-up ads, the truth is, if pop-up ads didn't produce revenue across the targeted population, there'd be no more pop-up ads. And no more pop-up ads would mean no more Facebook.

Saint Isaac of Nineveh, a desert father from the seventh century, advised younger disciples to be wary: "The *sight* of [worldly] things, their splendor and existence kindles in [our body] a desire for them."[70] So long as these things are kept at a distance, continues Isaac, they will cause us little trouble. But if worldly things are nearby, our affections resonate with a "strong power . . .

---

[68]Ibid., 38-39.

[69]Sendhil Mullainathan, "Hold the Phone: A Big-Data Conundrum," *New York Times,* July 26, 2014, www.nytimes.com/2014/07/27/upshot/hold-the-phone-a-big-data-conundrum.html?src=xps &abt=0002&abg=0.

[70]Isaac of Nineveh, *Mystical Treatises (Ascetical Homilies)*, trans. from Bedjan's Syriac Text with an introduction and registers by A. J. Wensinck (Amsterdam: n.p., 1939), 158.

to weaken the [Christian] strugglers and turn aside their mind."[71] Smart-phone users carry all the pleasures of the world in the palm of their hands. Is this wise? And to make matters worse, each phone is colluding with giant algorithms that conspire together to automatically send especially those ads that pique this user's lusts. Again Sloan wins; we lose.

Many readers will surely be surprised by grisly details about smartphones they were unaware of. There is a kind of bliss, isn't there, in remaining unaware—when one does not know, one does not "see." When one cannot "see," one cannot act. Prior to your reading the last few pages perhaps the smartphone did not stand out glaringly as an ethical minefield but blended seamlessly with the rest of our busy lives. In fact, we purchase smartphone family plans and congratulate ourselves for having done our children a "good" turn.

In addition to arguing that virtue ethics is concerned about what we can and cannot "see," I also argued earlier that the forming of habits is a simple fact of biology. When we do not form habits intentionally, they are formed for us. A recent study of eighteen to twenty-four year olds found that 5 percent (one in twenty) check their smartphones *once every minute*. Granted, that *is* extreme. But what is the average? The average wait time between cold checks is a mere ten minutes. Theologian and ethicist Jeff Vogel suggests we may be willingly colluding with the habit of frequent checking because we live lives "in pursuit of interruption." We want "something—anything—to happen." And with a smartphone we can generate our own interruption. Thus we acquire the habit of holding ourselves in the state of perpetual readiness to be distracted.[72]

Of course, not all of our habits are fallen into. I've also argued that human beings are built to form habits *intentionally*. The earliest Christians deliberately imitated Christ (1 Pet 2:21), imitated Paul (1 Cor 11:1), imitated Paul's disciple Timothy (2 Tim 2:2), imitated faithful leaders (Heb 13:7), imitated other con-gregations (1 Thess 2:14), and so on with each successive generation. By the fourth century, Athanasius wrote about the imitation principle this way:

One cannot possibly understand the teaching of the saints unless one has a pure mind and is trying to imitate their life. . . . Anyone who wishes to

---

[71]Ibid., 159.
[72]Jeff Vogel, "Manufactured Disruption: Why We Keep Checking Our Phones," *Christian Century*, June 24, 2015, 11-12.

understand the mind of the sacred writers must first cleanse his own life, and approach the saints *by copying their deeds*.[73]

Isaac of Nineveh observes:

> If the chain of Christians-imitating-Christians can provide us with any tips it would be this: Chief among the body-shaping activities that can counter covetousness is "fasting." Although serious fasting is not in vogue today, it once was. When fasting had been practiced by Christians for nearly a millennium, it was "known to every one" that fasting "is the fountain of all good." Indeed, it was common knowledge that fasting was the "strengthening of all the virtues" and is in itself "beautiful," since fasting "naturally excites vigilance unto God."[74]

The kind of fasting our forebears spoke of is not to be confused with skipping desserts or foregoing foods we deem yucky anyway. Fasting is the regular surrender of what we need to live. Food obviously fits. But what about the smartphone? Perhaps smartphone use fits this category too. (Then again, perhaps one cannot know until one tries to give it up.)

I find myself secretly hoping that the seventh-century theologian Isaac of Nineveh is exaggerating: "For fasting is a storehouse of all virtues. And he that despises it, makes all virtues totter."[75] I, for one, would rather face the day with "a full tank" than with hunger gnawing around the edges. So I consult another of the church fathers and find that Augustine of Hippo agrees with Isaac of Nineveh: "In this world we ought *not* to love fullness."[76] What am I to do? When my druthers goes head to head with the church fathers, whose druthers should I trust? It depends: Who am I? Of which people am I a member? And what sort of people ought we to be?

---

[73]St. Athanasius, *The Incarnation of the Word of God: Being the Treatise of St. Athanasius, De Incarnatione Verbi Dei*, trans. a religious of C.S.M.V, intro. C. S. Lewis (New York: Macmillan, 1947), 96, chap. 9, §57.

[74]Isaac of Nineveh, *Mystical Treatises (Ascetical Homilies)*, 160-61.

[75]Ibid., 161.

[76]Augustine, *Exposition on the Book of Psalms*, ed. A. Cleveland Coxe, Nicene and Post-Nicene Fathers, first series (Grand Rapids:. Eerdmans, 1989), 8:259.

# A Natural Law Response

*CLAIRE BROWN PETERSON*

**While virtue ethics and natural law ethics** are not equivalent views of morality, certain versions of these theories fit together quite naturally. One indication of this potential fit is the fact that Christian proponents of both theories can point to the same philosopher—Thomas Aquinas—as their most important historical defender. I would go so far as to classify the natural law ethic that I defend and the heart of Brad Kallenberg's preferred virtue ethic as complementary rather than competing views. Both of our views emphasize both the individual and the corporate dimensions of morality. Moreover, both views insist that morality concerns itself with every aspect of our humanity, "heart and mind, emotions and will, soul and [even] *body*" (Kallenberg). And both cite the incarnation—in which the second person of the Trinity took on every aspect of our humanity and lived as we were designed to live—as evidence of this multidimensional focus.

Virtue ethics places a great deal of emphasis on the importance of character and the way in which one's moral orientation, through habit, becomes a part of oneself so that changing one's moral orientation is not a simple matter of resolving to behave in a particular way in the future. As a natural law ethicist, I can agree with all of this. *Because* of the way humans are designed, if I have a problem with callousness, I cannot simply today decide to trade in my callousness for compassion and be done with my previous moral failing. It will take time and numerous small decisions (setting new habits) for virtue to replace vice, so that I come not only to act differently but also to see the world and other people differently. If I am to live as a human is designed to live, I must remember this fact as I consider my own moral development. In other words, natural law ethics will affirm that humans are not simply designed to perform particular actions on particular occasions; we are designed to cultivate and live out the virtues.

Given all of these points of consonance that I see between Kallenberg's Christian virtue ethics and natural law ethics, I can imagine a reader of this book asking me, "Well, then why do you call yourself a natural law ethicist rather than virtue ethicist?" My answer is that I actually *do* consider myself a virtue ethicist (as well as a natural law ethicist) but that I do not consider virtue ethics a standalone ethical theory. Virtue ethics requires a context, and that context is best provided by the natural law. No full-fledged theory of ethics is complete if it merely emphasizes the importance of developing and consistently acting out of good character traits. A full-fledged ethical theory that emphasizes the virtues also needs an explanation of

1. what *makes* a particular trait a virtue (as opposed to a vice or a morally neutral trait)

2. how to flesh out specific virtues (the theory should thus give us some indication of how to delineate generosity from prodigality, for instance)

To understand the importance of providing explanations of (1) and (2), consider the fact that both Aristotle and David Hume were proponents of moral theories that could be classified as types of virtue ethics, yet both figures considered humility to be not a virtue but a *vice* (Hume called it a "monkish virtue," a designation that was not intended to be complimentary!).[1] The question for Hume, Aristotle, Kallenberg, and any other virtue ethicist is, What rationale is being used to determine whether any particular trait— and by extension humility in particular—should be classified as a virtue, a vice, or neither? If no such rationale is forthcoming, we have been given no reason for thinking that the traits that the thinker in question calls "virtues" really are morally good or that the ones she labels "vices" really are morally bad. Thus, any ethical theory that emphasizes the virtues needs to do more than simply argue for the moral significance of stable character traits and provide a list of the traits that its proponent believes to be virtues. To be complete, the theory needs also to explain *why* its proponent's preferred

[1]David Hume, *Enquiries Concerning the Human Understanding and Concerning the Principles of Morals*, ed. L. A. Selby-Bigge, 2nd ed. (Oxford: Clarendon Press, 1902), 270.

traits are virtues and *how* we should understand particular virtues. (Thus, a rationale for classifying humility as a virtue should also help us at least begin to identify the key differences between humility and low self-esteem or even just low self-regard). This is what I am getting at when I say that a complete ethical theory needs to identify a context for the virtues.

The needed context, in my opinion, is best provided by the natural law. Thus, it is *because* humans are creatures designed for dependency on one another and worship of our Creator and Sustainer that humility is a virtue. Aristotle incorrectly classifies humility as a vice because, while he recognizes that the point of the virtues is to help us achieve our *telos*, he gets human excellence wrong. Aristotle's ideal man is a godlike figure who has moved beyond any initial need he may have had for other people. He has achieved greatness, and he glories in his own greatness and despises dependency (which is not to say he despises others who are dependent on him—he is happy to help others, but dependency on others is something he will no longer tolerate for himself).[2] From this recognition of his own great self-worth, Aristotle's ideal man sets his sights on the highest of human achievements and honors.[3] Aristotle recognizes that it is a problem if a person mistakenly *believes* he has achieved this state and is worthy of great honors when he is not,[4] but for Aristotle this simply means that not everyone who thinks he is great really is. It doesn't change the fact that the ideal man who has such worth will ideally also recognize it and glory in his own independence. Aristotle thus erroneously construes independence as the ultimate fulfillment of human nature when in fact to scorn dependency (even "only" one's own dependency and not that of others) is to scorn an essential feature of human nature.

Similar comments about the necessary connection between human nature and a proper understanding of particular virtues (and vices) could be made about a host of other virtues and vices. Thus, temperance in food and drink is not a matter of consuming an arbitrary number of calories per day. Temperance is rather fundamentally about approaching food in a way that is sensitive to our physical, social, and spiritual needs as human beings. The

---

[2] Aristotle, *Nicomachean Ethics,* 2nd ed., trans. Terence Irwin (Indianapolis: Hackett, 1999), 1124b.
[3] Ibid., 1123b.
[4] Ibid., 1123b, 1124a.

physical dimension explains why a temperate caloric intake for an Olympic swimmer would typically not be temperate for the rest of us. The social and spiritual dimensions explain why *simply* attending to one's own physical health does not suffice for a temperate approach to food. If I regularly insist on serving food that I like without considering the preferences of my guests, I probably have a problem with temperance even if the food in question is perfectly healthy and I consume only moderate amounts of it. Likewise, if I refuse to even occasionally fast a couple of meals to devote myself to prayer, I probably have a problem with temperance even if my overall food intake is not so much as to be physically unhealthy.[5] The physical, social, and spiritual dimensions of human nature thus all bear importantly on what genuine temperance looks like lived out.

While some virtue ethicists have turned to the natural law to identify the context for the virtues in the ways I have sketched here, other ethicists who place great emphasis on the virtues have looked outside the natural law and human nature for a context for the virtues. Consider the following accounts of what makes a character trait a virtue that depart rather widely from natural law ethics:

David Hume: A virtue is defined as *"whatever mental action or quality gives to a spectator the pleasing sentiment of approbation;* and vice the contrary."[6]

Julia Driver: "a virtue is a character trait that produces more good (in the actual world) than not systematically."[7]

Hume thus believes that what makes a character trait a virtue is widespread human approval: we get a warm feeling of approval when we think about the virtues and a nasty feeling when we think about the vices. The problem with such a theory is not hard to spot: widespread human approval may be a generally helpful *indication* of that which is morally good, but "we feel nice when we think of generous people; we feel angry when

---

[5]Consider Jesus' complaint to the dozing disciples, "So, could you not stay awake with me one hour?" (Mt 26:40 NRSV). Jesus was not claiming that there was anything physically unhealthy about taking a nap that evening. Rather, Jesus recognized the spiritual and relational dimension of the human person and was lamenting the fact that his disciples—and especially Peter—appeared to care more about their physical comfort than their relationship with him. This is a point that applies not only to sleep but also to food.

[6]Hume, *Enquiries Concerning the Human Understanding*, 289.

[7]Julia Driver, *Uneasy Virtue* (Cambridge: Cambridge University Press, 2001), 82.

we think of cruel people" does not reveal what about generosity is so very important as to make it a virtue and what about cruelty is so problematic as to make it a vice.

Driver's account is superior to Hume's in that "generosity tends to make the world a better place" is a more enlightening and plausible explanation of generosity's status as an actual virtue than Hume's "we tend to get happy when we think about generosity." Nonetheless, Driver's thoroughgoing consequentialist account of virtue is still inferior to a natural law–based account. If we were to discover that a generally optimistic disposition and a keen wit are both personal qualities that generally produce more good consequences than bad, it would not follow that those traits are actual *virtues*. A trait can be generally valuable without being an actual moral virtue. A virtue is *necessary* for human excellence. Developing one's wit is certainly one way to manifest excellence, but a keen wit is nonetheless not a virtue, because it is not strictly necessary for human excellence. A defender of Driver's view might respond that her account specifically defines virtues as those "character traits" that systematically produce more good than bad and that, even if wit systematically makes the world a better place, it is not technically a character trait and hence not a virtue. The problem with attempting to salvage Driver's account in this way is that it works only by presupposing a particular account of human nature. Such an account is needed in order to justify classifying generosity and cruelty, on the one hand, as actual "character traits" and optimism and wit, on the other, as "mere individual personality traits." A full account of morality thus cannot avoid the fundamental ethical issue of what is truly fulfilling of human nature.

Kallenberg himself is comfortable describing his view using the language of "human excellence" and "the human *telos*." Natural law theorists are eager to use the same language. What I have been at pains to establish is that the best way to account for what truly constitutes "human excellence" is by reference to human nature and therefore the natural law. We simply cannot get clear on what makes for an excellent human without getting clear on what humans fundamentally are and how they are designed to live. A virtue ethics that relies on natural law for the theoretical underpinning needed to identify and unpack the virtues is, for this reason, a promising theory. Meanwhile, a virtue ethic that attempts to avoid committing itself to a substantive picture of what it means to be human is going to struggle to explain why our bodily, social, and spiritual dimensions (fundamental features of our humanity) each have bearing on morality and, by extension, why a number of virtues (e.g., humility, faith, temperance) really are virtues.

# A Divine Command Theory Response

*JOHN HARE*

**To a large extent I agree** with Brad Kallenberg's chapter. But I think he sometimes exaggerates, and this has the result that though I agree with the points I think he is trying to make, I cannot endorse his expression of them. This is true in various small matters. For example, Socrates in the *Crito* is not "heroically individualistic," and Aristotle in *Nicomachean Ethics*, book 1, does not mean by "self-sufficiency" independence of others. But in this reply I will focus on the larger of the questions where I disagree at least with his formulation.

One important question is about bodily habituation. Kallenberg says, "A 'good nose' for telling good from evil is not something one is born with. It is not something one can simply turn on like a light switch. Rather, skilled judgment is developed slowly by bodily training." Sometimes this is true, and it is probably true that the body should never be ignored. But often the kind of training or habituation that is required is *not* bodily. This is sometimes obscured by Paul's use of the term *flesh* to mean sinful desires. We have to practice mortifying these desires, and sometimes this is a bodily discipline, but often it has much more to do with giving priority in our minds to some good rather than some other good—for example, giving priority to finishing reading a philosophy article over watching the next episode of an enjoyable television series.

A related point is about the definition of *ought*. Sometimes, it is true, our duty goes against our inclinations. But this is not because *ought* or *duty* is *defined* this way. I agree with Kant on this, that we are born with both a predisposition to good and a propensity to evil. We do sometimes *want* to do something that we also ought to do, and the goal of sanctification is to increase the number of times this is the case. Kallenberg says about Kant that Kant thinks actions are right or wrong "regardless of outcomes." But Kallenberg also says that "every kind of ethicist will insist that *both* action and outcomes are germane to serious ethical analysis." This seems to mean, assuming that serious ethical analysis is the analysis of right and wrong, that Kant is not a kind of ethicist. But I think Kallenberg means that Kant's view is that *intended* outcomes are what is considered by the good will. We should therefore concede to Kant that sometimes the outcomes we are naturally disposed to want are good ones.

The most important area where I disagree with Kallenberg's formulation is his discussion of the human *telos*. He says, "Virtue ethicists claim that if we had a clear grasp of the *telos*, moral obligation would be straightforward." Kallenberg gives the example of Wilt Chamberlain's claim to have slept with over twenty thousand women, which averages 2.3 women per day. Surely, says Kallenberg, we agree that dying without intimate friendship (which is precluded by a schedule of such heroic promiscuity) is not what human life is for. There might be disagreement here about whether a hermit's life could be a good human life, and I will return to this. But that is not my present point. My point is that we could know the *human telos* and not know our own *individual telos*. There are deep questions here in the metaphysics of individuation that need discussing. I agree with Duns Scotus that there is an individual essence, a "haecceity" or "thisness," which distinguishes one human from another. For example, what distinguishes Socrates from Callias is not, as Aristotle thought, his matter but his "Socrateity." A biblical image for this point is given in Revelation 2:17, where we are told that God has a new name for each one of us that will be given to us in heaven, written on a white stone. If this name gives intended character, in the way Peter means "rock," and Jesus means "savior," perhaps this name on the white stone is a name for the haecceity, the character into which we are called. Scotus holds that the individual essence is a perfection of the common essence, humanity, just as the common essence is a perfection of the genus, animality. Since he thinks that we are called to be co-lovers (*condiligentes*), entering into the love that is between the three persons of the Trinity, perhaps the individual *telos* into which we are called is a unique *way* of loving God. We can see Jesus, for example, in his dealings with Jairus, the ruler of the synagogue, and the woman with the hemorrhage in Luke 8, as taking each person through the temptations to deformation particular to each one of them, so that each can get further on the path to his or her unique destination.

Much more needs to be said about all this. But my point is that there are different good ways to be human. This is true, I think, whether or not we agree with Scotus about haecceity. If it is true, then the work for ethics is not done even if agreement is reached about the common essence, humanity, and its destination. The question is still open: Which of the good human ways of living is the right way *for me*? Here is just one example. It comes out of the tension that many readers feel between the beginning of Aristotle's *Nicomachean Ethics* and the end. What is the best life for a human being? Is it the life of virtuous action, especially the virtuous action of the statesman running the city? Or is it the life of the philosopher, whose contemplation would be disturbed by the exigencies of public office? Is it the *vita activa* or the *vita contemplativa*, the life of action or the life of contemplation? Much scholarly ink has been devoted to the exegesis of Aristotle on this question, and I do not intend now to go further into Aristotle's intentions. But surely it is plausible to say that both the active life and the contemplative life are good human lives. Perhaps it is a mistake to think that there has to be a single right answer to the question about what is the best human life. Perhaps two different kinds of human lives can be equally good. But this is not to say that the two lives are equally right *for me* or for the individual human being. Christianity has a great deal to say about discerning vocation. We should be able to talk about this discernment as *ethical* work, though it is also the work of listening to God's call. Gerard Manley Hopkins has a poem influenced by Duns Scotus, in which he says, "Christ plays in ten thousand places, / Lovely in limbs, and lovely in eyes not his / To the Father through the features of men's faces."[1]

This brings up a related question. I have just said that Christianity has a great to deal to say about vocation. Kallenberg talks about "our Christian

---

[1]Gerard Manley Hopkins, "As Kingfishers Catch Fire," in *The Norton Anthology of Poetry*, ed. Margaret Ferguson, Mary Jo Salter, and Jon Stallworthy, 4th ed. (New York: Norton, 1996), 1064.

tradition," "a peculiar Christian dialect," "a particular [Christian] pattern of communal living," and "a distinctive [Christian] manner in executing all practices." But this exaggerates the extent to which Christians have agreed in the interpretation of the sacred texts. It is better to allow that there are *different* Christian traditions, Christian dialects, Christian patterns of communal living, and Christian manners of executing the practices of, for example, medicine or law or education. To say this is not to deny the authority of Scripture but to allow for a plurality of faithful interpretations. It is true that we do not want to end up with "each to his or her own taste." But the question of the acceptable limits on interpretation is *itself* an ecclesiological question to which there have been in the history of Christianity, on my view, different faithful answers. Again, here is just one example, and it is one I have already mentioned. Kallenberg extols the example of St. Isaac of Nineveh, one of the desert fathers from the seventh century, whose *Ascetical Homilies* advised against the sight of (worldly) things, "because their splendor and existence kindles in [our body] a desire for them." But some of the desert fathers, including St. Isaac, were solitaries. Saint Simeon Stylites lived *by himself* on the top of a pillar. It is not my purpose here to try to adjudicate the question of whether such a solitary life is a good human life. My point is just that this has been one Christian tradition. It is also a tradition that other Christians, like Kierkegaard, have found aberrant. Kierkegaard, indeed, was against the monastic life in general, even in community, and he was quite typical in this of a Christian tradition that came out of the Reformation. We should be careful here because talk of a single Christian tradition, like talk of a single human *telos*, not only might be but has been used for oppressive purposes.

Finally, what about smartphones? I have resisted this technology for years, but have now given in. I see many of the same dangers that Kallenberg does. I see my students constantly checking, and I worry about their declining attention spans, their declining ability to wholeheartedly attend to other people, and their susceptibility to increasingly targeted advertising. I am also aware of the exploitation in other parts of the world that makes this technology available to us, and I hate the towers spoiling beautiful landscapes all over the world. But I have given in because there are also great *goods* associated with the smartphone. I retain the hope that it is possible to have and own one well, by practicing the sort of habituation that Kallenberg himself describes in the first part of the chapter. What are the goods here, what are the required ascetical practices, and what, if anything, does all of this have to do with divine command?

First, the good thing made easier by smartphones is the access to information. Being able to find the way to my destination without running into traffic is a good thing. Being able to check my calendar with all those on my committee is a good thing. Being able to send loving messages to my relative with cancer in a way where he is able to control when he reads the message is a good thing. The situation is thus mixed. So far I have just mentioned relatively trivial goods. But the great harm to developing parts of the world is matched by correspondingly great goods. Smartphones give access to medical information where there are no good hospitals, access to market information where there is no reliable stock market, access to downloads from political allies where the regime is oppressive and controls public meetings. A blanket condemnation is an exaggeration. Second, what are the ascetical practices? I can check the machine only three times a day, and I can briefly pray before I do so. I can refrain from social media. I can leave the machine behind when I go for times of spiritual refreshment. I do not intend these as general prescriptions but as fitted to resisting my own particular temptations.

Finally, this area seems to me to fall not so much within divine command as within divine permission, a difference I discuss in my book *God's Command*.[2] Divine permissions do not create obligations. I may be permitted to own a smartphone without having an obligation to own one. God gave permission to Adam and Eve to eat all the fruit in the garden except from one tree. They had an obligation not to eat *that* fruit, but they did not have an obligation to eat all the rest. There is more to say about why we should think God permits the use of the technology for the sake of the good things it allows. I want to end with a different point, going back to the claim about individual vocation. We should be open to the possibility that God will, through the Holy Spirit, *guide* us individually about whether owning and using this technology is right for us.

---

[2]John Hare, *God's Command* (New York: Oxford University Press, 2015). See chapter 2.

# A Prophetic Ethics Response

*PETER GOODWIN HELTZEL*

**Brad Kallenberg's presentation** of virtue ethics is admirable in many ways. First, he pays close attention to the "habit-formation process" as he argues for the *intentional* cultivation of virtuous habits in the lives of Christians. Second, he argues that virtue is best formed in Christian community, a needed emphasis in our individualistic culture today. Third, he makes a persuasive case that if we do not intentionally form habits, they will be formed for us by our consumer-driven technological culture. Fourth, he demonstrates that virtue ethics is deeply rooted in the Christian tradition.

Drawing on the wisdom of St. Augustine and Isaac of Nineveh, Kallenberg suggests fasting from iPhone usage because we are becoming a "covetous people"; however, I claim that an individual abstaining from smartphone usage does not adequately encompass the fullness of Jesus' teaching on fasting in the Sermon on the Mount (Mt 5–7), a template for prophetic ethics. While I have great appreciation for Kallenberg's virtue ethic, my central concern is that the conspicuous *absence of justice* in his virtue ethic blinds him from seeing the suffering of those wronged by injustice. In the spirit of James William McClendon, Kallenberg's "first and best ethics teacher," I suggest that Kallenberg's virtue ethic can be fortified through a deeper engagement with race as a theological problem in conversation with African American theological ethics.[1]

Jesus discussed fasting in the context of three spiritual disciplines in the Sermon on the Mount: almsgiving (Mt 6:2-4), praying (Mt 6:5-15), and

---

[1]Peter J. Paris has a new anthology of African American theological ethics that should be a part of every Christian's library. Peter J. Paris, ed., with Julius Crump, *African American Theological Ethics* (Louisville, KY: Westminster Press, 2015).

fasting (Mt 6:16-18).[2] Jesus' practice of fasting was shaped by the prophet Isaiah, who critiqued ceremonial fasting that is disconnected from justice:

> Is this the kind of fast I have chosen,
>> only a day for people to humble themselves?
> Is it only for bowing one's head like a reed
>> and for lying in sackcloth and ashes?
> Is that what you call a fast,
>> a day acceptable to the LORD?
>
> Is not this the kind of fasting I have chosen:
> to loose the chains of injustice
>> and untie the cords of the yoke,
> to set the oppressed free
>> and break every yoke?
> Is it not to share your food with the hungry
>> and to provide the poor wanderer with shelter—
> when you see the naked, to clothe them,
>> and not to turn away from your own flesh and blood? (Is 58:5-7 NIV)

For Isaiah, the primary purpose of fasting is to liberate the oppressed and end injustice (Is 58:6).

With the prophetic fire of Isaiah, Jesus challenges his disciples: "And whenever you fast, do not look dismal, like the hypocrites, for they disfigure their faces" (Mt 6:16 NSRV). Mirroring the melancholy mood of their Jewish forebears during the exile, the Pharisees intentionally looked "dismal" to draw public attention to their rigorous ritual of fasting on Mondays and

---

[2]My interpretation of Jesus' Sermon on the Mount is indebted to Glen H. Stassen's hermeneutic of transformative initiatives. David P. Gushee and Glen H. Stassen, "Doing, Not Dualism: The Transforming Initiatives of the Sermon on the Mount," in *Kingdom Ethics: Following Jesus in Contemporary Context*, 2nd ed. (Grand Rapids: Eerdmans, 2016), esp. 86-106, "The 'Practices of Righteousness' (Matthew 6:1-18)," 340-43. For a chart with the fourteen triads of the Sermon on the Mount, see table 5.5 in Gushee and Stassen, *Kingdom Ethics*, 102-3. Stassen argues that the Sermon on the Mount is structured around fourteen triads that we see illustrated in his discussion of fasting (Mt 6:16-18):

| | |
|---|---|
| Traditional Righteousness | "When you fast" |
| Sinful Pattern | "Practicing righteousness for show" |
| Transformative Initiative | "But dress with joy, and your father will reward you." |

See Glen H. Stassen, "The Fourteen Triads of the Sermon on the Mount: Matthew 5:21-7:12," *Journal of Biblical Literature* 122, no. 2 (Summer 2003): 267-308.

Thursdays (Lk 18:12).[3] In contrast, Jesus calls his disciples to anoint themselves with the oil of joyful justice, the heart of his teaching of the kingdom of God (Mt 6:17-18, 33).[4]

Instead of seeking public recognition, Jesus' disciples are called to imitate his example of fasting and praying in private, deepening their intimacy with God, whose Spirit empowers them to "do alms" *with* and *for* the poor.[5] Proclaiming the poor as "blessed" (Mt 5:3), Jesus says, "Blessed are those who hunger and thirst for righteousness, for they will be filled" (Mt 5:6 NSRV).[6]

In the spirit of this fourth beatitude, prophetic ethics sees fasting as a pathway to awaken a hunger and thirst for the liberating love and community-restoring justice of the God of justice (Is 61:8; Ps 37:28). To consider fasting only in order to cultivate personal virtue misunderstands the *political dimension* of fasting. From fasting in prison to fasting in prayer vigils during

---

[3]In fasting twice a week, the Pharisees went beyond the law, which only required fasting on the Day of Atonement (Lev 16:29; Acts 27:9). The Pharisees sought to secure their class status in the community through "disfiguring their faces" for public recognition, while not humbly recognizing the redemptive singularity of the promised Messiah, whose "appearance was so disfigured beyond that of any human being" (Is 52:14 NIV). I am indebted to Otto Betz, who explores the resonate echoes of Isaiah's prophecy in Jesus' teaching on the Sermon on the Mount. See Otto Betz, "Jesus and Isaiah 53," in *Jesus and the Suffering Servant: Isaiah 53 and Christian Origins*, ed. William H. Bellinger Jr. and William R. Farmer (Harrisburg, PA: Trinity International Press, 1998), 70-88, esp. 80-81.

[4]Baptized in the Jordan River by John the Baptist, Jesus himself was anointed by the Holy Spirit to bring forth justice to the nations (Lk 3:21-22; Mt 12:18). The life and messianic ministry of Jesus of Nazareth fulfill three prophecies of Isaiah, who promised a coming Spirit-bearer of justice (Is 11:1-16; 42:1-4; 61:1-11). German theologian Michael Welker writes, "The power and authority of the person who bears God's Spirit lie in the fact that this person establishes *justice, mercy and knowledge of God and gives them universal extension.*" See Welker's discussion of the Hebrew prophets and Jesus as Spirit-bearers for justice in Michael Welker, "The Promised Spirit of Justice and Peace," in *God the Spirit*, trans. John F. Hoffmeyer (Minneapolis: Fortress Press, 1994), 109ff. I discuss God's Spirit as the Holy Spirit of justice in "The Holy Spirit of Justice," in *The Justice Project*, ed. Brian McClaren, Elisa Padilla, and Ashley Bunting Seeber (Grand Rapids: Baker Academic, 2009), 44-50. On the prophetic charism of John the Baptist see Walter Wink, *John the Baptist in the Gospel Tradition* (Cambridge: Cambridge University Press, 1968).

[5]I appreciate R. V. G. Tasker's interpretation of almsgiving as "doing alms" as it emphasizes prophetic action instead of paternalistic benevolence. R. V. G. Tasker, *St. Matthew: An Introduction and Commentary* (Grand Rapids: Eerdmans, 1961), 71.

[6]David P. Gushee and Glen H. Stassen offer a prophetic amplification of the fourth beatitude: "*Blessed are those who hunger and thirst for a justice that delivers and restores to covenant community, for God is a God who brings such justice.*" Gushee and Stassen, *Kingdom Ethics*, 32. "An ethics of virtue must be subordinated to God's grace and deliverance, justice and righteousness, peace and presence," write Gushee and Stassen (p. 27). Gushee and Stassen accept virtue ethics as a component of their kingdom ethic. In contrast to the classical virtues of fifth-century-BCE Greece, biblical virtues are connected to the Jewish justice-centered prophetic vision that we see embodied in the Beatitudes in Jesus' Sermon on the Mount (Mt 5:1-12). See Gushee and Stassen, "Blessed Are You: Virtues of Kingdom People," in ibid., 21-42.

nonviolent direct action, Dr. Martin Luther King Jr. saw fasting as both a spiritual and political practice.[7]

While calling for the cultivation of virtues, Kallenberg does not clearly delineate which virtues Christians are called to cultivate, nor does he clarify the difference and relationship between the biblical virtues (e.g., faith, hope, and love) and the four traditional Greek virtues (courage, justice, temperance, and wisdom).[8] While offering an extensive discussion of the virtue of wisdom (*phronēsis*), Kallenberg's failure to mention the virtue of justice (*dikaiosynē*) is deeply disturbing.[9] Without justice as a moral norm, virtue ethics is susceptible to becoming a theological grammar of whiteness—the social power and privilege that white people gain through active participation in sinful social structures that mistreat and exclude people of color.[10]

While Kallenberg offers an insightful analysis of our moral habits and their physical embodiment in a technological world, our bodies are also drawn into a racial world. The public, almost ritualistic, nature of lynchings

---

[7]Fasting in jail was routine for Martin Luther King Jr., who was often imprisoned for his justice-centered activism. Solitary confinement offered him the ideal time to fast, meditate, and pray. In this sense King transformed jail cells into sacred space, where he would deepen his relationship with God and meditate on the next steps in the faith-rooted movement for justice. However, Dr. King never viewed fasting as simply a spiritual practice; it was also a prophetic *political practice*, identifying with the oppressed who hungered for justice (Mt 5:6; 25:42). Fasting was also deployed by Dr. King in community prayer vigils as a strategy of nonviolent direct action. Fasting was a powerful practice of *prayer*, building *embodied solidarity* among the activists who sought spiritual identification with those who they were advocating through a *faith-rooted organizing* campaign. In the context of prayer vigils for justice, fasting wove together the three strands of prophetic ethics: faith-rooted organizing, embodied solidarity, and prayerful presence (Mic 6:8). Dr. King's wife, Coretta, discusses his fasting in jail in Coretta Scott King, *My Life with Martin Luther King, Jr.* (New York: Henry Holt, 1983), 189, 211.

[8]Kallenberg is aware of the problem of the diversity of lists of virtue within the virtue ethics tradition, which he notes in "Mastering the Argument of MacIntyre's *After Virtue*," in *Virtues and Practices in the Christian Tradition: Christian Ethics After MacIntyre*, ed. Nancey Murphy, Brad J. Kallenberg, and Mark Thiessen Nation (Harrisburg, PA: Trinity International Press, 1997), 20.

[9]The recovery of a virtue ethics after Alisdair MacIntyre and Stanley Hauerwas has too often been juxtaposed with a justice-centered prophetic ethic. While seeking justice is central to Jesus' teaching of the kingdom of God and is central to the prophetic Baptist vision of Dr. Martin Luther King Jr., Stanley Hauerwas and many virtue ethicists in his wake have actively avoided discussing justice, so they can take a pass on difficult ethical issues like racism. See Bruce Ellis Benson, Malinda Elizabeth Berry, and Peter Goodwin Heltzel, "Stanley Hauerwas, Martin Luther King, Jr., and the Quest for Justice," in *Prophetic Evangelicals* (Grand Rapids: Eerdmans, 2012), 20-30.

[10]For a challenging introduction to the moral crisis of whiteness and what we can do about it, see Jennifer Harvey, *Dear White Christians* (Grand Rapids: Eerdmans, 1994).

unveils the racialization of whites in post–Civil War America.[11] What kind of formation led to the participation of men, women, and children in the public torture and burning of black Americans? Put differently, how does virtue ethics account for the implicit but essential ways our culture of whiteness affects the ways we answer the question "ought"? Or as the Killers pose the question in their song "Human": "Are we human or are we dancer?"

Race matters in Christian ethics. Race can be considered as a kind of technology that shapes what we see in the world and determines who remains unseen and why. Like technology, race constrains the mobility of bodies through a *classification* of color, *concealing* its relationship to centers of institutional power and *distracting* us from its covert operation. Since every institution in the United States was founded to legitimate and perpetuate white male power and privilege, faithful Christians should seek to understand how social structures benefit whites over people of color, where those structures came from, and how they are currently being administered.[12]

James William McClendon offers some important insights for a justice-centered virtue ethic that prophetically engages racism. McClendon uses the metaphor of a three-corded rope to describe the task of Christian ethics, focusing on three spheres of Christian existence: the *body*, the *social*, and the *resurrection* strands.[13] Raised in Louisiana, McClendon had a conscience sensitive to racial injustice. Justin Randall Phillips writes, "McClendon embodies the practice of thinking deeply about his own formation, moving beyond the shame of his segregated upbringing, and incorporating the

---

[11]From 1880 to 1940, white Christians lynched nearly five thousand black women and men in the United States. White Christians burned black bodies, including often dismembering their bodies and bones, and using their bones as keepsakes of the moment, all without an acknowledgement of the moral contradiction in the brutal act of lynching. Theologian James Cone argues that only through an honest confrontation with the lynching tree can American Christians authentically articulate and embody a theology of the cross. James Cone, *The Cross and the Lynching Tree* (Maryknoll, NY: Orbis, 2011).

[12]Three important recent works that analyze race as a theological problem are Brian Bantum, *The Death of Race: Building a New Christianity in a Racial World* (Minneapolis: Fortress Press, 2016); J. Kameron Carter, *Race: A Theological Account* (Oxford: Oxford University Press, 2008); and Willie James Jennings, *The Christian Imagination: Theology and the Origins of Race* (New Haven, CT: Yale University Press, 2010). I am grateful to Brian Bantum's suggestion of considering race as a form of technology within the modern West.

[13]See James William McClendon Jr., *Systematic Theology*, vol. 1, *Ethics*, 2nd ed. (Waco, TX: Baylor University Press, 2012), 49ff; James William McClendon Jr., "Three Strands of Christian Ethics," *Journal of Religious Ethics* 6 (Spring 1978): 54-80.

voices of prominent African Americans throughout his academic work."[14] McClendon starts his *Ethics* with a discussion of black bodies, affirming the inherent worth and dignity of African Americans and God's *presence* among them, even amid the scourge of slavery and segregation.[15] McClendon is concerned not only about the moral status of black bodies but lifts up the prophetic leadership of black faith leaders like Dr. King as moral exemplars who we are to emulate.[16] Dr. King found in the Old Testament two elements of prophetic faith: "man's own role and the role of the God of history, held together in productive tension . . . humanity that must act, and God who is acting."[17] In the spirit of Dr. King, McClendon argues that the *prophetic* "is *the* way—of Christian existence itself."[18]

Dr. King preached that "whenever Christianity has remained true to its prophetic mission, it has taken a deep interest in social justice. Whenever it has fallen short at this point, it has brought about disastrous consequences."[19] Within the virtue ethics tradition, Peter Paris has highlighted the importance of the virtue of justice coupled with a commitment to dismantle institutional racism.[20] The virtue of *justice* was central to the moral vision of the black church whose "primary mission has always been that of calling the nation to effect racial equality and justice (that is, the kinship of all peoples) within its border."[21] Starting with the wronged,[22] prophetic ethics seeks to

---

[14]Justin Randall Phillips, "Lord, When Did We See You? The Ethical Vision of White, Progressive Baptists in the South During the Civil Rights Movement" (PhD diss., Fuller Theological Seminary, 2013), 115.

[15]McClendon, "Black Religion as Embodied Ethics," in *Systematic Theology*, 1:86-90.

[16]James William McClendon Jr., "The Religion of Martin Luther King, Jr.," *Biography as Theology: How Life Stories Can Remake Today's Theology* (Philadelphia: Trinity Press International, 1990), 47-66.

[17]Ibid., 65.

[18]McClendon, *Systematic Theology*, 1:33.

[19]Martin Luther King Jr., "Social Ethics (Psalms)," in *Papers of Martin Luther King, Jr.,* vol. 2, *Rediscovering Precious Values, July 1951-November 1955,* ed. Clayborne Carson, Ralph E. Luker, Penny A. Russell, and Pete Holloron (Berkeley: University of California Press, 1994), 167.

[20]Paris identifies six African and African American moral virtues: beneficence, forbearance, practical wisdom, improvisation, forgiveness, and justice. Peter J. Paris, *The Spirituality of African Peoples: The Search for a Common Moral Discourse* (Minneapolis: Fortress, 1995), 130ff.

[21]Peter J. Paris, *The Social Teaching of the Black Churches* (Philadelphia: Fortress, 1985), 134.

[22]Nicholas P. Wolterstorff's prophetic ethic starts with the wronged because of his experiences with wronged people, including blacks and coloreds, in Potschefstroom, South Africa, and Palestinians in West Chicago, Illinois. Wolterstorff writes, "Not only was I emotionally moved, I felt that I had been issued a call from God to speak up for these wronged people." Nicholas Wolterstorff, "Two Awakenings," in *Journey Toward Justice: Personal Encounters in the Global South* (Grand Rapids: Baker Academic, 2013), 9.

right the wrongs through faith-rooted organizing guided by the moral norms of love *and* justice.[23]

When considering an ethical problem like the iPhone, prophetic ethics brings an anti-racist socioeconomic analysis and concrete organizing tools. Since Apple Computer is engaged in mining for "conflict minerals" in the Congo, we need to understand the function of racism in the colonization of West Africa in relation to the trans-Atlantic slave trade. Since Chinese workers are committing suicide in factories with low wages and unsafe work conditions, we need a systemic social and economic analysis to understand the alienation of labor and the sources of the financial exploitation. Communal *discernment* unveils "the lie" in Apple's practice and marketing vision.[24] Once we understand how "the lie" is used to justify systemic injustice, we can then follow the leadership of Congolese and Chinese workers in developing a faith-rooted organizing strategy with an on-the-ground strategy (e.g., unionizing the Congolese and Chinese workers) and a digital organizing strategy (e.g., creating an online petition that raises the issues of injustices and is presented to CEO Tim Cook at the next Apple shareholders meeting). I'm ready to fast from my iPhone if Kallenberg is willing to join in embodied solidarity with Congolese and Chinese workers in a campaign for worker justice that has a concrete "ask" for Tim Cook.

Fasting from our iPhones is a start, but our fasting should be connected to the work of justice in solidarity with those who have been wronged who we are fighting for. Fasting from one's smartphone may help cultivate one's personal piety; however, prophetic ethics reminds virtue ethics that personal piety alone is unable to materialize God's justice in the world.

---

[23]Alexia Salvatierra and I introduce the principles and practices of faith-rooted organizing in our book *Faith-Rooted Organizing: Mobilizing the Church in Service to the World* (Downers Grove, IL: InterVarsity Press, 2014). The cry for justice of actual oppressed people is the starting place for prophetic ethics. Salvatierra and I discuss the priority of the perspective of the poor in "Our Starting Place, the Call of the Poor," in ibid., 42-64.

[24]See Alexia Salvatierra and Peter Goodwin Heltzel, "The Lie, the Divine Truth and the Issue that Reveals," ibid., 66-67. Alexia Salvatierra and I write, "The discernment process begins with the identification of a lie that is believed by the majority of the people in a given society at a given historical moment. This lie is commonly used to justify systemic injustice and evil. In the civil rights movement, a number of leaders determined that this big lie was the belief that some people were worth more than others. Among other things, this lie has been used to justify slavery, in the assumption that some people were born to serve and others to be served" (ibid., 66).

# 2

# Natural Law

*CLAIRE BROWN PETERSON*

**Natural law ethics** is the theory that morality is rooted in central truths about who we are as human beings.[1] By "morality" or "ethics" I don't mean what we might call "societal expectations" or "culturally accepted morality." Natural law ethics does have something to say about why societies tend to praise and expect some behaviors and attitudes while criticizing and condemning others, but the primary concern of natural law ethics is not what societies think. Rather, natural law ethics, like the other theories in this book, is fundamentally a theory of what we might call true morality—how human beings really ought to live and relate to one another (and to God and other creatures), something individuals and even whole societies can get wrong. According to natural law ethics, the answer to the question of how we ought to live (true morality) is rooted in facts about the sort of creature we are, what God created when he created human beings.

How might morality be "rooted in" facts about "the sort of creature we are"? In the first place, morality is made *possible* by the fact that human beings are creatures capable of recognizing things as good and enjoying freedom of the will regarding if and how we pursue these goods. If one takes away these abilities, it no longer makes sense to say that human beings are

---

[1]The natural law tradition in ethics is extensive, finding its roots in Aristotle and the Stoics and including numerous adherents in both the medieval and modern periods. Identifying a core conception of morality that is endorsed by all of these adherents is probably impossible. Thomas Aquinas is usually considered the central figure in the natural law tradition, and his influence is obvious in the theory of natural law that I am putting forth. Still, this paper is not an exercise in Thomistic exegesis. My main purpose is simply to put forward a general theory of morality that is philosophically defensible, true to Christianity, and obviously at home within the natural law tradition.

obligated to live in particular ways. In the second place, the very *content* of
ethics (how we ought to live) is largely determined by facts about who we
are: the specific needs, limitations, capabilities, and purposes we have as
human beings. C. S. Lewis makes this point in *Mere Christianity* when he
states, "In reality, moral rules are directions for running the human
machine."[2] Lewis calls this set of instructions various things: "the Law of
Human Nature," "the Law of Nature," and the "Law or Rule of fair play or
decent behavior."[3] Following the natural law tradition of ethics, I will be
calling it "the natural law." There are certain things all humans need simply
to survive, others that we need to thrive (individually or as communities),
and others that we need to exercise our intended roles vis-à-vis one another,
the creation, and God. But these "things we need" are not limited to specific
objects such as food, water, and oxygen. Certain ways of ordering our own
thoughts, behaviors, and desires are also necessary if creatures like us are to
thrive and fulfill our diverse roles in God's kingdom. These necessary "ways
of ordering" our lives furnish the content of ethics. Love, forgiveness, mutual
respect, and empathy (all elements of the natural law) are not built into our
DNA in the sense that these things come easily to us, but love, forgiveness,
mutual respect, and empathy are essential to our full-fledged development
individually and as communities. Their absence or diminishment in our lives
is no mere absence. Their absence is rather an actual privation: a lack of
something that ought to be, and this is why the natural law theorist will
include love, forgiveness, mutual respect, and empathy among the many
elements of the natural law.

In spelling out just how the natural law turns out to be "directions for
running the human machine," Lewis uses the analogy of a fleet of ships. If
the fleet is to succeed, three things are required: the ships need to be cooperating with one another (and not, say, running into one another); each
individual ship needs to be in proper working order; and the ships need to
be on course to the correct destination.[4] Humans, too, have needs on the
individual, social, and transcendent levels; the natural law indicates how we
are designed to operate on each of these levels so we can thrive as the beings

---

[2] C. S. Lewis, *Mere Christianity* (New York: HarperSanFrancisco, 2001), 69.
[3] Ibid., 4, 5, 6, respectively.
[4] Ibid., 71-72.

God created us to be. As Lewis notes, the social level is the most obvious
level at which morality dictates how we must behave if we are to live well:
we can all see that none of us will succeed in a society in which we are per-
petually at odds with one another.[5] But natural law ethics agrees with
Lewis that "not hurting" one another is neither the whole of ethics nor the
whole of the question of whether we are living well, just as the fleet of ships
can hardly be assumed to be well-functioning simply because the boats
aren't running into one another.[6]

Given that the purpose and justification of the natural law is to enable
human beings to fulfill all of their God-given purposes, natural law has
historically been thought of as an element of divine providence.[7] "Providence" or "divine providence" simply refers to God's way of working out
his purposes in the world. According to the natural law tradition, when it
comes to most parts of creation, God's way of working out his purposes
is largely deterministic. God tells the sea, "Thus far shall you come, and
no farther" (Job 38:11), and the ant is governed not by its own conscious
reason but by instinct.[8] God could have created us so that we behave like
ants—instinctively, easily, nonreflectively cooperating with one another to
create the human analogs of ant hills (engineering marvels, to be sure,
even if not reflectively designed by the ant!). But that is not what God
does with us.

In the case of humans, God does have a plan of how we are to live, but
God has not created us so that we automatically follow that plan. What
is more, God's plan for us is more open-ended than his plan for the sea
or the ant in the sense that part of the plan itself involves humans using
their creative and reflective powers to form their lives and societies within
very complex and diverse environments. If you want an image of this sort
of directed openness, consider the way Ilúvatar ("the One," the creator)
commissions the Ainur ("the Holy Ones," the "offspring of [Ilúvatar's]
thought") to (sub)compose the music that will become a world in J. R. R.
Tolkien's *The Silmarillion*:

---

[5]Ibid., 72-73.
[6]Ibid., 73.
[7]See Thomas Aquinas, *Summa Theologica* I-II.91.2, 2nd rev. ed., trans. Fathers of the English Dominican Province (New York: Benzinger, 2008), available at www.newadvent.org/summa.
[8]All Scripture references in this chapter will use the New Revised Standard Version.

And it came to pass that Ilúvatar called together all the Ainur and declared to them a mighty theme, unfolding to them things greater and more wonderful that he had yet revealed; and the glory of its beginning and the splendor of its end amazed the Ainur, so that they bowed before Ilúvatar and were silent.

Then Ilúvatar said to them: "Of the theme that I have declared to you, I will now that ye make in harmony together a Great Music. And since I have kindled you with the Flame imperishable, ye shall show forth your powers in adorning this theme, each with his own thoughts and devices, if he will. But I will sit and hearken, and be glad that through you great beauty has been wakened into song."[9]

According to a natural law conception of ethics, God created human nature with a particular "theme" in mind for us and for the universe. The specificity of the theme means that not just any music we might choose to make with our bodies, minds, and hearts will do. Nonetheless, we are given a great deal of freedom—and even called to exercise such freedom—in using our own powers (some generally human, others more individual) to "adorn" this theme. The theme is thus intended to allow for improvisation. Our capacities for creativity can be used rebelliously, but to use creativity is not inherently rebellious. Indeed, to fail to use one's creative powers in nonexplicitly specified ways may itself be a kind of rebellion, a way one "scorns the good gifts of a loving God."[10] What all of this means is that divine providence looks very different in the lives of creatures like us who have been given the tremendous (if admittedly limited) creative and reflective capacities that we have than it does in creatures lacking the sort of free agency humans have been given. The natural law doesn't specify our every action, because that is not how creatures like us were designed to live.

This point about theme and variation applies not only at the level of how individuals are to lead their individual lives but also at the level of how societies ought to function. More than one way of organizing society can be honoring of human nature.[11] Still, not just any way of organizing society is compatible with natural law. A society's total structure must honor basic

---

[9]J. R. R. Tolkien, *The Silmarillion*, 2nd ed. (New York: Houghton Mifflin, 2001), 15.

[10]I take this phrase from Mark Noll, *The Scandal of the Evangelical Mind* (Grand Rapids: Eerdmans, 1994), 23.

[11]For more on this point, see Jean Porter, *Nature as Reason: A Thomistic Theory of the Natural Law* (Grand Rapids: Eerdmans, 2005), 333-42.

facts of human nature. There is a reason that depriving an infant of physical touch does long-term damage to that child. There is a reason that emotional abuse cannot be undone by simply reminding victims that, unlike "sticks and stones," words don't break bones. The reasons have to do with how we are built. We are not built to be hermits; we are built for relationship. We are not built to be immune to the power of language; we are built to harness the power of language in ways that build one another up, a difficult lesson if ever there was (Jas 3:1-12)! We are built so that we crave purpose and relationship with God. Significantly, there are many ways to structure a society that are cognizant of our very real and diverse human needs, but social movements and individual actions that ignore who we are and what we need to flourish violate the natural law and undermine their own aims.

## HUMAN NATURE AND HUMAN PURPOSES

I have been emphasizing that an important commitment of natural law ethics is that the very content of ethics—how God created us to live—is intricately connected to the sort of creature we are. Natural law theorists often make this point by saying that ethics is grounded in something they call "human nature." However, the phrase "human nature" is today used in many different ways, and it is important to get clear on what natural law theorists mean by "human nature" when they say that ethics is rightly grounded in human nature. The short answer is that by "human nature" natural law theorists roughly mean "the perfect definition of a human being."

Note that natural law theorists do *not* mean by "human nature" what we often mean today when we make a comment such as "It's no surprise that he exaggerated his accomplishments; that's just human nature." When we make comments like this, we are treating human nature as equivalent to sin nature or selfishness, a perversion that *feels* normal and even natural to us because we live in the fallen world that we do. But it is worth pointing out that *human nature* and *sin nature* are not equivalent to one another, that a person can be fully human and thus have a complete human nature without following or even having sin nature. Indeed, this was true of the first Adam up until his fall and of the second Adam (Jesus) all throughout his life. The first humans were fully human all the way up until the time that they sinned, and the sinless Jesus was (and is) fully human his entire life on earth and afterward. Thus, sinful nature and selfishness are not part of the perfect definition of a human being. Sinfulness and selfishness are not required for full-fledged humanity. This truth highlights the problem with saying that human beings are inherently sinful. Sinfulness and selfishness *are* serious afflictions to which all fallen humans are subject, but sin does not give us our very definition. What is rather the case is that our selfish tendencies are so pervasive and powerful that we forget that the sin nature we have inherited is actually a *perversion of* human nature rather than *divinely created human nature* itself. The divinely created human nature—what God created us to be—grounds the content of right living, according the natural law ethics, not sin nature!

To be sure, even though we know that human nature and sin nature are not the same things, it can be hard to tease out the difference between the two, given that our first lessons in "who humans are" come from looking at the imperfect human beings around us. Exposure to such consistent selfishness can cause quite a bit of confusion. J. Budziszewski uses the analogy of a broken foot to explain the implications for natural law:

> The Fall does not deprive us of our nature—a broken foot still has the nature of a foot—but our nature is not in its intended condition. For natural law, this is no insignificant consideration. If we had never seen healthy feet, it might have taken us a long time to discover that broken feet were broken.... In the meantime we might have taken their broken condition as normative. Even if we grasped that something was wrong with our feet, we might have misunderstood what it was. We might have thought that feet are bad by nature, or that they are good but corrupted by shoes. Apart from revelation we make the same mistakes about human nature.[12]

Thus, even though how we are to live is based on who we are as human beings, and even though all human beings have some sense of how we regularly deviate from how we really ought to live (thus, the natural law is, at least to some extent, "written on the hearts" of all of us [see Rom 2:14-16]), sin makes much of this hard to recognize. We know something is wrong, but our diagnosis can quite widely miss the mark. This is why we

---

[12]J. Budziszewski, *The Line Through the Heart: Natural Law as Fact, Theory, and Sign of Contradiction* (Wilmington, DE: ISI Books, 2009), 53.

need what is known as special revelation in addition to general revelation.[13] "General revelation" refers to the knowledge that God has made available to almost all humans. It includes the knowledge we get when we look out into the ordered natural world around us, but it also includes the knowledge we get when we look inward and feel the gnawing of our consciences when, for instance, we make a cruel remark about a younger sibling. "Special revelation" refers to knowledge that God has communicated at a specific time and place. For Christians, the central instance of special revelation is the Bible, the Christian Scriptures. Budziszewski's point is that as fallen human beings we can no longer look around ourselves or in ourselves to get the full picture of who we were created to be. Scripture is needed because it clarifies what sin obscures.

In what follows, I will be using the term *human nature* to refer not to sin nature (real though that is) but to something even more fundamental that all human beings share. When the second person of the Trinity (the Son) became incarnate, he took on human nature and lived in a way that showed us the perfect fulfillment of human nature. Thus, as I am using the term, *human nature* is something common to all humans, including Christ, but it is something that only Christ has perfectly honored and lived out.

With this vocabulary in mind, I will restate the two claims about natural law that I made at the beginning of this chapter. First, the possibility of ethics is rooted in human nature (specifically, the fact that we are creatures capable of cooperation, discernment, rationality, will, and so forth). Second, the very content of ethics is rooted in human nature. The first statement is a familiar one and amounts to the claim that certain facts about the way humans were created explain why morality makes sense for us but not for (at least most) other animals. A frog or a lion may hurt someone, but neither the frog nor the lion should be blamed for what it does. This is the case because frogs and lions do not have all the capacities needed to function as moral agents. The second statement, though, is less familiar. Why should facts about human nature, including the *imago Dei* (one fundamental element of our human nature), our particular physical makeup (another element of our human nature), and our social and emotional forms of life (yet

---

[13]See Aquinas, *Summa Theologica* I-II.91.4.

other elements of our human nature) have implications for how we ought to live? I stated earlier that human nature, as I will be using the term, means "the perfect definition of what it means to be a human," but I also keep talking about how our human nature is something we ought to live out and fulfill. But, you might ask, how can we fulfill or live out our definition? Isn't a definition just a *fact* about what we are rather than a *set of values* to which we should try to conform?[14]

According to natural law theorists, the facts about what we are and value claims about how we should behave are more tightly connected than they may at first appear.[15] One way of drawing this connection we have already seen: what humans are determines what they need to flourish, and needs have value implications. When a psychologist claims that because young (human) children need physical stimulation for their developing brains and cannot easily connect media content with the three-dimensional world, and that solo viewing of television is not good *for* them and should be avoided, the psychologist is tapping into this fact-value connection.[16] Another way that who we are informs how we should live focuses less on what is good for us and more on what is fitting of us. A friend of mine once suggested the following slightly silly but easily grasped example. Imagine a nanny for a royal family who says to the young prince and princess who have been placed in her charge, "My dears, *royal* children do not pick their noses!" If the nanny takes the time to say this, you can bet that some royal child is in the process of proving her wrong by doing exactly what the statement, taken at face value, claims royal children don't do. So, why might the nanny make such a statement? The answer, of course, is that the nanny is tying the children's identity (children of royalty) to a set of values. It's a way of telling the children to live up to who they are. They will be royal children whatever

---

[14]This question is an application of David Hume's complaint that no rational argument may deduce what *ought* to be (value) from what *is* (fact). David Hume, *A Treatise of Human Nature*, bk. 3, pt. 1, sec. 1.

[15]A more detailed discussion of how evaluative facts are presupposed by ordinary, naturalistic descriptions of human beings can be found in Philippa Foot, *Natural Goodness* (Oxford: Clarendon Press, 2001); and Michael Thompson, *Life and Action: Elementary Structures of Practice and Practical Thought* (Cambridge, MA: Harvard University Press, 2008).

[16]The American Academy of Pediatrics recommends against media use for children under eighteen to twenty-four months and further recommends only selective, limited media use facilitated by a caregiver for children two to five years. "Media and Young Minds: Council on Communications and Media," *Pediatrics* 138 (November 2016), DOI:10.1542/peds.2016-2591.

manners they adopt, but there are certain ways they can act that are befitting of their royal identity and others that are not. According to natural law theory, similarly, we don't cease to be human if we violate the natural law, but certain ways of living are befitting of a creature made in the image of God, and other ways of living are not. Natural law theory goes further still and insists that the ways of living that are befitting of us are also good for us, and not just individually but on a cosmic scale.

## FROM HUMAN NATURE TO NATURAL LAW

So far, much of what I have said about the natural law and human nature has been framed at a fairly general level: we were created with specific—but not exhaustively specific—purposes; those purposes are part of who we are; the natural law tells us how creatures like us must live if we are to achieve those purposes; and to live in this way is to both glory in who we (really) are and to glorify God by playing the role he has for us in creation. I now turn to getting more specific about human beings and their purposes and how those purposes connect to the natural law.

A large set of human purposes concerns enjoyment of the diverse goods of human life that almost everyone can recognize. Such goods include friendship, humor, scientific understanding, storytelling, artistic achievement, engineering, gardening, good food, romance, and athletic achievement. These goods of human life point to an important way in which who we are has something to say about how we should live: humans are created to pursue and enjoy these goods and help one another do the same. Following the natural law helps us to do so at the social level in ways that almost all humans, religious and nonreligious, Christian and non-Christian, can recognize. Trust, trustworthiness, generosity, gratitude, empathy, patience, self-control, and forgiveness are essential for societies to flourish with respect to the apparently "secular" human goods previously listed. This is true both because humans have a difficult time achieving many of these goods of human life when they are proactively hurting one another but also because we are so dependent on one another that "not hurting" one another isn't enough. To achieve the ordinary goods of human life, we need one another's active cooperation and respect. This mutual dependency isn't a fact about human beings that is to be lamented, but it is one that must be accepted,

even embraced, if we are to live well. And because we are so dependent on
one another, human beings need the natural law to guide their behavior with
respect to one another.

We also need the natural law to guide our lives at the individual level. A
lack of self-control and empathy is obviously bad for society, but it is also
bad for the individual insofar as it cuts the individual off from a whole range
of the goods of human life. To be sure, even a selfish, hot-tempered, lazy
person can enjoy many good things in life (good food, simple pleasures, and
certainly life itself, for example), but such a person's life on the whole is likely
to be lacking when it comes to some of the greatest human goods. The
natural law is good for us individually and as a society, and one need not be
a Christian to see how much of this works. Consider, for instance, the value
*for the individual* that researchers in the social sciences see in gratitude, generosity, and forgiveness.[17]

Even though many aspects of "the good life for human beings" are recognizable apart from the special revelation of Scripture, not all of them are.
Moreover, there may not always be a perfectly neat line dividing what we
can know through revelation and what we can know through the light that
God has written on the hearts of all humans. Part of the problem, as I see
it, is that much that God has "written on the hearts" of all humans may be
obscured for particular individuals, sometimes through the fault of the
individual (as when I rationalize my own wrongdoing) but sometimes due
to factors over which the individual has no control. The latter might occur
in a case in which a person is born into a society where a particular sin is
so widely accepted and normalized that it does not occur to that person to
question it.[18] I suspect that most societies have a few such cultural blind
spots. If the sin in question is *not* considered acceptable in most other

---

[17]On gratitude see Robert A. Emmons, *Thanks: How the New Science of Gratitude Can Make You
Happier* (New York: Houghton Mifflin, 2007), esp. 19-55. Regarding generosity see Christian
Smith and Hilary Davidson, *The Paradox of Generosity: Giving We Receive, Grasping We Lose* (New
York: Oxford University Press, 2014). On forgiveness see Loren Toussaint and Jon R. Webb,
"Theoretical and Empirical Connections Between Forgiveness, Mental Health, and Well-Being,"
in *Handbook of Forgiveness*, ed. Everett L. Worthington Jr. (New York: Routledge, 2005), 351-57. I
am not suggesting that the research on gratitude, generosity, and forgiveness (or any other moral
trait with overall benefits to the individual) indicates that the traits in question are always unambiguously good for the individual. There may well be personal costs associated with these traits, at
least in some contexts.

[18]Aquinas, *Summa Theologica* I-II.94.6.

societies, then it seems that the knowledge of that sin does not in general require the special revelation of Scripture. Nonetheless, for the individuals in the specific society in question, special revelation may well be needed.

I do not wish to get bogged down dividing those aspects of the natural law that are "written on the heart," those that are written only in Scripture, and those that are written in both. I will, however, now be turning explicitly to Scripture, particularly to the creation accounts, and what those accounts say about who we are and how that connects to how we are to live. Some of the claims of Scripture that I will be mentioning are arguably available even to those who have no access to Scripture (e.g., the claim that human beings were created for worship of or friendship with the divine). The reader is invited to ponder which claims can be appreciated only by those who have access to Scripture and which are things a present-day Paul might appeal to as common ground with non-Christians.[19]

In Genesis 1, we witness humans created in the image and likeness of God (Gen 1:26). The psalmist glories in this divine gift, marveling:

> When I look at your heavens, the work of your fingers,
> the moon and the stars that you have established;
> what are human beings that you are mindful of them,
> mortals that you care for them?
> Yet you have made them a little lower than God,
> and crowned them with glory and honor.
> You have given them dominion over the works of your hands;
> you have put all things under their feet,
> all sheep and oxen,
> and also the beasts of the field,
> the birds of the air, and the fish of the sea,
> whatever passes along the paths of the seas.
> O LORD, our Sovereign,
> how majestic is your name in all the earth! (Ps 8:3-9)

It is worth asking with the psalmist why God has crowned humans with "glory and honor" in this way. What purpose might God have for us that explains the gift of the *imago Dei* (literally, "the image of God")? I am

---

[19]I am referring to the fact that Paul begins his discussions with non-Jews with what they already know as true rather than with the Jewish Scriptures, which they do not accept.

doubtful that there is only one right answer to this question. God may have many reasons for endowing us with the *imago Dei*. Moreover, one of the reasons may simply be "because God saw that a creature with the powers of human beings would be a very good creature and accordingly chose to create such a creature." But another set of reasons explaining our possession of the *imago Dei* concerns God's specific purposes for us, purposes that are crucial to explore if we are to understand our identity. Some of these divine purposes we have already discussed in the section on the secularly recognizable goods of human life: friendship with one another and different forms of creative engagement with the physical world. Let's consider two other divine purposes for human beings that Christianity recognizes.

According to Christian teaching, one of God's major purposes for human beings is to have relationship with us. God has some sort of relationship to all of his creatures, but the relationship God wants with humans is deeper, personal, hence the need for us to be persons, personal creatures, with certain capacities. This relationship is most commonly described as love; Jesus once used the language of friendship (Jn 15:12-17). Love and friendship with God require a creature elevated in its capacities, bearing God's own image. One specific capacity humans need for this friendship is freedom, not only the freedom of whether to respond affirmatively to God but also the freedom of how to live out that love once the "yes" has initially been given, a living out that is itself constitutive of the "yes." We want our friends to affirm and live out their commitments to us not just freely but in their own words and ways. God wants the same from us, and we do this when we use the powers God has given us to "adorn the mighty theme."

A second purpose God has for humans that partially explains the gift of *imago Dei* concerns God's intended role for humans within the economy of creation. Specifically, both Genesis and the psalm quoted above indicate that human beings were intended to be caretakers of God's world. Consider the following two passages, the first from the creation account of Genesis 1, the second from the account in Genesis 2.

> Then God said, "Let us make humankind in our image, according to our likeness; and let them have dominion over the fish of the sea, and over the birds of the air, and over the cattle, and over all the wild animals of the earth, and over every creeping thing that creeps upon the earth."

> So God created humankind in his image,
> > in the image of God he created them;
> > male and female he created them.

> God blessed them and God said to them, "Be fruitful and multiply, and fill the earth and subdue it; and have dominion over the fish of the sea and over the birds of the air and over every living thing that moves upon the earth." (Gen 1:26-28)

> In the day that the LORD God made the earth and the heavens, when no plant of the field was yet in the earth and no herb of the field had yet sprung up—for the LORD God had not caused it to rain upon the earth, and there was no one to till the ground; but a stream would rise from the earth, and water the whole face of the ground. . . . The LORD God took the man and put him in the garden of Eden to till and keep it. (Gen 2:4-6, 15)

Note that both passages tie the creation of humans to some role to be played in creation: in Genesis 1, humans, as created in God's image, are to "fill the earth and subdue it," and for that reason they are given "dominion" over the other creatures. In Genesis 2, humans are to "till and keep" the garden that God has planted. Note that in both passages humans have a job, and that job pertains to caring for what God has made. This is important because occasionally one hears work disparaged as if it were the product of the fall, not part of our ultimate purpose. However, Scripture indicates that work is not a product of the fall any more than procreation is—both are part of God's original intent for humans. What the fall did change is our relationship to both of those purposes—work becomes toil and childbearing becomes painful (see Gen 3:16-19). Sin makes a crucial part of our human nature and the fulfillment of the natural law a source of pain. Living into our purpose now feels oppressive.

It is important to note that our creation-care purpose to "till and keep" the garden and "fill the earth and subdue it and have dominion" over its various creatures is not a command to be domineering. The interpretation of authority and dominion as self-serving exploitation is itself a manifestation of sin—a fact that the humble servant Jesus, who is Lord, impresses on us. Humans—who were created for friendship with God, relationship with one another, enjoyment of the goods of life, and care of creation—have responded by abusing their power (and by extension the very image of God) and attempting to dominate everyone and everything in their paths. I am reminded of the unfaithful servant in one of Jesus' parables: the servant in question is put in charge of his master's property and the other servants, but instead of taking care of either he beats his fellow servants and gets drunk (Mt 24:45-51; Lk 12:42-48). The problem with this servant is not merely that he hurts his fellow servants but also that he neglects the master's work,[20] and this is true even if we remember that the servant was given a great deal of discretion regarding how to accomplish that work.

## KNOWLEDGE OF THE NATURAL LAW: THE SIGNIFICANCE OF THE HEART AND THE NECESSITY OF DISCERNMENT

The natural law theory of ethics helps make sense of an otherwise surprising treatment of moral principles that we see in Scripture, especially but not exclusively in the New Testament: the expectation that humans are capable of knowing much of how they ought to live apart from explicit divine in-structions in the form of special revelation. Thus, Gentiles who lack the revelation of Scripture are said to have the law "written on their hearts" so that they can be held accountable when they violate what they are capable of seeing is right (Rom 2:15). No one's knowledge is perfect, of course. As I stated before, all cultures and all individuals will have their blind spots, some of them self-imposed (as when we try to define ethical behavior in a way that is especially convenient for ourselves or our own interest groups). Still, when an individual can sense in Jesus the person she ought to be, that indi-vidual is drawing on her knowledge of the natural law, imperfect though that knowledge may be.

Perhaps even more interestingly, natural law theory helps explain why even those who have access to the law in Scripture are expected to under-stand how to apply that law to a host of situations that Scripture does not explicitly address. When Jesus' disciples pick grain on the sabbath and are accused of violating the law of the Old Testament, Jesus could have de-fended his followers through a simple legal argument about how picking a

---

[20]This point becomes especially clear when one contrasts the unfaithful servant with the faithful one, who is specifically praised for attending to his work (Mt 24:46-47).

few heads of grain is not technically work and hence does not fall under the sabbath commandment. But that isn't the path that Jesus takes, at least not directly. Instead, Jesus likens what his disciples are doing to a case of a person being justified in doing what a law explicitly forbade. When David and his companions were hungry, Jesus says, they ate food that the law explicitly stated could be eaten only by priests (Mk 2:23-28). Note that it is clear in this case that if David is justified (as Jesus assumes he is), technical reasons will definitely not suffice for explaining why. David and his companions *clearly* ate the bread of the Presence (not, say, a few leftover crumbs). David and his companions were *clearly not* priests, and the Levitical law that reserves the bread for the priests includes no stated exceptions (Lev 24:9). What justified David and his companions was not a technical matter of what qualifies as bread but a recognizable higher need. David had fled for his life, and the bread of the Presence was the only bread available without raising suspicion (1 Sam 21:6).[21] In summing up his response by saying "the sabbath was made for humankind, and not humankind for the sabbath" (Mk 2:27), Jesus indicates that human beings both can and should form judgments about such higher and lower needs in the context of human life. The law and how to honor and obey it must be understood within the context of our ultimate human good because, as humans are capable of seeing, the law is ultimately created for that context. In criticizing the Pharisees for criticizing him, Jesus seems to be saying what he often says to them: I'm right about this, and even if you don't take my word for it, you should be able to see that I am right about it!

My interpretation of Jesus as saying to the Pharisees, "You should have known better than to criticize my actions for breaking a law while deliberately ignoring both the point of my actions and the point of the law," may seem too quick. In particular, one might ask *how* the Pharisees should have known to consider these things. Isn't the move from rule following (without reference to the point of the rules) to considered judgment in light of the rules and their point a New Testament move? One reason for thinking that

---

[21]The full story is even more complicated: David tells the priest he is on a secret mission from the king and that is why no one must know where he is. In reality, David is hiding from the king, who wants to kill him. So, we have not only the priest making the judgment of what to do about the bread but David deciding to lie to the priest to preserve his own life. See 1 Sam 19:11–21:9.

this is not how we should interpret the law of the Old Testament is one we have already seen: the example of David and the bread of the Presence and the assumption that the original intended audience of those passages could understand why David's actions were justified. Another reason is that, even at the time of Jesus, people who were not yet sure what to think of him knew enough about the law to know that the question "Which commandment is the first of all?" was a sensible one (Mk 12:28), which indicates they knew that discernment was crucial for correct application of the law. And it's not an accident that Jesus' answer to this question makes reference to the two most important parts of our ultimate purpose: loving God and loving one another (Mk 12:29-31). Interestingly, the person who asked this question also seems to have anticipated this answer (Mk 12:32-33).

How might a person have come to see that loving God and neighbor are the two greatest commandments? Perhaps by fulfilling another command from the Old Testament, one specifically concerning how the Israelites were to treat the law:

> You shall put these words of mine in your heart and soul, and you shall bind them as a sign on your hand, and fix them as an emblem on your forehead. Teach them to your children, talking about them when you are at home and when you are away, when you lie down and when you rise. (Deut 11:18-19)

Thus, even in the Old Testament, the Lord wants not just compliance with but love for and *understanding* of the law (hence the command to "talk about" the law at every place and time), a love and understanding that presupposes that there is something to be understood, a rationale. That rationale is built into our nature.

## NATURAL LAW AND MORAL GUIDANCE

For many of life's choices, natural law ethics offers what might be called nondeterministic guidance. What this means is that applied natural law may allow for a wide range of actions to qualify as good. For instance, if you are deciding between two careers likely to take you in very different directions with regard to your influence in the world, your proximity to your family and the community where you grew up, your pay, and the sorts of experiences you are able to have, it is entirely possible that natural law ethics will not tell you which path to take. What natural law ethics is more likely to emphasize is the importance of recognizing the factors potentially at stake in your choice and how you can responsibly inhabit whichever path you choose. This is essentially the point from the earlier discussion of the Tolkien quote and the idea of humans as commissioned to "adorn the mighty theme." We have freedom in how we "adorn the theme" in our lives, and that means that different life choices can be very good.

The freedom that natural law ethics offers can make some people uncomfortable. Morality isn't about freedom; it's about what we have to do, even if we don't particularly like it, a person might think. One might be worried that natural law ethics makes our choices arbitrary or that its guidance is likely to be abused. I want to address each of these concerns. I will begin with the worry that morality is about what we have to do, not what we want to do. On the picture I have painted, ethics is not solely or even mostly about getting us to do cumbersome tasks that we would be better off avoiding but nonetheless must do. Nonetheless, I think there is something very right about this sentiment that ethical behavior is often not especially fun and goes against what we want at the time. Often, our own sin is the reason that our ethical obligations clash with our desires (sin has corrupted our very desires), but sometimes the clash arises simply because living up to our nature can result in the loss of a real good for us. Fulfilling one's duties as a parent of young children can mean giving up a regular sleep schedule for long periods of time. (Imagine having triplets!) People have lost their lives and their livelihoods by virtue of following Christ. These losses are real, and they are sometimes demanded. I cannot imagine how difficult it must be for a persecuted Christian to stand firm in the faith, but loving God above all else—our highest purpose—requires standing firm. So, natural law ethics does recognize difficult moral demands in some situations and not just wide open paths. Even though submitting to these demands can result in a genuine, sometimes grieve-worthy loss for a person, precisely because our ultimate end is union with God and union with other humans, these genuine losses will never be ultimate. It will never be the case that a person's life would have been better on the ultimate scale if only he had violated the law of his nature.

Let's tackle the second concern regarding the level of freedom in natural law ethics: Does such freedom make our choices arbitrary? The idea, I take it, is that because several paths are (often) all deemed to be good (e.g., in the case of the person deciding between two different careers) it follows that it doesn't matter which path one chooses; one might as well flip a coin. Natural law theorist Mark Murphy addresses this worry by pointing out that the reason that natural law allows multiple paths is that natural law can recognize the distinct goods available on each path.[22] But the fact that applied natural law enables one to recognize all these distinct goods among which one must choose makes *arbitrary* the wrong word to describe the choice a person must make concerning these goods.[23] To reference our earlier music analogy, the fact that a composer need not follow one set path to compose a beautiful piece of music does not make that musician's specific decisions in composing her piece arbitrary! So too the person deciding between two different career paths is not acting arbitrarily when he thinks carefully about both paths and chooses one even though the other could have also been good. Moreover, even though multiple paths can each be good, this does not mean that every path or every way of pursuing a potentially good path is good. As Murphy notes, each of us must form a life plan and consider how our choices fit within that plan.[24] All the notes on the piano may be able to be put to use in playing a specific theme, but once I have committed to a particular composition style, some uses of those notes may no longer fit. Paying attention to these big-picture considerations is itself an aspect of using our human capacities for their intended purposes.

What about the concern that the freedom the natural law recognizes is liable to be abused? I think it must be admitted that even though natural law certainly does not say "anything goes," lots of people may point to it as an excuse for doing whatever it is they want on a particular occasion, and this is a way the theory may be abused. To be sure, every ethical theory, even one with the strictest of rules, is subject to abuse. Jesus told us to love our neighbor as ourselves, and someone unsurprisingly responded by asking Jesus to define *neighbor*. No doubt, the asker was already busy crafting his own definition of *neighbor*, one that would conveniently get him (the asker)

---

[22]Mark C. Murphy, *Natural Law and Practical Rationality*, Cambridge Studies in Philosophy and Law (New York: Cambridge University Press, 2001), 248.
[23]Ibid.
[24]Ibid.

off the hook (Lk 10:25-29). It's a lawyer's trick that we have all deployed. This is also the reason that even though the present-day United States has some of the most specific legal code in human history, US court rooms still see fights over how those codes apply in particular cases, each side conveniently insisting on its own definitions, interpretations, and (by extension) legal rightness. Moreover, strict legal codes have their own special form of abuse, known as legalism, in which fences are set up around the law to protect against abuse. Paradoxically, those fences added to the law sometimes wind up undermining the original intent of the law.

Given all the ways a person can attempt to twist a law or ethical theory to justify her own preferred course of action, I think the real concern one ought to have with natural law is not over what will happen if it is applied by a person who wants only to rationalize her own behavior but what can sometimes happen when even honest people try to apply it. Sometimes honest people will apply the natural law and mistakenly conclude that a particular path is good when it is not, and arguably a more specific set of rules could have avoided this problem. I admit that this is a potential complication of the level of freedom allowed in the natural law. Recognizing such difficulties, natural law theorist Jean Porter notes that we must admit that we can never avoid our need for divine grace and mercy at the level of our imperfect applications of natural law. We are left with the justified hope

> that God will at least not relegate our efforts to meaninglessness, or look upon them with indifference—they will be assessed in the light of God's own wisdom and love, and whatever is good in them will be preserved. At the end of the day, we must hope for this judgment for others and for ourselves, remembering that in God justice and mercy are one.[25]

## NATURAL LAW AND A MORAL DILEMMA

With the understanding that natural law does not always provide specific moral guidance (but may), we can take a look at how one might use natural law theory to think through a moral dilemma. Consider the case of Anthony, a man in his mid-twenties who has been working full-time for the past three years as a personal trainer and assistant manager of a health club. He

---

[25]Porter, *Nature as Reason*, 400.

loves working with clients to help them set and achieve their goals, and his clients seem to like working with him as well. Indeed, Anthony has one of the highest retention rates of any trainer at the club. About a year ago the club where he works was bought by a larger regional company, and this has not been good for Anthony's pay. The new company has shifted to a commission-driven pay system. Anthony now receives a small monthly base pay plus a bonus for every new training or membership contract he sells beyond a certain level, and a further bonus for contracts sold once he reaches an even higher level. The upshot is that in order make much income at all, Anthony has to sign up a lot of new people every month; most of the time he comes up short. Meanwhile, the new company regularly runs sales-coaching sessions to help employees raise their sales and by extension their commissions. Anthony finds many of the suggested tactics downright manipulative and dishonest. He has noticed, though, that the workers with the highest commissions are the ones who are best able to pull off these tactics. To make a little more money, Anthony has started using some of the less extreme deceptions himself, avoiding the more extreme ones but still feeling dirty in the process. He feels especially bad when the people in question become not just club members but his own personal training clients. To be successful, he needs the people he is training to trust him, and he is beginning to feel unworthy of that trust. What Anthony cannot control are the unjust practices that the new management is starting to use on anyone who signs a contract, including his clients. Some of his clients are complaining that the club is adding extra fees mid-contract and making it nearly impossible for members to cancel their memberships. Anthony feels used when he thinks about what the club is doing to his clients and to him, and he is considering quitting. Unfortunately, he has no other job lined up and only six weeks of living expenses in the bank, some of this past year's leaner paychecks having slowly eaten into his savings.

How would natural law ethics offer guidance on how Anthony should respond to this less than ideal situation? The deceptions and actions of the new health club management are clearly unjust.[26] The question for Anthony

---

[26]The fact that no governmental authorities have intervened to declare the health club's tactics illegal does not mean that the tactics are just. In the first place, there is a difference between what the law allows and what is truly just. In the second place, illegal actions may occur without an authority

is how to respond to this unjust situation with the limited power he has. How would the natural law suggest Anthony think through his situation? He might begin by identifying the different feelings and concerns he is experiencing, and honestly assessing which of these feelings and concerns come from good and important aspects of human nature and which are the effects of sin, whether individual or cultural. For instance, Anthony is almost assuredly concerned about having a job, paying his bills, and supporting his interests, and these are good concerns to have. Society would have big problems if most of us stopped working or started ignoring our financial obligations. Still, it cannot be right to make the fulfillment of a monetary obligation (such as paying rent to a landlord) so important that one is willing to deceive other people to do so. Avoiding bad faith cannot be the justification for acting in it! So, if he stays at his job, Anthony is going to have to fight the strong incentive to deceive. Considering he has already had some struggles fighting that temptation, if he stays, he will need to come up with some practical steps he can take to avoid that temptation. If he quits, he needs to think carefully about how he can find a job capable of meeting his needs and obligations, and what the bottom line is on the income he requires to do so.

While Anthony's desires to work and to fulfill his financial obligations are very good and human, it's also possible that Anthony's concern to be self-sustaining is *too* strong. While we were all made to work and thus contribute to our own care, we were also all made to depend on one another. In our society, however, men especially are socialized to think that their identity is connected to their ability to make money and that there is something shameful in relying on other people to carry them for a time. While Anthony certainly shouldn't assume that other people can help him out through a potential period of unemployment without checking first, having such a conversation, hard as it may be, should be something to which he is at least open. The fear of such a conversation should not be driving his decision. Humility is hard, but it's a virtue befitting our fragile human nature.

---

stepping in and declaring the actions illegal. Thus, the fact that a company is behaving in a particular way (and has lawyers advising it as it so behaves) does not mean that the company's actions comply with the law. It can take years for a company's illegal activities to gain the attention of the courts. It can take multiple lawyers with access to thousands of documents to know what is legal, what is illegal, and what is likely (or unlikely) to be successfully prosecuted. For the rest of us, the questions we must answer, now, are, "what is moral?" "what is just?" and "what role will I play?"

Another good thing that Anthony is feeling is enjoyment and satisfaction in his work as a personal trainer. We were created for good work, and it's wonderful that Anthony is finding fulfillment in work that helps others strengthen their bodies. If Anthony decides to leave his current job, he will need to look at the likelihood that he will eventually be able to find work that is as meaningful and fulfilling of his own particular gifts. While meaningful work is not a deal-breaker, its loss should be recognized as a real loss, something not to be eagerly embraced even though giving it up may be, all things considered, the right decision. Moreover, the loss should not be perceived as a loss only for Anthony. If he really is doing good work, it's also a loss for his clients and the community.

Finally, it's very good that Anthony cares not only about the physical well-being of his clients but also whether they are being treated fairly, and not just by him but by his company. The natural law isn't a game of how to make sure our own hands always technically stay clean so that if we do it, it matters, but if the company does it, it does not. We invest ourselves in our employers, and so we should care what those employers are doing (and what they are using us to do). Such concern is an aspect of our social nature. So, just as being a part of his clients' physical strengthening is something that should bring Anthony joy, being a part of their deception, even an unwilling part, should concern him. Indeed, to be an *unwilling* part is to be *concerned*. Like doing meaningful work, working for a company that deceives isn't necessarily a deal-breaker (consider extreme situations), but working for such a company still always matters and should always count. The actions of groups are responsible for both many of the greatest human accomplishments as well as the most damaging ones. We have to care what our groups do, and that concern has to be capable of informing our behavior. If the "concern" is incapable of informing our behavior, we can hardly be said to truly love our neighbor (1 Jn 3:17-19).

With all of these desires and concerns (and their connection to what it means to live up to one's humanity) explored, Anthony's needed course of action is coming into focus: in all likelihood, he needs to quit. His work environment has already taken a toll on his love of neighbor (consider his increased willingness to manipulate), and the new company is using him and his colleagues to take advantage of people. If you're interested, I know a person who was in a situation very similar to Anthony's, and that is exactly what my friend did: he quit, unsure of where he would land but sure he needed to get out more than he needed financial security or even independence.[27] Anthony does have another option, though, albeit a potentially more difficult one: he could stay at his present position and be "salt and light" (Mt 5:13-16) where he is, *respectfully* explaining to his superiors why he is unwilling to use the sales tactics they suggest, *respectfully* explaining his concerns about how they are treating customers, and *respectfully* advocating on customers' behalf as best he can. He probably won't make much money; he might lose his position anyway; and he'll probably feel extremely uncomfortable and unsure of himself the whole time. If he could keep it up for a time, though (perhaps until another job becomes available), he would be doing very good work. He would be living as one who reflects the image of God in an imperfect world.

## WHAT DIFFERENCE DOES GOD MAKE?

When discussing explicitly Christian theories of ethics, my students (most of them Christians) often ask, what difference does God make to this theory? Behind this question, I think, is the intuition that whatever ethical theory is correct must honor the rightful place of the Christian God as Alpha and Omega, beginning and end (see Rev 22:13). Such an intuition fits well with natural law ethics according to which God, as the very creator of human nature, is the author of the very foundation of ethics. The story of human beings I have told is a story according to which human beings were created by God to enjoy the specific goods of human life, to live in community with one another, to be God's own friends, and to be caretakers of the earth. All of these purposes hold true for us only because God created us in a very particular way, writing these purposes into who we are and enabling us to recognize them. Take away the Creator and you take away the creature; take away the creature and you take away natural law.

Having recognized that both the truth and knowledge of how we should live derive from our Creator, we need to clarify that a person can nonetheless

---

[27]The name and some details have of course been changed, but the main features of the case are true to life.

be aware of much of the natural law without being aware of the Christian
God. Much of the natural law is "written on our hearts" in a deep way so
that not being a Christian and even being an atheist or an agnostic need not
remove one's awareness that we have certain obligations with respect to how
we are to treat one another and the world around us. One need not be
thinking about our Creator to appreciate the value of many of the goods of
human life, including knowledge, friendship, art, and mental and physical
health. One need not be thinking about Christianity to recognize the way
in which community is needed for the achievement of these goods. In other
words, the human good and our knowledge of it both come from God, but
precisely because God imprints such knowledge on all humans, not just the
religious, it is available to nontheists.

Even though natural law ethics makes God, as Creator, the source of
ethics, there is a way in which natural law ethics can at least seem not to
make God sufficiently important. It is absolutely impossible for us—or anything else—to exist without God. And yet we seem to be able to imagine a
world without God, even something very much like *this* world without God.
We can entertain the supposition that God does not exist and that we and
all the things around us—animals, trees, water, matter itself, the laws of
physics—have simply arisen by chance. Once we are entertaining this idea,
we can further ask, If this admittedly impossible situation of life without
God were true, would there still be ethical truth, or would morality be a
series of groundless recommendations for how humans should live? The
answer to this question is what leads some people to think that God is not
important enough to ethics on the natural law theory.

Now, asking questions about the impossible is bound to lead to some
baffling statements, and it may be that we should simply say, "There is no
saying what would be true in the absolutely impossible (and not just highly
unlikely) scenario in which God fails to exist." If that is your inclination, you
can ignore what follows. Not everyone has that inclination, though, and I
will say that although I recognize the strangeness of the question, I tend to
think that we can meaningfully ask the question, what follows about ethics
if we somehow find out tomorrow that atheism is true? While different
natural law theorists will give different answers to this question, I think the
answer is that some things would still be objectively ethically good and

others would still be objectively ethically bad. There would still be certain ways of living that would be good for us and other ways of living that would be bad for us, just as exercise and sleep would still be recognizably conducive to our physical and mental health. Humans would still need cooperative, respectful societies (and friendships and families) to thrive and achieve recognizable human goods. Such a need would support a common rationale for assisting and respecting one another. So, in my opinion ethics survives in an impossible but hypothetical godless universe.

Even though ethics survives in this hypothetical situation, at least on the natural law theory that I have sketched, I think we must admit that the surviving moral principles, especially their point, would be impoverished. In the first place, our purpose is radically impoverished if there is no God: without God, friendship with the creator of the universe is off the table, and that is an incalculable loss. So, without God, our longing for the divine is a pipe dream, and our eyes will need to lower their aim significantly.

A second impoverishment of morality in a godless universe is that even though humans would still need one another and would in that sense remain social creatures, we also would be somewhat at odds with one another and thus become somewhat antisocial creatures. When I say we would "become" antisocial creatures, I am not making a prediction of how people would behave in a godless universe. Instead, I am making a statement about what sort of life would actually be good for us in a world without God. If there is no providential God who created all of us with our common nature, then it is unlikely that aiming at your good will always be of benefit to me. In well-functioning societies, aiming at your good will often be to my benefit, especially when the two of us are closely connected. Friendship and familial relationships are probably some of the highest goods in a godless world, so forgiveness, sacrifice, and love would remain crucial for living well. The problem is that friendship and all the other goods of a godless world can be achieved only by those who are alive, and the necessities of life (e.g., health care) are often in limited supply. Human beings would need to work with one another to acquire these necessities, but they would also need to work against one another, eyeing one another with suspicion, to ensure sufficient access for their own friends and families. So, while rational human beings would remain allies in some respects, they would become competitors in other respects. The first to lose out in such a competition would be the weakest and those relationally distant from the strong.[28] Note that the issue is not that it would make no sense to recognize the weak as having value in a godless universe. I think humans can rationally be viewed as having value even if we are cosmic accidents rather than specially created in the image of God. It is rather that bare survival would sometimes require ignoring the value of the weak and distant or otherwise viewing the weak and distant as threats.

Finally, even if it made sense to a particular individual to love all of her neighbors, even her weak and distant neighbors, as much as she loves herself, the idea that humans might ever become capable of such love is irrational without reference to God. If there is no God, the law of nature we feel in our hearts mocks us as we realize that we are entirely too selfish to ever come close to real compliance.[29] So, according to natural law ethics, if we can meaningfully talk about what would be true in a godless universe, the answer is that ethics would survive but in an impoverished form. We could characterize such impoverishment as disappointed hope: no hope for contact with the divine; no hope for extreme transformation and healing; no hope that we can cheer for the ultimate good of all human beings.

Natural law ethics is a moral theory that has an extensive history of support in the Christian moral tradition. If I have done my job, the heart of that theory should now be clear: Christian natural law theory states that human beings are dependent, physically embodied creatures made in the image of God to care for creation, enjoy life with one another, and experience friendship with God. That's who we are, and the natural law tells us what it looks like to live in a way that is fulfilling and befitting of who we are. While I do not think that Scripture teaches any specific ethical theory, I also hope that natural law's consonance with Scripture has at least started to become clear. We see that fit not only in the creation accounts that I have discussed (provided simply that one takes those accounts seriously and reverently; no literal interpretation is presupposed) but also in the story of salvation that runs through the whole of Scripture. If the way we are to live

---

[28]This includes most nonhuman creatures (who tend to be both relationally distant from us and weak in comparison to us).

[29]Note that the *existence* of God is not enough to solve this problem; we need a God who will heal us.

is fundamentally connected to the type of creature we are, it should not be surprising that the type of creature we are is also essential to the way of salvation in which the Son of God became a full-fledged human being, living perfectly as a human being.

# A Virtue Ethics Response

*BRAD J. KALLENBERG*

There is much to be commended in Claire Brown Peterson's chapter on natural law. One strength of her account is the way it easily overcomes the so-called naturalist fallacy. The naturalist fallacy was the name given to David Hume's complaint that there is no legitimate way to move from *fact* to *value*, from *is* to *ought*, from *description* to *prescription*. But as Philippa Foot, Alasdair MacIntyre, and others have shown, the language of "ought" is already bound up with the description of what a thing is *for* (its aim, intent, purpose, or *telos*). If the *telos* of a clock is timekeeping, then it *ought* to keep time well. Why? Because that is what it is *for*. And Peterson argues that both *what sort* of animal *Homo sapiens* is and the various social *roles* we occupy are sources from which we can begin to make out the human *telos* and thus our moral obligations.

I also commend Peterson for her attention to specifically religious sources for learning the human *telos*, the book of Scripture as well as the book of nature. Peterson is clear that Scripture does not mandate one particular theory of ethics. Thus, while it is true that following the natural law is good for us, so is obeying the divine command, developing virtue, and righting social injustice. Each of us four authors is after the construction of the most coherent model we can build, one that makes sense of all the data—both the data we live and the data we glean from revelation. In this basically affirmative spirit I want to offer suggestions (more than criticisms) regarding ways in which her model could be strengthened.

First, although this present book treats natural law separately from virtue ethics, I think it makes more sense for Peterson to treat them of a piece.

After all, Aquinas put them together. It is interesting to note that the massive 3,012-page *Summa Theologica* devotes 159 pages to the topic of virtue but only six pages to natural law per se.[1] However, both natural law and virtue are a part of the bigger conversation. And I think that the kind of conversation Aquinas is having is particularly important for Peterson's very biblical model. For while natural law admittedly has some conceptual roots in Stoicism, what Cicero developed is decidedly *non*-theological when compared to that which the medieval theologians constructed.

Peterson's account may be further strengthened by resisting two temptations. The first temptation to resist is the urge to ontologize, which is so common among natural lawyers. What do I mean? There is an ever-present tendency among natural law thinkers to reify the terms of their explanation, mistakenly thinking that by turning every noun into a *thing* explanations thereby become more solid. Plato, and to some extent Aristotle, had a habit of treating human nature (*physis*) as a *thing*. But contemporary science doesn't speak this language. Speak of "human nature" to scientists and they are apt to mistake the term as referring to the human genome (a move that threatens to entail physical determinism). "No," we insist, "human nature is *not* merely physical." And then we get tongue-tied, employing apparent oxymorons (such as "immaterial substance") while living as if we don't believe it.[2] The concept of "human nature" as a some*thing* vanished from the academy some time after the Enlightenment.[3] But is this a problem? Do we really need to make human nature or natural kinds into *things* in order to employ natural law ethics?

One philosophical theologian, the late Herbert McCabe, offers us a way to think about natural kinds and laws that avoids the morass of medieval ontologies.[4] Rather than insist that our human nature is a real entity, he

---

[1] The "Treatise on Virtues" is found at I-II.49-67 (93 pages) but also relevant is II-II.47-56 on practical reasoning (42 pages) and questions 58-61 on the virtue of justice (24 pages), not to mention Thomas's discussion of vices or the theological virtues. The entire "Treatise on Law" in II-II.90-94, which covers divine and human law as well as natural law, spans only 20 pages.

[2] The tendency of contemporary Christians to live as thoroughgoing materialists, what Charles Taylor calls the "buffered self," is discussed in his blog devoted to his massive *The Secular Age*. See Charles Taylor, "Buffered and Porous Selves," *The Immanent Frame*, September 2, 2008, http://blogs.ssrc.org/tif/2008/09/02/buffered-and-porous-selves.

[3] See the introduction to Bas C. van Fraassen, *Laws and Symmetry* (Oxford: Clarendon Press, 1989).

[4] Herbert McCabe, *Law, Love and Language* (New York: Continuum, 2004).

advises us to simply let our ordinary language-use show us what it makes sense to say. For example, when we kick the tires of a car, we normally say, "I kicked the tire." But if I intentionally kick your shin, you'd ordinarily say, "Stop kicking *me!*" rather than "Stop kicking the shin of the leg."[5] Our language shows our tendency to treat a machine, even a complex one, as an aggregate of parts. But we treat an organism, whether a person or a leopard, not as an aggregate of pieces (arms and legs or paws and claws). The way we talk shows that we naturally treat a living organism as a unit, an organic whole. We don't need to fret about the thingy-ness of *physis*; we can build a perfectly good model by attending to how we ordinarily speak.

Reliance on language (rather than overdependence on ontology) for making discriminations is not to say matters are thereby quite easily done! But treating human beings as a machine (as in C. S. Lewis's colloquial metaphor) is to get off on the wrong paw, er, foot. Peterson is sensitive to the fact that if God were to treat us like the sea ("Thus far shall you come, and no farther"), we effectively would be machines. Of course, if we were machines, reading our *telos* off our mechanical functionality like we do with a mechanism would be relatively straightforward. The fact that we are *organisms* means that discovery of our God-given *telos* requires more of us than investigation of the machine and its parts.

The second temptation that lurks around the edges is the temptation to secure agreement by nailing down definitions. Now, Peterson doesn't actually attempt this. She writes that "by 'human nature' natural law theorists roughly mean 'the perfect definition of a human being.'" But from what soil might such a definition grow? Lost to us forever is the Edenic pre-fall state of perfection with freedom (*posse peccare*; lit. "able to sin"). We are all post-fall and have two options. Prior to grace human nature is corrupt, damaged in every fiber. Although human nature is not as bad as it can be, theologically speaking, Augustine explains that before we meet Christ, nothing we might do or be in this state is without sin (*nonposse nonpeccare* or "not able not to sin").[6] After we meet Christ, grace abounds for the Christian. We

---

[5]Herbert McCabe, "Soul, Life, Machines and Language," in *Faith Within Reason*, ed. and intro. Brian Davies (New York: Continuum, 2007), 123-49.
[6]See chap. 33 of Augustine's "On Rebuke and Grace," New Advent, accessed October 26, 2016, www.newadvent.org/fathers/1513.htm. See also chap. 118 of his *Enchiridion*.

then have freedom but not perfection; we no longer *must* necessarily sin (*posse nonpeccare*; "able not to sin"). And, according to Augustine, in this state redeemed human nature will remain until our resurrection, after which our nature is perfected and "permanentized" (*nonposse peccare*, "not able to sin"!). From which of these four states is "the perfect definition of a human being" to be drawn?

Peterson appears sensitive to the fact that our attempts to read human nature off of actual human persons is distorted by the fact that the human specimens under observation are imperfect, distorted by sin. Moreover, *we* who are doing the reading are as flawed by sin as are those we study. Christ, of course, is the exception "who in every respect has been tested as we are, yet without sin" (Heb 4:15 NRSV). So why not take our moral bearings from Christ instead of a putative "perfect definition"? God did not send us a definition; he sent his Son. We have not been given a definition; we have been given a Savior who is also our example (1 Pet 2:21). In sharp contrast to perfect definitions, examples and analogies and paradigms and images require training for us to get the hand of imitating.

Peterson is cognizant of the fact that black-and-white answers are not what the natural law normally provides. She argues instead that natural law gives "open-ended" and "nondeterminative" guidance. On the one hand this leaves Peterson open to the complaint: "Then what good is natural law? Isn't natural law in the end unhelpful since it only can supply general stuff like 'I don't have wings, therefore I ought not jump off roofs'?" On the other hand, I think Peterson could have made much more of the fact that the open-endedness of natural law prescriptions makes demands on us as disciples: "pay attention to *how* [*pōs*, particle expressing manner] you listen," Jesus warns (Lk 8:18). For this reason, I find counterproductive the tendency to (1) presume *physis* is a stable *thing* that can be (2) captured in a perfect definition. Both aspects bewitch us into imagining that any ethical ambiguity is merely exegetical (as if the definition needs only fine-tuning or closer examination) rather than the result of the cloudiness of our eyesight. Peterson comes close to what I'm trying to say when she paraphrases Jesus' argument with the Pharisees, "I'm right about this, and even if you don't take my word for it, you should be able to see that I am right about it!" The questions I take Jesus to be asking are threefold: "Do you see? If not, why not?" and "What will it take for you to become able to see?" Peterson asks these very questions and answers with the tandem answer "love and understanding." So far, so good! However, Peterson concludes that the presence of "understanding" in the pairing implies that there must be *something* to understand and "that rationale is built into our nature." What Peterson does not address—again this may be the fault of space limitations—is the way love (a character virtue that began as a gift) *transforms one's nature*, including the mind that understands. At least that is the way the early fathers understood the action of love and the semi-mutability of "nature."[7]

I was surprised to see Peterson sail past the Scylla and Charybdis of faulty ethics without ever discussing the role that practical reasoning plays. Consider: say an engineer is faced with a technical design problem. At that moment two things are not true. First, it is *not* true that there exists only one correct solution (the Scylla). It is equally *not* true that in falling short of the single, answer-in-the-back-of-the-book correct solution, "anything goes!" (the Charybdis). Between those two false options lies the real work of practical reasoning (what engineers call "design reasoning" and the New Testament calls practical wisdom [*phronēsis* rather than *sophia*]).[8] Peterson could strengthen her model by explaining how practical reasoning, and the attending virtue "savvy" (*phronēsis* or *prudentia* [Latin]),[9] may be nurtured via the gritty practice of following Christ. Interestingly, another natural law thinker, Martin Rhonheimer, has taken the view that natural law refers not to the *content* of moral positions (neither the claims, reasons, nor warrants) but refers rather to the *process* of practical reasoning.[10] As it is the nature of stone to fall to the ground, human beings reason out what to do. The real problems facing Christian ethics are the noetic effects of sin and the impaired state of our moral eyesight.

---

[7]This action was referred to as "theosis," the way we become godlike insofar as we are "partakers of the divine *physis*" (*genēsthe theias koinōnoi physeōs*) (2 Pet 1:4).

[8]See Brad J. Kallenberg, *By Design: Theology, Ethics and the Practice of Engineering* (Eugene, OR: Cascade Books, 2013).

[9]Herbert McCabe, "Aquinas on Good Sense," *New Blackfriars* 67, no. 796 (1986): 419-31.

[10]Martin Rhonheimer, "The Cognitive Structure of the Natural Law and the Truth of Subjectivity," *Thomist* 67, no. 1 (2003): 1-44.

# A Divine Command
# Theory Response

*JOHN HARE*

I have more disagreement with Claire Brown Peterson than with the other two authors, and that is to be expected because she and I are defending different accounts of what Christians should say about what makes something morally obligatory. My main difficulty with her chapter is that she uses many different terms for the relation between morality and human nature, and it is not clear in the end what her claim is about this relation. Here is a partial list, in the order of occurrence in her text. Morality is "rooted in central truths about who we are as human beings"; "the very *content* of ethics (how we ought to live) is largely determined by facts about who we are"; "these necessary 'ways of ordering' our lives furnish the content of ethics"; "the very content of ethics—how God created us to live—is intricately connected to the sort of creature we are"; "ethics is . . . grounded in human nature"; "our social and emotional forms of life . . . have implications for how we ought to live"; "certain ways of living are befitting of a creature made in the image of God." This sort of list shows that there are stronger and weaker ways of expressing the relation between morality and human nature.

In the history of the discussion of this question, there have been at least two main views. One is that of Aquinas, whom Peterson says she is following (though her paper is not an exegesis of Aquinas), and one is that of Scotus, whom she ignores. The difference between the two lies exactly in how strong a relation they hold to obtain between morality and human nature. Scotus says that the second table of the law (the commandments that Moses brought down from Sinai) fits, but is not deducible from, our nature. Moreover, God can "dispense" from it—for example, in the case of the binding of Isaac, the Hebrew midwives, and the command to Hosea to take Gomer as his wife. The second table deals with our obligations to the neighbor, and the first table with our obligations to God. Scotus holds that the first table is necessary, known to be true "from its terms," and so is natural law strictly speaking, whereas the second table is natural law only in an extended sense. If we go back to the list of the ways Peterson expresses the relation between morality and human nature, we can see that about half of these ways would be acceptable to Scotus and half would not. He would be perfectly happy with saying that the law is intricately connected to our nature and that our form of life has implications for how we ought to live. But he would deny that the moral law can be *deduced* from our nature or that we would know "from its terms" the proposition that humans ought to live by it.

Why does this matter? It matters because it affects how we see our relation to God and to our own sin. Peterson is clear that when she says morality is grounded in nature, she does not mean our sin nature but our created nature. The problem is how we are going to tell, without begging the relevant question, what our created nature is. By "begging the relevant question" I mean that "created nature" is not going to be any help in identifying how we ought to live if we have to already know what our obligations are in order to identify our created nature. Peterson refers for help with this question to Philippa Foot, and in particular her book *Natural Goodness*.[1] This book is illuminating with respect to just this point about "begging the question." Foot's project is to tell a "natural history story" about human nature that will enable us to deduce conclusions about moral goodness from premises about the characteristic form of life of the human species. The main problem with her account is that she treats our nature too much as a single package and is accordingly too optimistic in her account of practical rationality as sensitivity to the reasons this package gives to us. Our nature does indeed give us reasons, but some of them are good and some of them are bad. We therefore need some way to discern *which* reasons given us by our nature we should follow. Foot is not herself a Christian or a theist. She

---

[1]Philippa Foot, *Natural Goodness* (New York: Oxford University Press, 2001).

does not have an account of the fall. So her deduction is from human nature as we observe it.

Consider the example Peterson takes from Budziszewski, that a broken foot still has the nature of a foot. If we had never seen healthy feet, he says, we might have taken the broken condition as normative: "Apart from revelation we make the same mistakes about human nature." But what is this revelation? It is primarily God's commands, both in the Hebrew Scriptures and primarily, for a Christian, in the teaching of Jesus. We learn that we are to love our enemies, for example, in the Sermon on the Mount and in the parable of the good Samaritan. Foot's book is illuminating because it shows what happens when we do not have this revelation to appeal to. She gives us an account of our "natural ends," and Rosalind Hursthouse expands on Foot's account by saying that there are four of these ends, two that we share with plants and two that we share with (some) nonhuman animals.[2] The two that we share with plants are survival and reproduction. The two that we share with (some) nonhuman animals are pleasure (or the absence of pain) and the well-being of our social group. These are, she says, the natural ends against which we can measure whether some human life is a naturally good life, and there is no fifth such end. But the problem here is that this account of our natural ends is inadequate for the project of deducing our moral obligations from it. These ends conflict in practice, and the appeal to human nature as we observe it does not settle these conflicts. We sometimes pursue survival, reproduction, pleasure, and the advantage of our group by lying, stealing, and committing genocide. Foot and Hursthouse are not, like Larry Arnhart,[3] trying to argue that impartial benevolence is not found in our biology or in the inclinations we supposedly share with the hunter-gatherers who formed most of our evolutionary history, and therefore it is not obligatory. My point is just that they *do* want to preserve the obligation of impartial benevolence, but their theory does not give them the resources to deduce it from our nature as they define this. We will get a sufficiently rich account of nature to allow this deduction only by building our moral obligations into our account of *created* human nature. And this begs the relevant question.

---

[2]Rosalind Hursthouse, *On Virtue Ethics* (New York: Oxford University Press, 1999), 204-5.
[3]Larry Arnhart, *Darwinian Natural Right: The Biological Ethics of Human Nature* (Albany: State University of New York Press, 1998).

The problem is not just that a natural law ethic might be "defined in a way that is especially convenient for ourselves or our own interest group," which Peterson concedes. The problem is that it *has* repeatedly been so defined. Aristotle's own ethics is a paradigm case, including the privilege he gives to males and to Greeks. But there is a dismal history of this kind of special pleading, based on a self-serving account of human nature. I am not saying that nothing at all can be discerned from human nature without building revealed moral obligations into our picture of it. Paul's words about Gentiles, that "what the law requires is written on their hearts" (Rom 2:15 NRSV) teaches that all humans are accountable to God and cannot plead ignorance as an excuse at the final judgment. But Paul does not tell us the *content* of what is revealed in this way to all. Presumably the whole law is not revealed, but just enough so that they are without excuse. But what this "just enough" is, we are not told. In my remarks on Peter Heltzel's chapter, I spent some time on the Greeks in order to try to illustrate a "Gentile" ethical system (in particular an account of the competitive goods) very different from that revealed in the teaching of Jesus. We should be modest about the extent to which humans just as humans know the moral law.

Peterson discusses the case of the Pharisees who, Jesus implies, should have known that it was all right to pick grains of wheat on the sabbath, in the same way that David and his companions ate the showbread because of a "higher need." How should the Pharisees have known this? Because, Peterson replies, they should have known that the highest commandment is to love God and the neighbor. But note the structure of this reply, with which I agree. God commands (in Deut 11:18-19) that we take the divine commands and bind them as a sign on our hand and fix them as an emblem on our forehead. What has priority here in knowing how to rank duties, when they conflict, is a previously revealed command. I do not want, however, to imply that God's commands are to be found only in Scripture. I agree with Karl Barth that the paradigm divine command is to an individual in a particular set of circumstances. One of Peterson's omissions is that she locates human freedom in the space that natural law allows, as in the case where a person is deciding between two different careers, both of which are declared good by natural law, as though that space were empty. But she does not mention a place here for a Christian's prayer for guidance by the Holy

Spirit. I do not mean that she denies such guidance. But God's command is, I think, *often* given when considerations of natural law (in Scotus's extended sense) and guidance from Scripture do not settle the question. It is true that we have freedom to obey the command or to reject it. But this freedom is not in a vacuum.

What should a divine command theorist say about Peterson's excellent example of Anthony the personal trainer, who is being pressured by the gym to engage in immoral practices? I agree with her conclusion. He should either quit or remain where he is as "salt and light," which will be uncomfortable and will probably not last very long. But *why* should he do this? Peterson says it is because "it cannot be right to make the fulfillment of a monetary obligation (such as paying rent to a landlord) so important that one is willing to deceive other people to do so." Again, I agree. But how do we know this cannot be right? Do we know it because it goes against our nature to deceive in order to have a place to live? Peterson would say that such deception might fit our "sin nature" but not our "created nature." But how do we know this about our created nature? Surely it is because we have defined our created nature as precluding moral wrong, and we have defined moral right in terms of telling the truth. And we know we ought to tell the truth because we have been so commanded.

One final point. Peterson defends the view that there would still be ethical truth even if (impossibly) God did not exist, though she says this would be an impoverished world because we would not reach our proper end of union with God, and because in situations of scarcity we would need to work against one another, and because we would not have divine assistance to lead a good life. But my position, like Elizabeth Anscombe's,[4] is that there would not be moral *obligation* at all, because there would be no final divine obligator. If we had to rely on what we knew about creation without God's revealed commands, we could still recognize some things as good and bad. But the good things would be in conflict with each other, and there would not be anyone with sufficient authority to tell us which good things were, so to speak, trumps.

---

[4]Elizabeth Anscombe, "Modern Moral Philosophy," *Philosophy* 33, no. 124 (January 1958): 26-42.

# A Prophetic Ethics Response

*PETER GOODWIN HELTZEL*

**Claire Brown Peterson introduces** natural law ethics through music, sharing a story from J. R. R. Tolkien's *Silmarillion*. God the Creator in Tolkien's mythology of Middle Earth, Eru Ilúvatar, invites his creatures to sing "Great Music," harmoniously adorning the theme.[1] Peterson conceives of morality as analogous to a musical motif that humans are invited to sing with improvisational creativity. Like Eru Ilúvatar, God the Creator is an improviser and we too are invited to improvise in achieving our life calling.

My heart was "strangely warmed" when I heard Peterson's invocation of improvisation, for *improvising for love and justice* is the central task of prophetic ethics.[2] But the question is, What is the musical motif that we are to be improvising on? While introducing the concept of morality as a music motif, Peterson never clearly states what natural law's major motif is.

Prophetic ethics has two primary objections to natural law ethics. First, nature is ambiguous. Second, Christians are called to be conformed to Christ, not conformed to nature. Rooted in Holy Scripture and energized by the Holy Spirit, prophetic ethics is a *Christ-centered* ethic.

---

[1]J. R. R. Tolkien, *The Silmarillion* (New York: Houghton Mifflin, 1977), 15.

[2]Improvisation is innovation through collaboration that we see manifest in jazz music. As jazz musicians study the standards so they are prepared to improvise in live performance, Christians study the Word and the world so they can be led by the Holy Spirit to improvise for love, justice, and peace. For my discussion of improvisation in theological method see Peter Goodwin Heltzel, "Improvising: A Jazz Approach to Theology," *Resurrection City: A Theology of Improvisation* (Grand Rapids: Eerdmans, 2012), 13ff; The most important methodological work on improvisation in the field of Christian ethics is Samuel Wells, *Improvisation: The Drama of Christian Ethics* (Grand Rapids: Brazos, 2004); Anabaptist theologian Ryan Andrew Newson explores the role of the ecclesial community in ethical discernment in his "Ethics as Improvisation: Anabaptist Communal Discernment as Method," *Mennonite Quarterly Review* 87, no. 2 (April 2013): 187-205.

Since nature is ambiguous, natural law is not sufficient as a Christian ethic.[3] Whether in the medieval cosmos or the Copernican cosmos, every concept of "nature" is constructed and based on the cultural, scientific, and religious wisdom that we project on it from our subject position in a particular cultural-linguistic community within a historical horizon.[4] Because of the ambiguity of nature, discerning and conforming one's life to the natural law is inadequate as a comprehensive ethical paradigm when our understanding of nature is constantly changing.

While ambiguity is defined as an uncertainty of meaning, it also has a second meaning: a lack of decisiveness resulting from a failure to make a choice between two alternatives. The Protestant Reformers saw the human heart as divided because of humanity's fall into sin. Martin Luther speaks of humans as "simultaneously sinner and saint." John Calvin writes, "the contagion of sin has run riot through every part, nothing pure and free from all defilement will be found in us."[5] Since sin impairs our minds from seeing the Creator's fingerprints in creation, Calvin argues that we need the "spectacles" of Scripture to discern the gracious action of God in the world amid the brutal predatory instinct of the natural world and the moral paradoxes of the human heart.

Natural law ethicists do not take the fall seriously enough. As a result of sin, humans have a predisposition toward selfishness, conflict, and violence. Natural law ethics overestimates humanity's ability to rationally discern our ethical course through an innate comprehension of our natural purpose. While each of us has a song to sing, there are many like Melkor, the Dark Lord, in Tolkien's *Silmarillion*, whose music of "discord" produced conditions for the Great Music to falter and founder "in a sea of turbulent sound."[6] Instead of pursuing justice and love, humans, like Boromir of Gondor, are too often seduced by the ring of power.

---

[3]Christianity needs a full recognition of the problem of ambiguity in public Christian ethics today. See David Tracy, *Plurality and Ambiguity: Hermeneutics, Religion and Hope* (San Francisco: Harper & Row, 1987).

[4]Alister McGrath, *Nature: A Scientific Theology* (London: T&T Clark, 2001), 1:137-38. McGrath offers an insightful account of the social mediation of nature in chapter three, "The Construction of Nature," 81-134.

[5]John Calvin, *The Gospel According to St. John 1-10*, Calvin's Commentaries, trans. T. H. L. Parker (Grand Rapids: Eerdmans, 1993), 66.

[6]J. R. R. Tolkien, *The Silmarillion* (New York: Houghton Mifflin, 1977), 16.

As a result of the fall, the shalom of creation has been shattered. All of nature is out of balance, including our own moral compass. When people look to nature as a moral guide, they usually get what they are looking for. "Nature does not teach. . . . Nature will verify any theological or metaphysical proposition," writes C. S. Lewis in his classic *The Four Loves*.[7] Nature as a source of ethics at best is ambiguous and at its worst can be downright dangerous.

When Adolf Hitler and the Nazis commandeered the language of the "natural" to support the Aryan ideal, Karl Barth and Dietrich Bonhoeffer signed the Barmen Declaration in 1934, affirming that Jesus Christ "is the one Word of God" and rejected other sources of revelation, including natural law. When Peterson argues that the "natural law" is the "the perfect definition of a human being," she unveils an unreachable, prior state of humanity before the fall that is not relevant to anyone living in the world today. Peterson thinks about nature as it *ought to be* rather than *what it is* in its current fallen condition. Since we know nothing about the *prelapsarian* state of humanity that was experienced by only Adam and Eve before the fall, we can easily fall prey to injecting our own moral content into this archetype of "perfection" (e.g., patriarchy, white supremacy, Western imperialism). Given humanity's selfish quest for power and nature "red in tooth and claw," as Alfred Lord Tennyson expresses it in his poem "In Memoriam A. A. H." (1850), it is never a good idea to "let nature take her course."

Through God's common grace in creation there are some internal moral sources like *conscience* within humans, but even conscience is muted and marred without the special grace of Jesus Christ. Inspired by a dream of beloved community, Dr. Martin Luther King Jr. saw the conscience as a *strategic* moral resource for his doctrine of human dignity. In his "Letter from Birmingham Jail," King answered eight white pastors' "anxiety over our willingness to break laws" and makes a clear-cut a distinction between just and unjust laws:

> An unjust law is a code that is out of harmony with the moral law. To put it
> in the terms of Saint Thomas Aquinas, an unjust law is a human law that is
> not rooted in eternal and natural law. Any law that uplifts human personality
> is just. Any law that degrades human personality is unjust. All segregation
> statutes are unjust because segregation distorts the soul and damages the

---

[7]C. S. Lewis, *The Four Loves* (New York: Harcourt, 1960), 20.

personality. It gives the segregator a false sense of superiority, and the segregated a false sense of inferiority.[8]

King argues that just civil laws are rooted in the eternal moral law, which Aquinas describes as the "natural law." As a prophetic personalist ethicist, Dr. King considers a law's effect on the diminishment or flourishing of human personality as a test of whether the law is just or unjust.

With his back up against the wall of a prison cell, King eclectically draws on every ethical concept he can get his hands on to systematically dismantle racist segregation laws. Rhetorically, King knew that invoking Aquinas's natural law would appeal to Catholics, multifaith leaders, and secular activists. Through nonviolent direct action protest, he sought to "arouse the conscience of the community over its injustice." King believed that all humans have a conscience, an innate sense of right and wrong, which is why he had faith in the moral conversion of white moderate Christians.

King's appeals to the conscience and the natural law reflect God's common grace, a loving provision for all creatures in the community of creation. As Patrick T. Smith and Fabrice Jotterand write, "According to Calvin, even though the moral, natural, or inward law is affected by sin, it, nevertheless, remains as *a gift* to human beings. The result is that God, in his common grace . . . restrains sin through these natural mechanisms that are part of human nature as such."[9] Through the Christian doctrine of common grace the conscience and moral law can be viewed as *good gifts* to all God's children as we work together for the common good.[10] While King deploys natural law on a strategic *ad hoc* basis, it is not programmatic for prophetic ethics. While God's common grace provides humans good gifts to restrain evil, Christ Jesus offers humanity saving grace and an ethical model to emulate in the walk of costly discipleship.

---

[8]Dr. King goes on to argue that segregation statutes "gives the segregator a false sense of superiority, and the segregated a false sense of inferiority." Martin Luther King Jr., "Letter from Birmingham Jail," *A Testament of Hope: The Essential Writings and Speeches of Martin Luther King Jr.*, ed. James M. Washington (New York: HarperCollins, 1986), 293. The letter was published April 16, 1963.

[9]Patrick T. Smith and Fabrice Jotterand, "Toward a Common Grace Christian Bioethics: A Reformed Protestant Engagement with H. Tristram Engelhardt, Jr.," *Christian Bioethics* 20, no. 2 (2014): 237; italics added.

[10]For an insightful introduction to the Christian doctrine of common grace see Vincent E. Bacote, *The Political Disciple: A Theology of Public Life* (Grand Rapids: Zondervan, 2015); and Richard J. Mouw, *He Shines in All That's Fair: Culture and Common Grace* (Grand Rapids: Eerdmans, 2001).

Prophetic ethics is a Jesus-centered ethic. It is concretely realized in the life, death, descent, resurrection, and ascension of Jesus Christ. Peterson writes, "when an individual can sense in Jesus the person she ought to be, that individual is drawing on her knowledge of the natural law, imperfect though that knowledge may be." Christian ethics is not about drawing on our own internal knowledge of natural law but about having our whole life *fundamentally reoriented* by the incarnation, life, death, descent, resurrection, and ascension of Jesus Christ through the power of the Holy Spirit.

*Jesus of Nazareth*, not nature, is the center of gravity in prophetic ethics. Starting his ministry by rolling out the Isaiah scroll, Jesus comes singing an inspiring song of jubilee justice, inaugurating a new socioeconomic order.[11] More than an embodiment of natural law, Jesus is love incarnate. From Gethsemane to Golgotha, Jesus shows us what love looks like in a life dedicated the flourishing of others, especially the least and the lost (Mt 25:31-46). In his crucifixion on a Roman cross, Christ disarmed the powers and principalities (Col 2:13-15). Through Jesus Christ's death and resurrection, we are saved *by* grace, saved *from* sin, and saved *for* life-giving witness, marked by love, justice, and peace.

Only through God's grace in Jesus Christ can we strongly image the goodness of God through the power of the Holy Spirit. Jesus Christ is "both the model of and means to our becoming the image of God."[12] Through the *full humanity* of Jesus Christ our true purpose as humans made in the image of God is fully revealed, and through his full *divinity* we are transformed into the likeness of God through the power of the Holy Spirit. Following Jesus, we need to respect all creatures and their activities as an embodied expression of our reverence to our living and loving God.[13] Prophetic ethics calls us to be conformed to Christ so we can be Spirit-led prophets of transformation who build beloved cities in light of the coming city of God (Rev 21:2).[14]

---

[11] André Trochmé, *Jesus and the Nonviolent Revolution*, trans. Michael H. Shank and Marlin E. Miller (Scottdale, PA: Herald Press, 1956), esp. 48-52.

[12] Kathryn Tanner, *Christ the Key* (Cambridge: Cambridge University Press, 2010), 58.

[13] For a thoughtful discussion on the respect for others as creatures, see Kathryn Tanner, *The Politics of God: Christian Theologies and Social Justice* (Minneapolis: Fortress, 1992), chap. 5.

[14] See my discussion of building beloved cities with reference to Dr. Martin Luther King's theology of "beloved community." Peter Goodwin Heltzel, "Building the Beloved City: Howard Thurman and Martin Luther King, Jr.," in *Resurrection City: A Theology of Improvisation* (Grand Rapids: Eerdmans, 2012), 90-120.

# 3

# Divine Command Theory

*JOHN HARE*

This chapter will first state a form of divine command theory and then reply to four objections. The theory is, very simply, that what makes something morally wrong (or morally forbidden) is that God forbids it, and what makes something morally right (or morally obligatory) is that God requires it. There is a relation claimed here between moral obligation and divine command. The first part of this chapter focuses on clarifying the two terms in this relation—namely, moral right and wrong and divine command—and the nature of the relation that is claimed between them—namely, *making* right and wrong. The second part describes and replies to the objections. The main concern of divine command theory is that we remember to love God's law and God's command. Christians are prone to emphasize God's grace and to say that they are not under the law (Gal 4:5). But they need to remember that despite our repeated failures to live by the law and the command, and despite the need to be forgiven for this failure, the law and the command are the presupposition for the rest of the narrative of redemption. Psalm 119 is an extended expression of the gratitude of a people who would otherwise, without God's revelation, go astray like lost sheep. God's sovereignty is manifested in selecting the path we are to follow to our destination as co-lovers when we enter into the love that is between the persons of the Trinity, and then in revealing to us by command what is the right and the wrong way to live in this world so as to follow this path.

## MORAL RIGHT AND WRONG

The first term in this relation, moral right and wrong, will be treated here in a Kantian way. There is no necessity about this. One could have a divine command theory about moral rightness and wrongness construed in a utilitarian way, for example, or a virtue ethics way. But it will be helpful to have a particular account in mind, and Kant's account is appropriate because he teaches throughout his published work that we should recognize our duties as God's commands.[1] It is important to see that the divine command theory I am proposing is a theory about right and wrong, and not a theory about good and bad. The reply to the second objection to the theory (the objection from arbitrariness) will depend on this point. The theory is not that God's command makes something *good*. This does not mean that God is irrelevant to the theory of the good presupposed here.[2] The good, in the sense of the excellent, might be what resembles God, as in Robert M. Adams's theory.[3] Or, if this cannot capture all cases of excellence, we may need to add some additional clauses. The good sometimes is what draws us toward union with God, or sometimes what expresses God's character or manifests it (without resembling it). The purpose of the present chapter does not require going further into this question. The point is just that the good can be essentially related to God without this being a relation to divine *command*. But the theory posits an essential relation of moral *right and wrong* to God's command. The account of moral right and wrong that is presupposed is Kantian in the sense that Kant gives us a philosophically more precise way to formulate the principle that is already present in some of the world's religions that we should love the neighbor as we do our self. The formulation is in terms of what Kant calls "the categorical imperative," which he thinks is the supreme principle of morality and which he in turn explains in terms of a number of different

---

[1] E.g., Immanuel Kant, *Religion Within the Boundaries of Mere Reason*, 6:154; and *Critique of Practical Reason*, 5:129. References to Kant will be by the volume and page number of the Berlin Academy Edition (Berlin: George Reiner, later Walter de Gruyter, 1900–). But Kant is not himself a divine command theorist in the sense I am proposing, because he does not think divine command *makes* something right and wrong. At least in the second *Critique* and subsequently, he does not think he can give an account of the ground of moral obligation, and simply starts from what he calls "the fact of reason" that we are under the moral law. His view is that we should determine by the categorical imperative procedure what is right and wrong, and we should then attribute this to divine command, because it is only if it is divine command that we can hope in a rationally stable way for the union of virtue and happiness, which is our highest good.

[2] Here, and at many places in this chapter, there is a fuller account that is being abbreviated. The fuller, book-length account is given in John E. Hare, *God's Command* (Oxford: Oxford University Press, 2015).

[3] Robert M. Adams, *Finite and Infinite Goods* (Oxford: Oxford University Press, 1999), chap. 1.

formulations or formulas. We can take two of these as paradigmatic and explain them briefly as follows.[4]

The first formula is that if the prescription of an action is to be morally permissible, we have to be able to will that prescription, together with the reason for it, as a universal law. To will a prescription as a universal law requires that we be able to eliminate in principle all reference to the agent herself or any other particular persons or times or places. In the same way physical lawfulness requires that *any* stone of a certain mass thrown with a certain velocity will break *any* window of a certain degree of fragility at *any* time and *any* place where normal conditions apply; we need to be able to eliminate reference to any individual stone or window or time or place. Kant holds that it is inconsistent to will an end or goal and will the destruction of a required means to that end. He then gives the example of a false promise (a promise the agent does not intend to keep). It is inconsistent to will as a universal law the prescription of a false promise to pay back a loan, so as to get the money without subsequently having to give it back, because if anyone at any time is permitted to make a false promise for such a reason, the institution of promise making (which is itself a required means to making a false promise) is destroyed.

The second formula is that if the prescription of an action is to be morally permissible, the agent has to treat humanity, whether in herself or in any other person, always at the same time as an end and never merely as a means. To treat a person as an end and not merely as a means requires at least sharing his purposes if the fulfillment of those purposes is affected by the agent's action and if those purposes are themselves morally permissible. To share a person's purpose is to make his purpose my purpose. For example, I am required to treat my enemy this way since my enemy is a human being. I do not have to share his immoral purposes—for example, his purpose to do me harm—but his other purposes (to have friends, pleasure, etc.). I have to make my own purposes to the extent I will secure them by what I do.

---

[4]I am giving a reconstruction of Kant's account at *The Groundwork of the Metaphysics of Morals*, 4:421 and 4:430. In *God's Command*, I make two objections to Kant's account as described here. First, I argue that there are *particular* moral judgments, where the terms in the prescription are not necessarily universalizable except for the term in the action position (since what is prescribed even in a particular moral judgment is an action of a certain *type*). Second, not all inclinations should be construed as directed toward the agent's pleasure or satisfaction.

There are various obscurities in this account of the two Kantian formulas, but it is not necessary to try to sort them out for our present purposes.

## DIVINE COMMAND

So far we have an account of the first term in divine command theory—namely, the morally right and wrong. The second term is divine command. The purpose of commands is for the speaker to effect change in the world through the expression of her will. It is useful to distinguish as the Christian scholastics did between five kinds of divine prescription, though this should not be taken as an exhaustive list.[5] These five are named in a Latin dactylic hexameter: *praecipit et prohibet, permittit, consulit, implet*. God gives precepts, prohibitions, permissions, counsels, and directly effective commands. Both precepts and prohibitions create obligations. They are issued with authority, and some kind of sanction is envisioned for noncompliance, ranging from blame to punishment. The notion of authority here needs some explanation. The term as used in connection with human commands is not unambiguously normative, because human commands can be issued with both proper and improper authority. In this way the term *authority* is like other "thick" value terms that take up the criteria for their application into their meaning, and combine them unstably with the evaluation, so that it is possible to find cases where the criteria are approximately met, but the evaluation is the opposite of the usual. For example, if the criteria for politeness include deference to the opinions of others, it is possible to find people who are *too* deferential and thus too polite. What then is rightful or *proper* authority? Joseph Raz says that one person is practically authoritative over another in a certain domain only if the first person's dictates bring about to some extent the reasons for action that the other has in that domain.[6] Objectively, when God commands a person to do something, this brings about a reason for acting in accordance with the command, even if, subjectively, the person does not acknowledge this reason. There is an analogy with the authority of the state, as Kant construes this. Kant holds that we have a reason to obey

---

[5]William of Ockham, *Ordinatio*, dist. 46, q. 1.

[6]Joseph Raz, *The Morality of Freedom* (Oxford: Oxford University Press, 1986). See also Mark Murphy, *An Essay on Divine Authority* (Ithaca, NY: Cornell University Press, 2002), 8-16. But I disagree with Murphy's view that God's commands do not have objective authority for nonbelievers, though the nonbelievers have reason to accept such authority.

the laws of the state because the state upholds external freedom, which is the freedom of action that expresses in the world our internal freedom of choice (which Kant thinks is valuable in itself). The state provides what he calls "a hindrance to the hindrances" to this freedom by providing those who would interfere with our external freedom a motive for refraining from this interference.[7] Even an anarchist who does not acknowledge the authority of the state has an objective reason, on this view, to obey the laws—namely, the value of internal and external freedom. To apply the analogy, we can make use of the scholastic distinction between God's three roles as sovereign. When God commands something by legislative authority, implemented in God's executive and judicial authority, there is an objective reason for obedience from the union of wills (divine and human) that is expressed in such obedience and which is good in itself.[8] The idea that obedience to God is a union of wills that is good in itself is defended in the following reply to the first objection to divine command theory—namely, the objection that it creates a vicious regress of justification.

To say that some kind of sanction is envisioned for noncompliance is not to say that the *motive* for compliance should be to avoid the sanction. In the Kantian analogy of obedience to the state, the motive should be respect for freedom, but the existence of the sanction provides a motive for those who are *not* motivated by such respect. There is a reply here to the objection that divine command theory makes obedience to the moral law self-serving by basing motivation on hope of reward or fear of punishment.[9]

The other three kinds of divine prescription do not create obligations to do something from the prescription of it. Permissions are different from precepts because if a person is given a precept she is permitted to comply but is not permitted not to comply. If a person is permitted, she is permitted both to do the thing and not to do it. God tells Adam, "You may freely eat of every tree of the garden; but of the tree of the knowledge of good and evil you shall not eat" (Gen 2:16-17 NRSV), following a permission with a

---

[7]Immanuel Kant, *The Metaphysics of Morals*, 6:396.
[8]Francisco Suárez, *De Legibus*, 2.15.20.
[9]Kant himself is sometimes taken to make this objection, but he does not. He objects to a *version* of divine command theory—for example, in Crusius—that gives a wrongful place to fear of punishment. But the objection does not apply to all theories that say we should recognize our duties as God's commands. See John E. Hare, *God's Call* (Grand Rapids: Eerdmans, 2001), chap. 3.

prohibition. The topic of whether there is a separate category of divine *counsels* has been controversial. I have argued that God can use imperative sentences to give us advice or invitation, where these speech acts do not create obligation and there is no sanction envisioned for noncompliance.[10] A person can receive a call from God to a new way of life, even though there is nothing wrong with the old one. If we were to attribute emotions to God, we would say that God was disappointed when we declined, and not that God was angry. But this is anthropomorphic language. Perhaps an ingredient in the picture is that a call is often accompanied by the offer of a gift. On the Roman Catholic picture of the three evangelical counsels, which seems wrong if taken as a complete list of counsels, the call to chastity is accompanied by a gift from God to make that way of life livable in an excellent way. The refusal of the call is in such a case the refusal of the gift, and an appropriate *human* response to the refusal of a gift is disappointment. Finally, directly effective commands do not need to have any language-using human recipient. God says, "Let there be light," and there is light (Gen 1:3; see also Ps 33:9; Gen 1:22). God effects something directly by commanding it. It is important to see that this category of prescription places *creation* in the category of something commanded. If God's commands that produce our obligations are themselves constrained because of God's love by the human nature that God created, as I will concede in reply to the second objection (from arbitrariness), this does not take us outside God's commands to something else constraining God. Rather, God creates by command and sustains creation by command, and then commands us with one of the other types of divine prescription in a way that is consistent with that creative command.

## THE RELATION BETWEEN MORAL OBLIGATION AND DIVINE COMMAND

So far we have dealt with the two terms of the relation claimed by divine command theory between moral obligation and divine command. But what is the relation itself? In what sense does God's command *make* something right or wrong? I am going to reject two proposals that are current in the

---

[10]Hare, *God's Command*, 2.1.5.

literature and then propose a third. The two proposals I am rejecting are Philip Quinn's suggestion that the command *causes* the obligation, and Robert Adams's suggestion that the command *constitutes* the obligation.[11] Causation seems wrong because it suggests two different *events* (one always coming after the other under physical law, as throwing the stone is followed by breaking the window). And constitution seems wrong because obligation is not a natural kind like water, which is constituted by two hydrogen atoms and an oxygen atom. The command is not an ingredient of the obligation. Here is a third proposal. A king can make a law by declaring, "The king wills it" (*le roi le veult*).[12] This is an "explicit performative," in John Austin's terminology, like "I promise."[13] There are many other cases, such as a priest's baptizing by saying "I baptize you in the name of the Father, the Son, and the Holy Spirit." In all these cases there is an internal conceptual connection between the *producing* and what is *produced*. There may be a suspicion that we are here deriving an obligation illegitimately from a fact—namely, that God commands something.[14] But in the promising case, I am committed to the judgment "I ought to do x" when I have promised to do x because I endorse the institution of making promises. In the divine command case, I am committed to the judgment "I ought to do x" when God commands x because of the necessity of the judgment that God is to be obeyed. This necessity is the topic of the reply to the first objection to divine command theory (the objection from vicious regress), and we will come to it shortly.

Before we get to that, however, there is a reply here to a different objection to divine command theory proposed by Nicholas Wolterstorff.[15] He denies that all moral obligations are generated by God's commands because, he says, some are generated by *human* commands—for example, a parent's command to a child to clean up his room. But we should see divine command

---

[11]Philip Quinn, "Divine Command Theory," in *Guide to Ethical Theory*, ed. Hugh LaFollette (Oxford: Blackwell, 1999), 54-55. Adams, *Finite and Infinite Goods*, 250.

[12]This is current practice in Great Britain.

[13]J. L. Austin, *How to Do Things with Words*, ed. J. O. Urmson (Oxford: Oxford University Press, 1962), 69. "Saying 'I promise that' (if happy, of course) makes it a promise, and unambiguously a promise."

[14]See Jon R. Searle, "How to Derive 'Ought' from 'Is,'" *Philosophical Review* 73 (1964): 44. And see the reply in R. M. Hare, "The Promising Game," in *Essays in Ethical Theory* (Oxford: Oxford University Press, 1989), 130-44.

[15]Nicholas Wolterstorff, *Justice: Rights and Wrongs* (Princeton, NJ: Princeton University Press, 2008), 271-73.

theory as operating in answer to the question why we should hold ourselves under those obligations. Granted, for example, that if I have promised to take my children out for lunch, and I have an obligation to keep my promises, then I have an obligation to take them to lunch. There is still the question why I should keep my promises. To draw the implication from my having said "I promise" to my obligation, I need to endorse the institution of promising, and the fact that God requires this faithfulness of me gives me a reason for this endorsement.

## OBJECTIONS TO DIVINE COMMAND THEORY

We come now to the first of four objections to divine command theory, and the responses to these four will consume the rest of this chapter.

*First objection to divine command theory.* The first objection is that divine command theory gives us a vicious regress. If I say, "I ought to keep my promises because God commands me to do so," surely I then have to answer the question, "Why should I do what God tells me to do?" Perhaps the answer is "Because I am grateful to God for all God's gifts, including the gift of my life." But then surely I have to answer the question, "Why should I have an obligation of gratitude?" At this point there seem to be three options, none of them good. Either I go on giving new justifications forever, or I say, "Because God commands it," but then I am stuck in a circle; or I say, "I just do have such an obligation, and there is no further ground to be given," but then I have denied that God's command is what makes things obligatory, at least in this case.[16]

There is a reply to this objection, using a distinction Duns Scotus draws between natural law strictly speaking and natural law in an extended sense. He thinks that the command to love God given in the first table of the Ten Commandments is natural law strictly speaking; that is, it is known to be true just by knowing its terms (or follows from propositions known in this way).[17] But he thinks the second table, which concerns our various duties to the neighbor, is natural law only in an extended sense. It is true, but only

[16]Stephen Darwall raises this objection in *The Second-Person Standpoint: Morality, Respect, and Accountability* (Cambridge, MA: Harvard University Press, 2009), 104-9, using a text from Ralph Cudworth, and there is a similar objection in Leibniz, *Opinion on the Principles of Pufendorf.*
[17]Scotus, *Ordinatio* 4, dist. 17.

contingently so. With respect to the first table, Scotus holds that we know that if God exists, God is supremely good, and we know that what is supremely good is to be loved. Similarly Ockham says, "It is because God is the greatest good that He is to be loved above all."[18] It is also true that we know that to love God is at least to obey God. This is because to love God is at least to will what God wills for us to will.[19] One way to show this is to appeal to the second formula of Kant's categorical imperative discussed earlier: for me to treat another person as an end in herself (Kant calls it "practical love") is to share her morally permitted purposes to the extent that these are affected by what I do. To love God is to share God's ends as far as we can. But our love for God is different in this way from our love for human beings. In the case of our love for God there is a disproportion since we are finite beings and God is infinite. Loving God is not simply to repeat God's will in our will, because there are things God wills that God does not will for us to will.[20] So what we are to repeat in our wills is God's will for our willing. But willing what God wills for our willing is obedience. So it is necessarily true not just that God is to be loved but that God is to be obeyed. The first objection is that we get a vicious regress of justification: either justifying each claim by another one *ad infinitum* or getting stuck in a circle or denying the central thesis of divine command theory. But if I justify the claim that the moral demand is a proper demand on me by saying that God's command makes things obligatory, I am not terminating the justification in something that *itself* requires justification, except in as far as I have to justify the claim that God exists. This means that divine commands do not generate *all* our obligations, because there is one important exception—namely, the very obligation to obey divine commands. But this is not a troubling exception once one accepts the necessary truths that if God exists, God is to be loved and God is to be obeyed.

**Second objection to divine command theory.** A second objection to divine command theory is that it makes morality arbitrary. If God's command makes things right and wrong, would not torturing babies be right if God

---

[18]William of Ockham, *In Sententiarum*, 1, 4.

[19]Ibid., 2, 7.

[20]See Scotus, *Ordinatio* 1, dist. 48. Experience suggests that God can will for us to will that someone we love should stay alive, and for us to do what we can to save her, even though God wills for that person to die.

commanded it? This objection is sometimes tied to Plato's account in the *Euthyphro* of Socrates's question, Is the holy holy because it is loved by the gods, or do they love it because it is holy?[21] Socrates is clear that he thinks the answer to this question is the second alternative, that the gods love the holy because it is holy. This answer has seemed to many philosophers to be fatal to divine command theory. If the gods love the holy because it is already holy, then they do not produce its holiness by loving it. I have elsewhere tried to show that Socrates does not actually give an argument for the key premise (at 10d4) that the gods love the holy because it is holy.[22] He simply gets Euthyphro to agree to this without an argument and then proceeds with an elaborate argument that from this premise we can see that the holy and the god-loved are not the same. If we try to find in the dialogue an argument for the key premise, the best candidate is from the earlier discussion about why the gods fight with each other. Socrates and Euthyphro agree (at 8e4) that dispute among the gods (and also between humans) is because some see justice in an action and some see injustice. There is an implicit appeal here to some kind of theory of Forms. But the dialogue is weak support for the opponent of divine command theory because the opponent needs an explicit argument that the gods love the holy because it is holy, and the dialogue does not in fact provide one.

There is a reply to the objection from arbitrariness, using a distinction referred to at the beginning of this chapter between what is obligatory and what is good (where both of these require reference to God in their account, but in *different* ways). We can say that what God commands is good, and the goodness is not produced by the command. This does not, however, make God's command redundant, because only those good things that are commanded are obligatory.[23] There are two seemingly opposite priority relations between what is obligatory and what is good. On the one hand, the good has priority over the obligatory because everything that is obligatory is good, though not vice versa. This is what Aristotle might call "priority in

---

[21]Plato, *Euthyphro* 10d-f.

[22]John E. Hare, *Plato's Euthyphro* (Bryn Mawr, PA; Bryn Mawr Commentaries, 1985).

[23]This solution to the Euthyphro problem is already worked out in J. L. Mackie, *Ethics: Inventing Right and Wrong* (Harmondsworth, UK: Penguin, 1977), 229-32, though Mackie does not believe that God exists. Another influential treatment is by Adams, *Finite and Infinite Goods*, chap. 11. I do not agree, however, with his treatment of the binding of Isaac.

account" since the proposed account is that something is obligatory if it is a good thing that God commands. For example, God commands us not to lie, because truthfulness is good, but there are many good things that God does not command (for example, should I play the violin or the viola?) and we are left free to choose between them. On the other hand, the obligatory has priority to the good because the good things that God selects as mandatory for us are, so to speak, trumps. This we might call "priority in practice." For example, we are not permitted to escape from the obligation of truthfulness just because there is some small good thing that a lie would make possible for us.[24]

We can now ask the question whether God's selection of some good things to require of us rather than other good things is constrained by the nature God has given to us. It might seem that such a constraint would be inconsistent with the sovereignty of God. This is one of the two main issues between divine command theory and natural law theory. The other main issue is whether we should be eudaemonist (i.e., whether we should say that everything we pursue is properly pursued for the sake of our own happiness [*eudaimonia* in Greek is traditionally translated as "happiness"]). It is not the purpose of the present chapter to get into a sustained discussion of natural law theory, but it may be helpful to give a rather brief account of the main defect of eudaemonism, which is that the most conspicuous versions of the theory are unacceptably self-regarding. Duns Scotus takes from Anselm the distinction between the affection for advantage (*affectio commodi*), which is directed toward the agent's own happiness and perfection, and the affection for justice (*affectio justitiae*), which is directed toward what is good in itself, independently of any reference to the agent. For example, the agent can will that, if it is God's will, she should be damned for the sake of the glory of God. Scotus thus gives an account of *two* basic springs of motivation, not (as in eudaemonism) just one. He is not saying that there is anything wrong with the affection for advantage. He thinks we will always have it, even in heaven, and we were created to have it. But the key question,

---

[24]The divine command theory defended in *God's Command* does not claim that there is an *absolute* duty to tell the truth, even in cases like that of the Dutch householder in World War II who was hiding a Jew and was asked by the Nazi officer whether there was anyone else in the house. But it suggests there is an overridable presumption that a prescription to tell a lie is not a divine command.

since there are two basic drives and not just one, is how we rank them; the affection for justice is supposed to be the "first checkrein" on the affection for advantage.[25]

In the ancient world, there were versions of eudaemonism that attempted to escape the objection that the theory is unacceptably self-regarding. I will give two conspicuous examples: first, the Epicurean suggestion that we should include the agent's sympathetic pleasures in the account—namely, the pleasures she gets from the pleasures of others. The trouble is that our sympathies are limited. We do not sufficiently care for those who are not related to us by kinship or friendship, and sympathetic pleasures will not get us to Kantian morality.[26] A second example is the Stoic suggestion that the idea of reason brings impartiality with it, and so our good as *rational* beings requires that we follow the moral law. The trouble is that there does not seem to be anything irrational about preferring oneself, unless we already build impartiality into the account of reason, but that begs the question. Aquinas held (following Aristotle) that every human being acts necessarily for *one* end, our own perfection or happiness, but he also held that the distinctive mark of charity is the love of God for God's own sake, and the love of the neighbor for the neighbor's sake.[27] To make these claims consistent requires that we believe in a necessary concurrence of interest between ourselves and our fellow creatures and "the fellowship of God's friends."[28] But while a Christian should believe that God in providence brings about such concurrence, it is presumptuous to claim a *necessary* concurrence rather than one mediated by God's free grace. Finally, if we identify our happiness as entering into God's loving that is itself self-transcending, we might think we could solve the problem of unacceptable self-regard.[29] But if this suggestion is that our interest becomes *purely* not self-indexed, the theory is now unacceptably self-neglecting. We need to retain *both* fundamental sources of motivation, and our nature is to be forced into a ranking of the two that retains them both.

[25]Scotus, *Reportatio* 2, dist. 6, q. 2, n. 10.
[26]For more argument, see Hare, *God's Command*, 3.3.1.
[27]Aquinas, *Summa Theologiae* I-II.1.5, 6, 8, and II-II.23.5.2 and 31.1.
[28]See Jean Porter, "The Desire for Happiness and the Virtues of the Will," *Journal of Moral Theology* 3, no. 1 (2014): 18-38.
[29]This is Jennifer Herdt's suggestion, in her Warfield lectures at Princeton Theological Seminary in 2013.

There is not a necessary connection between natural law theory and eudaemonism. In Islam, the Mut'azilites, such as Abd al-Jabbar, held *both* that the moral law, knowable by our reason independently of special revelation, is the standard by which special revelation is to be judged, *and* that the right in all of its aspects attract us in itself, intrinsically, and not because it leads to a benefit for us as agents of the action.[30] On the other hand, al-Ash'ari held a type of divine command theory that was consistent with eudaemonism. But in the Christian discussion of these matters, the pairing has usually been that natural law goes together with eudaemonism and deductivism (namely, the view that our moral obligations can be *deduced* from human nature), and divine command theory goes together with the denial of these.

A divine command theorist does need to have something to say about the relation between divine command and human nature. We have already seen that Scotus denies that the second table of the Ten Commandments is natural law strictly speaking, and this is because we do not know it "from its terms." This means that the moral law cannot be *deduced* from human nature, because we do not know just from our being human that we have obligations to refrain from murder, theft, lying, and so on. On the other hand, Scotus maintains that these laws *fit* our nature exceedingly well. What is this "fittingness" relation? I suggest that we can see the fittingness in terms of appropriateness to our end, which Scotus says is to be "co-lovers" (*condiligentes*) of God, entering into the love that is between the members of the Trinity. I would add, though this goes somewhat beyond Scotus, that the end of each one of us is a *unique* kind of love of God. Scotus gives the prohibition of theft as an example of the contingency of the second table.[31] Private property is presupposed by the commandment but is not essential to human beings. Scotus says we were not created with it, the church gave it up at Pentecost temporarily, and we will not have it in heaven. Moreover, even at times that we did have the institution of private property, God could and did "dispense" from the prohibition on theft, as with the despoiling of

---

[30]See Hare, *God's Command*, 6.1.1. There are also contemporary versions of natural law theory that are not eudaemonist, such as Mark Murphy, *Natural Law and Practical Rationality* (Cambridge: Cambridge University Press, 2001).

[31]Scotus, *Ordinatio* 3, suppl., dist. 37. See also Bonaventure, *De Perfectione Evangelica* 2.1. The Ten Commandments should not be taken in this discussion as an exhaustive summation of the moral law.

the Egyptians in Exodus under the threat of the plagues. With respect to the prohibition on murder, we can ask whether God could command the killing of the innocent, if they stay dead once killed (contrary to Scotus's understanding of Abraham's belief that Isaac would come back to life, in the story told in Genesis 22). Mark Murphy poses a dilemma here.[32] Let us call facts about moral obligation "moral facts" and facts about God "divine facts." We can then ask whether every moral fact is contingent (including the fact that killing the innocent is wrong), given the maximal set of nonmoral and nondivine facts. If we say yes (the first horn), this seems to make the nonmoral, nondivine facts morally inert, as though the moral necessitating or obliging comes out of God's will or command just by fiat. If we say no (the second horn), this seems to mean that even if, as divine command theorists, we deny that *we* are obliged directly by the nonmoral, nondivine facts, God *is* so constrained, and this seems very odd.

Here is a suggestion about how to navigate between the horns of this dilemma. We can assume, first, that there is an overridable presumption against taking something to be a divine command if it is inconsistent with our good as pilgrims (*viatores*, i.e., those on the way, *in via*). Because of the divine love, God will command only what is good, and so what is either constitutive of or conducive to our end. But one thing characteristic of being pilgrims is that our whole life prepares us for the unique kind of love of God that is our destination. We should assume, therefore, that it is not right to end a life prematurely. Another characteristic feature of being pilgrims is that we receive communications from God about how we are to live, and we make the pilgrimage together with other people with whom we communicate in language. But communication requires that we be able to trust God's and each other's sincerity; this is the plausible part of Kant's argument in the *Groundwork* that it is incoherent to will the prescription of a false promise as a universal law. The form of argument here is transcendental; it argues from the conditions of possibility of some fact that is taken as basic, here the fact that we are recipients of God's call and embedded in language-using community, to conclusions about what we (and God) have to be like to make this possible. But then it reverses direction and asks what

---

[32]Mark Murphy, *God and Moral Law: On the Theistic Explanation of Morality* (Oxford: Oxford University Press, 2012), 121-24.

constraints are placed on what we can take to be divine commands by the fact that we are this kind of people.

None of this implies that moral law or moral obligation is deducible from human nature, even in the case of the prohibitions on killing the innocent or on lying. This is because of the social character of law and obligation. Thus Aquinas holds that law, including natural law, has to be laid down by a lawmaker since law is an ordinance of reason made by one who has care of a community.[33] We are obligated *to* someone or *by* someone. The opposite of "obligatory" is "forbidden." This does not mean that we should derive the agent's obligation from the goodness to the agent of the relation that would be damaged by violating the obligation. This would just be another form of eudaemonism. But we can agree with Robert M. Adams that where there is a violation of an obligation, one "may appropriately have an adverse reaction to it."[34] The question is, *who* is it whose appropriate reaction is here in question? Adams argues that the best candidate is God, since other humans are in various ways disqualified (for example, by limited information and limited sympathies). Moral obligation requires not just a presumption against doing something but an obligator of a particular sort, and deducibility from human nature and nondivine facts alone has to be denied.

We can now return to Murphy's dilemma. The first horn proposed that if God is free to command what God wants, the nonmoral and nondivine facts are inert. But if, as I have argued, God is constrained though not determined by facts about our nature as pilgrims, these facts will not be inert. The second horn of the dilemma proposed that it is odd to say that *we* are not obligated by the maximal set of nonmoral, nondivine facts (where these include facts about our nature), but *God* is so constrained. The response is that this is not odd at all. We and God are different. Both God and we are constrained by the nonmoral and nondivine facts, and neither God nor we are obligated by those facts. But we are obligated by God's commands. God does not require an obligator at all, but *is* the obligator. Even in those cases of moral law (if there are any) in which God's command is constrained by the nonmoral, nondivine facts, we are not obligated by those facts but by God's command.

---

[33] Aquinas, *Summa Theologiae* I-II.90.3.
[34] Adams, *Finite and Infinite Goods*, 233. See also Thomas Carson, *Value and the Good Life* (Notre Dame, IN: University of Notre Dame Press, 2000), 239-48.

***Third objection to divine command theory.*** The third objection to divine command theory is that it makes us infantile, simply recipients of and responders to commands from someone else. We can call this the objection from heteronomy, using Kant's term, for Kant has the argument already mentioned against a Crusius-type divine command theory that proposes that we should be motivated simply by God's power to reward and punish us. Kant says that such motivation is heteronomous (taking the law, *nomos*, from somewhere else, *heteros*, and not autonomously taking the law from oneself, *autos*). Surely we do not want, as Philip Kitcher puts it, to be "in the position of the functionaries who defended their participation in acts of massacre and genocide" by saying they were following the orders of a leader wiser than themselves.[35]

The understanding of Kant's notion of autonomy needs to be corrected here. But more importantly, we need to think about the human response to divine command or divine call. When we do this, I suggest we will find that the response is free and takes a good deal of adult and difficult processing if it is to be done well. First, Kant's idea of autonomy is not that we *create* the law but that we will it as a law for ourselves. We do not create the law, because the law is necessary, in the same way (he says) as it is necessary for a triangle to have three angles. On Kant's conception not even God creates the moral law, though God creates the obligation in accordance with the law.[36] Humans have the freedom, however, to accept the law as a law for themselves or to reject it. There is much more to be said about this idea of human freedom than this chapter has space to describe. I will focus on five features of the phenomenology of receiving divine command, and my goal is to illustrate the complexity of the processing required. I will discuss features of what I will call "direct" divine prescription, which is a divine gift often given in prayer and which can present itself immediately *as* an "extraordinary" divine gift (perhaps there is an auditory sensation) or much more often as an "ordinary" part of our reflection that we then recognize as God speaking to us rather than our simply working out what to do ourselves. Both of these may be God's direct commands or counsels or permissions. I am here disagreeing with Kant, who distrusts what he calls "fanaticism" and

[35]Philip Kitcher, *The Ethical Project* (Cambridge, MA: Harvard University Press, 2011), 169.
[36]Kant, *Metaphysics of Morals*, 6:227.

thinks we should work out what we ought to do by the categorical imperative test and then attribute the resulting prescription to God because we think God has authorized the procedure and is sovereign of the universe in the three roles already described.[37] He thinks Abraham should not have taken to be God's command the prescription to take his son up Mount Moriah and kill him.[38] Any divine command theorist has to have something to say about why we should not take it to be God's command that we should hijack an airplane and fly it into a skyscraper.

One important response to the Abraham story is to say that we are not now in Abraham's position, exactly because of Abraham's story. We are the recipients of a narrative in which God progressively reveals how we are to live. Abraham had to learn two different things, separated in the story by the unusual divergence between God's command and God's will. Abraham had to learn obedience through the test, but he also had to learn that he was not to demonstrate his devotion to God by killing his son. The story replaces child sacrifice with animal sacrifice. We now know this second thing because it was revealed to Abraham. We also learn from the story of the revelation of the Ten Commandments on Mount Sinai. Christians learn especially from the revelation of God in Jesus Christ—for example, in his widening of the covenant to include the Canaanite woman in Matthew 15 and the widening of love of neighbor to include love of enemy in Matthew 5.

So the first thing for a divine command theorist to say about the reception of divine commands is that they have to be held against or within the whole arc of the narrative within which God has revealed how we are to live. This means holding ourselves accountable to the sense of Scripture as a whole. The second thing to say is that the receiver has to check these commands against the wisdom of the present community in which she lives. The third thing is to point to five features of the phenomenology of receiving a direct divine command: clarity and distinctness, external origin, familiarity, authority, and providential care.[39] Together, these five features give us a significant additional constraint on what we should take to be a divine

---

[37]Kant, *Religion Within the Boundaries of Mere Reason*, 6:201.

[38]See ibid., 6:186-87, and (in a different account in some key respects) Kant, *The Conflict of the Faculties*, 7:63.

[39]More detail about all five of these is given in Hare, *God's Command*, 5.3.3. The list should not be taken as exhaustive.

prescription. An outside observer who does not herself belong to the tradition can still agree that divine prescriptions appear this way within the tradition. The conjunction of the features does not, however, *guarantee* that the prescription comes from God. Mental hospitals contain many people who would (delusively) claim their experiences meet these conditions. But *no* phenomenological test can guarantee ethical correctness unless it builds the ethical terms into the test.

By "clarity and distinctness" I mean that what one takes to be a command stands out from the blur or cacophony of indistinct evaluative impressions that pervades much of our experience. A divine prohibition has, to use a visual analogy, a black line around it, or, to use an aural analogy, a divine precept has a resonance to it, though it does not have to be loud. This is only true, however, if we are receiving properly (here an ethical term is built into the test). Karl Barth puts this by saying, "From God's side nothing is hidden at this point."[40] It does not follow that, from *our* side, what we receive is completely distinct or unambiguous. Another description of this feature of the reception is that it resists our attempts to ignore it; it is persistent and not easily shaken. But again, we can undermine this. As Martin Buber puts it, we can plug wax into our own ears.[41] We are not, therefore, excused from obedience by our lack of hearing.

The second feature of the phenomenology is that the command presents itself as having an external origin. This can be true immediately, if the experience is "extraordinary," or after reflection, if the experience is "ordinary," in terms of the distinction made earlier. Again, we can be deceived about this, but the "voice" that is heard seems different from our own voice and different from what we are accustomed to produce out of our own resources. This is close to the third feature, which is that the command comes in a voice that, though different from our own, is still familiar. A person learns through experience to trust this voice. She obeys the command on one occasion, even if she is not given the reason for it, and she subsequently sees the fruit of this obedience. She takes this memory with her into her next encounter and trusts that obedience a second time will be fruitful as it was the first. This

---

[40]Karl Barth, *Church Dogmatics* II/2, ed. and trans. G. W. Bromiley and T. F. Torrance (London: T&T Clark, 2009), 704.

[41]Martin Buber, *I and Thou*, trans. Walter Kaufmann (New York: Scribner, 1970), 182.

means that the proper reception and recognition of divine command standardly requires practice. We *learn* what this voice is like by consistently listening for it and obeying it, and this takes a life of discipline. This is one reason the objection from infantilism or heteronomy misses its mark. What is normative is a lifetime of response, not the immediate response to a single momentary input, and the ability to respond in this way is characteristic of maturity. The fourth feature is that the commands carry about them a sense of conviction or authority. We have the sense that we will be held accountable for our response. Here the connection theologically is with the idea of God as judge "who sees both our actions and also ourselves, the heart from which they proceed."[42] This is the evaluative correlate of persistence, as described in relation to the first feature of the phenomenology. Persistence, we might say, is a matter of power; the "voice" is not easily ignored. But this could be true of some annoying jingle that one cannot get out of one's head. The point of authority as opposed to mere power is that one perceives the voice as *deserving* to be attended to or heeded, whether it is in fact attended to or not.

The most important feature of the phenomenology is the fifth—namely, that the command appears to come from a loving or merciful source.[43] Anything that we take to be a divine command has to be consistent with the character, the providential caring, of the God who is supposed to be communicating with us. There is an *experience* of being loved, even though being loved is not reducible to experience. Duns Scotus distinguishes three motivations we might have in loving God.[44] The first and best is independent of any relation to us; we simply want God to have everything good (whether this includes our salvation or not). The second loves God for the sake of our union with God, our becoming co-lovers. The third loves God for the sake of the satisfaction we get from the union. This third is the least, but it is still a great good to have this satisfaction, and it is an experience of which we get a foretaste in this life. We should expect to find that the command of God comes to us, even when it is hard, from a source that loves

---

[42]Barth, *Church Dogmatics* II/2, 637.

[43]Aquinas, *Summa Theologica* I-II.90.4; a law "is nothing other than a certain dictate of reason for the common good, made by *him who has the care of* the community and promulgated" (emphasis added).

[44]Scotus, *Ordinatio* 3, suppl., dist. 27, art. 3.

us. We should also expect that the command is consistent with our loving our neighbors, since God's love is for all of God's creation.

***Fourth objection to divine command theory.*** The fourth objection is from pluralism; we live in a pluralistic world in which there are many people who do not believe in the God we believe in, or in any god at all. How can we ground moral obligation in the command of God and at the same time maintain moral relations with those who do not believe in God? One central figure in this discussion is Richard Rorty, and his notion that anyone who invokes God's will in a public conversation in a democracy is unavoidably a "conversation-stopper."[45] We should base our recommendations for our life together on premises that we can all accept, he said. He had no objection to religious people using God's name within their religious communities, but he thought they should exercise the self-discipline of keeping that name in that place.

One way to respond to this objection is to point out that Rorty himself modified his position. He came to characterize his remarks as "hasty and insufficiently thoughtful."[46] He conceded,

> Both law and custom should leave [a believer] free to say, in the public square, that his endorsement of redistributionist social legislation is a result of his belief that God, in such passages as Psalm 72, has commanded that the cause of the poor should be defended. . . . Attempts to find rules that are neutral between the two sides [of the *Kulturkampf*] are pretty hopeless. So is the attempt to say that one or another contribution to political discourse is illegitimate.

There are several points here. One is that there is something repressive about refusing the believer permission to use her deepest beliefs in public discourse while allowing the atheist free rein. A second point is that there is no workable way to base political life on a foundation neutral between believers and nonbelievers that is still rich enough to generate good public policy.

There is a third point not explicit in the quote from Rorty but implicit in it. The point is made explicitly by Jürgen Habermas.[47] A pluralistic society

---

[45]Richard Rorty, "Religion as Conversation-Stopper," *Common Knowledge* 3 (1994): 1-6.
[46]Richard Rorty, "Religion in the Public Square: A Reconsideration," *Journal of Religious Ethics* 31, no. 1 (2003): 141-49.
[47]Jürgen Habermas, "Secularism's Crisis of Faith: Notes on Post-Secular Society," *New Perspectives Quarterly* 25 (2008): 17-29.

*needs* the resources of religious commitment on the part of some of its citizens in order to sustain its own democratic values. Rorty does not think he can give a ground or justification for the appeal to human rights, although he is wholehearted in his use of this appeal. It is not clear that there is any nonreligious ground. Perhaps this does not matter, and we can take moral obligation as a primitive, what Kant calls a "fact of reason."[48] But the trouble with this suggestion is that moral obedience is *fragile*; duty presents us with the need to do what we do not have an inclination to do, or at least not sufficient inclination. In the example I mentioned in the first section of this chapter, we are required to treat even our enemies as ends in themselves. Another example, which I do not have space to describe in more detail, is that morality requires those of us in the richer parts of the world to make sacrifices in our standard of living in order to support at least subsistence in the poorer parts of the world.[49] On those occasions where there seems to be a choice between duty and happiness, it helps us do our duty if we see some reason or ground or justification for this. This is true not just at the level of the individual but at the level of the society as a whole. Divine command theory, which makes the grounding in God's commands explicit, can contribute to the fabric of moral obedience in a pluralistic society.

How then should we reply to the objection that divine command theory makes moral conversation impossible between believers and nonbelievers? Here it is useful to return to the analogy with water, mentioned earlier in connection with the denial that divine command *constitutes* moral obligation. Suppose what makes something water is the combination of two hydrogen atoms and one oxygen atom. People who do not know this can converse perfectly well about water. Indeed, they have done so for thousands of years. Water is what fills lakes and streams and falls from the sky as rain. In the same way, if we suppose that what makes something morally obligatory is divine command, people who do not know this can converse perfectly well about moral obligation. We have moral obligations not to lie or murder or steal. All of this can be known by people who do not believe in God. Indeed, a robust account of general revelation would hold that God

---

[48]Kant, *Critique of Practical Reason*, 5:31.
[49]I have described this argument at greater length, as well as some objections to it, in John E. Hare and Carey B. Joynt, *Ethics and International Affairs* (London: Macmillan, 1982), 163-83.

reveals to everyone enough of these truths about obligation so that everyone can be held accountable, whether they believe in God or not.

## SUMMARY

To sum up, it may be helpful to look back briefly over what this chapter has tried to accomplish. We started with an account of divine command theory, the theory that divine command is what makes things morally obligatory, explaining the two terms *moral obligation* and *divine command* and then explaining the nature of the relation between them. Moral obligation was given a Kantian account, but this was not essential to the theory. There could be (indeed there have been) divine command consequentialist accounts and divine command virtue accounts of obligation. Divine command was explained in terms of a distinction between five types of divine prescription: precepts, prohibitions, permissions, counsels, and directly effective commands. Precepts and prohibitions create obligations. They are issued with authority, and some kind of sanction is envisioned for noncompliance, ranging from blame to punishment. The account of authority (borrowing from Joseph Raz) was that one person is practically authoritative over another in a certain domain only if the first person's dictates bring about to some extent the reasons for action that the other has in that domain. God's commands have proper objective authority because obedience to God is good in itself. Finally, the relation between the two terms is that divine command does not cause or constitute moral obligation, but God's commands are explicit performatives, like the phrase "I promise," which brings about an obligation just by its utterance in appropriate circumstances.

The chapter then considered and responded to four objections to divine command theory: the objections from vicious regress, from arbitrariness, from heteronomy, and from pluralism.[50] The reply to the objection from vicious regress was that justifying moral obligation by God's command does not terminate in something that itself requires justification, because, if God exists, it is necessarily true that God is to be obeyed. The reply to the objection from arbitrariness was that God selects from the probably infinite number of good things that might lead us to our proper end those things

---

[50]The list is not intended to be exhaustive. An excellent account of other objections can be found in C. Stephen Evans, *God and Moral Obligation* (Oxford: Oxford University Press, 2013).

to require, and only those things are obligatory. The reply to the objection from heteronomy was that autonomy does not mean creating the law but making it a law for oneself; the moral law already exists, but appropriating it (and so responding to divine command) requires a mature use of human freedom, and this response was given a phenomenology in terms of five features: clarity and distinctness, external origin, familiarity, authority, and providential care. Finally, the reply to the objection from pluralism was that democratic society, so far from banishing religiously based contributions to public discussion, actually needs this contribution, and such discussion between believers and nonbelievers is not impeded but is in fact helped by the divine command theorist's account, which offers a basis for obligations felt by believers and nonbelievers alike.

# A Virtue Ethics Response

*BRAD J. KALLENBERG*

**John Hare has delivered** a very tight, philosophically coherent account of moral obligation. Moral obligation, he explains, is neither *caused* by the command of God nor *constituted* by the command of God. Rather, moral obligation is *internally related* to the command of God. Relying on distinctions by J. L. Austin, Hare explains that when an imperatival speech-act leaves the mouth of God it is called a "divine command"; when we successfully "uptake" (or understand) that same speech-act, it is called "moral obligation." Same speech-act, two different labels depending on which end of the communication trajectory we are referring to.

There are three specific difficulties I have with Hare's model, minor difficulties that might be simply a function of the word limits placed on each of us as authors. For all I know, the questions I have may have been dealt with already in one or more of Hare's many writings. So I will briefly mention these three and then move on to my primary concern.

First, Hare's model appears to be a model of ethics for the lone individual. Textually speaking, this flies in the face of the fact that the vast majority of scriptural imperatives are delivered in the plural (to "y'all" as a group) rather than in the singular (to "you there wearing the green shirt," as an individual). The exceptions are those commands given to exceptional individuals in unique situations: Abraham at the foot of Mount Moriah, Moses in the Midian desert, the rich young ruler on a dusty road. Unfortunately, it has become standard fare (especially since Descartes, but also dating back before Martin Luther to Duns Scotus) to do philosophy in the first person singular: What am *I* to do? How am *I* to know?

The manner in which we moderns instinctively read individualism back into Scripture puts the lone individual under tremendous burden. I've heard sermons in which the Great Commission's imperative to "go make disciples" (given to the disciples *as a group* [Mt 28:18-20]) is paired with the Old Testament command that ends with the sanction: "their blood I will require at your hand" (given to the prophet *as an individual* [Ezek 3:18]). Obviously, this is a manipulative misuse of Scripture. But I fear the root error is the same as Hare's. No appeal to a fivefold phenomenology will release the lone individual from the burden that ensues when plural commands and singular commands are conflated. I wish Hare had made clear the difference between the bindingness felt by an individual under the strictures of a command and that sense of obligation experienced by members of a group living under a canon. But, as I say, perhaps Hare has dealt with this elsewhere.

Second, if, as Hare claims, God "can use imperative sentences to give us advice or invitation, where these acts do not create obligation," then how are we to tell which is which? This is an ad hoc loophole that cannot help but lead to *ethical minimalism* by which we—scratch that—by which *I* am only ever bound to the really, really obvious commands. Apparently Hare assumes Austin's speech-act theory can come to his rescue. If I hear a divine command *as a command*, then that simply shows I have already sensed the pinch of moral obligation. But once again we are back to the lone individual who, for all we know, may have cotton in the ears as well as a log in the eye (Mt 7:3-5).

Third, Hare's Kantian account has a suspiciously generic flavor. He writes, "To will a prescription as a universal law requires that we be able to eliminate in principle all reference to the agent herself or any other particular persons or times or places." But hold on a minute! One of the central points of Austin's speech-act theory, which Hare relies on, is that one's comprehension of a speech-act *necessarily* requires attention to the very particulars (character, relationships, time, situation, context, dialect, etc.) being discarded.

For example, consider what goes into understanding the following historical sentence, "In the absence of women, men will not burn." In order to judge whether it is true or false, one must first figure out what is being talked about. The sentence means one thing if spoken by an abbot of an

all-male monastery arguing for continued cloistering of monks. In surprising point of fact, the sentence was spoken in the context of the Treb-
linka concentration camp and indicated that the male corpses just would
not burn without an adequate ratio of female corpses in the same oven since
the females, emaciated as they were, had a higher percentage of body fat,
which enabled adequate combustion.[1] Quite a different meaning. Context
matters, as does our skill in reading particulars. J. L. Austin delighted in
thinking up examples like the one I supplied to show there is no such thing
as an act of communication shorn of all particulars. If someone were to
retort that the meaning of a sentence transcends all particulars, it would
make sense to ask, "So tell, me what is the 'meaning'?" One quickly sees that
it is impossible to describe the so-called meaning of a sentence "without
simply repeating the sentence."[2] If we take language seriously, we must also
take seriously all the particulars that come with language. Navigating all
the moving parts—not only context but also character, relationships, time,
situation, dialect, and so on—requires a set of special skills, *habitual* skills
cultivated over a long time and assisted by others who are better at it than
we. We call this set of virtues "fluency."

I turn then to what I take to be a central difficulty in Hare's model: Why
ought we assume that the Christian moral life is all about *commands*? Recall
that by Hare's account there are many goods in life among which the individual ranges freely. Moral obligation, by Hare's account, is that subset of
those goods that are explicitly commanded by God.

But why assume it is all about God as *Commander*? Granted, the God
Christians worship is called "lawgiver," "judge," and "king" (Is 33:22). But is
he not also called shepherd, Father, gardener, potter, Redeemer, fortress,
Savior, rock, portion, glory, co-laborer, the lifter of our heads, *and so on*?[3]
God is pleased to be called by *many* names and occupies *many* roles. To
restrict it all to a single name or role is to get something wrong.

---

[1] Steven T. Katz, "Technology and Genocide: Technology as a 'Form of Life,'" in *Historicism, the
Holocaust and Zionism: Critical Studies in Modern Jewish Thought and History* (New York: University
Press, 1992), 213.

[2] This poignant truism comes from Ludwig Wittgenstein, *Culture and Value*, ed. G. H. von Wright
and Heikki Nyman, trans. Peter Winch, English translation with the amended 2nd. ed. (Oxford:
Basil Blackwell, 1980), 10e.

[3] Ian Thomas Ramsey, "Talking of God: Models Ancient and Modern," in *Christian Empiricism*, ed.
Jerry H. Gill, Studies in Philosophy and Religion (London: Sheldon Press, 1974), 120-40.

If anything, *communication* should be the governing figure for Christian ethics.[4] After all, John 1:1 does not read "In the beginning was the *Command*, and the *Command* was with God, and the *Command* was God." Rather, it reads "In the beginning was the *Word*." Jesus, who is our archetype and Savior, displays for us the richness of what our relationship with God is to be (Jn 13:5; Heb 12:2; 1 Pet 2:21). The biblical figure for that relationship is *language*. The field of communication obviously includes some explicit commands. But it necessarily involves much, much more.[5] In fact, the word *communication* itself connotes the "much, much more." The word derives from *co* and *munus*, which is to say "shared world." If Jesus is the Word and if communication is taken as the central image, Christian ethics is centrally concerned with this question: What does it mean to share a world with the God who has adopted us into "the love that is between the members of the Trinity"? It is not that commands are irrelevant, it's that making commands the whole story distorts the picture.

We—together—as church are referred to as "the bride of Christ," and he who is Word, Lamb, and Savior has also taken the name Bridegroom. So let me use the image of marriage as a path into further discussion. Suppose I die prematurely. My wife of thirty-seven years insists that she alone can deliver a fitting eulogy (*eu* + *logos* = good word), one that accurately summarizes my good points. During the funeral she stands and proclaims to the gathered group, "Brad was a man without fault, because he did absolutely everything I commanded." You must admit, that would not be much of a eulogy!

Flourishing human relationships are clearly far more nuanced than that which can be spelled out in advance by commands. A happy marriage is better expressed by a mutual striving to be pleasing than merely obedient. And what holds for the nuanced relationship inside a marriage holds for nuanced relationships in all walks of life, including our nuanced relationship with God.

Just as we occupy many nuanced roles with each other, so too God is pleased to reveal himself to us in manifold roles, and we learn to relate to him accordingly. The Christian moral life does not happen only in those

[4]For extended treatment see chapter 3 of Herbert McCabe, *Law, Love and Language* (New York: Continuum, 2004).
[5]The "much more" of the entire field of communication is the necessary backdrop without which a command will not be properly understood. If in human interaction I hear the words "Drop and gimme twenty!" How am I to know this isn't a joke?

moments we relate to God as Commander. Moreover, insofar as Jesus is the Word who fully reveals the Father, then there is no good reason to take the wonderful breadth and variety that is language and elevate a single speech-act, the command, into a place of dominance. This is not to say that Hare's model of Christian ethics is incorrect, but I am saying it is incomplete.

By looking at the breadth of field of the marriage relationship, I am suggesting the divine command model is "spatially" restricted, so to speak. I think it is also "temporally" restricted. Commands themselves are not static. Commands are self-transformative over time. Consider this mundane example: "Every day run five minutes longer than is comfortable." First, the command is fuzzy. "How far must one run?" Well, one has to determine when discomfort sets in. "Does this refer to the period after about ninety seconds, when all the ATP is depleted from the muscles but before the body shifts into aerobic mode?" Hmm, maybe or maybe not. "So, should one endure into the third and fourth minutes before starting the five-minute countdown?" Surprisingly, one gets used to that initial pain so that by week three one will think, *This isn't so bad!* So, one should begin the countdown clock after seven minutes? Maybe.

The point is that "discomfort" will happen later and later with each successive week of running. Obviously, one is slowly getting in shape. But something else is happening as well: the person is learning to endure pain. As their pain threshold rises, they discover that "discomfort" has become a petty thing, something not worth troubling about. Eventually, when runs begin to exceed six or seven miles a surprise happens: endorphins kick in (the so-called runner's high), and the pain vanishes for several, perhaps many, more miles. At this stage of the game, say six months into training, would we say that this person is "intentional" about obeying the initial command? Not at all. The person has changed through time; the person has *become* a runner, the command has become *internalized*, and the five-minute countdown is now *irrelevant* to the sheer joy of long-distance running.

Hare has described the moral life in terms of divine commands. But to identify the moral life with that which is commanded is to take a freeze-frame snapshot *at the very beginning* of a journey that is itself constituted by ongoing character transformation and friendship building. Hare's model does not give a complete picture of what the remainder of the journey, which has become a long-distance race, will be like.

# A Natural Law Response

*CLAIRE BROWN PETERSON*

**John Hare's preferred** divine command theory involves the following three basic commitments:

1. Certain actions can be objectively good or bad even if God does not command those actions.

2. Any action, whether that action be good, bad, or neutral *apart* from God's command, *becomes* obligatory once God commands it (and wrong once God prohibits it).

3. No action is obligatory unless God has commanded it (and no action is wrong unless God has prohibited it).

I will raise no objections to commitments (1) and (2). Indeed, I agree with (1), and I would put the point in the following way: Jesus commanded his disciples to love one another as he had loved them, but this new commandment did not *make* such love good. Such love was good even before Jesus commanded it, which is why one need not recognize Jesus' divinity in order to recognize his goodness and in particular the goodness manifested in his love for others. Certainly none of Jesus' early companions reasoned, "This Jesus guy is God incarnate; I also noticed that he commanded us to love one another as he has loved us. Therefore, it must actually be good to love people the way he has loved us. But of course no one can surpass Jesus in loving *like Jesus*; therefore, Jesus must be very good!" Rather, Jesus' followers typically saw the goodness of his love, justice, and mercy first and his divinity only later. The divine command theory that Hare has presented can recognize all of this since it speaks of divine commands as creators of *obligation*, but *not of goodness*. As Hare acknowledges, the goodness of the action exists prior to God's command that the action be performed.

Commitments (2) and (3) speak specifically of the relationship between divine commands and obligations: (2) states that *whenever* God commands a course of action, that action is obligatory; (3) states that *only* actions that are so commanded by God are obligatory. I will not here object to (2). We are all familiar with the phenomenon of an otherwise optional act becoming obligatory due to the command—or even merely the request—of the right sort of person. If the state tells me to file my taxes by April 15, I incur an obligation to file my taxes by April 15, even though there is nothing intrinsically compelling about this date on its own. If my husband asks me to pick up a jar of peanut butter on my way home, then I ought to do so, even though without his request it would be perfectly fine for me to arrive home *sans* peanut butter. Even actions that would ordinarily be bad and wrong can become right and obligatory as a result of the commands (or requests) of the right sort of authority. When I have people over for dinner, it would normally be wrong for me to withhold the best food from some of my guests—but not if one such guest asks that I not place any scallops on his plate. The guest need not even tell me why he does not want scallops on his plate for me to incur such an obligation. Certainly, if an unexplained request or command from a dinner guest can create an obligation, a command from God can do the same. Moreover, divine command theorists are right to point out that a clear command from God creates such an obligation even if (as in the scallop example) we do not know why God is commanding (or prohibiting) this particular action. The command is sufficient.

My primary objection to divine command theory concerns commitment (3): I do not think that commands from God are the only way or even the typical way in which human beings incur moral obligations. Commitment (3), recall, states that an action must be commanded by God in order to be obligatory. To understand the significance of this claim, note that a command (or prohibition) is a specific type of *communication*. Thus, Hare characterizes a divine command as a certain type of divine "speech act." A divine command is thus not simply a true statement about what God wants or desires or thinks best at the level of human action. In the first place, what God most wants for me when it comes to my behavior (i.e., how God wants me to act) may not be a command, because it may not have been revealed to me. In the second place, even if such information has been revealed to me, it does not follow that God has commanded me or anyone else to behave in this way. That is, it doesn't follow from the fact that *I know God would want me to do X* that *God has issued me a command (direct or indirect) to do X.* Note that the distinction between divine precepts and prohibitions that Hare introduces acknowledges this difference. According to Hare's divine command theory, only divine precepts (commands to humans to act in particular ways) and prohibitions (commands to humans not to act in particular ways) create actual moral obligations. Divine counsels (God's advice, revealed to us) do not create such obligations. Certainly, for divine command theory, divine will (what God wants of us) does not create such obligations, and neither do the very reasons that explain God's will, even if we are capable of recognizing those reasons.

Contra divine command theory, I hold that we can—and often are—obligated to behave in specific ways even if God has not commanded us so to act. Humans certainly should attend to and obey God's commands, but we should also seek knowledge of what is good (or bad) and of what courses of action are most fitting of our divinely created human nature. Our access to such knowledge alone—apart from any knowledge of whether God has also commanded the course of action in question—can yield genuine moral obligations. I have often heard people speak about discerning what God would or does want or how it would be best for them to behave considering various factors in their life situations, but rarely have I heard someone say that God told her that she *must* do something (although occasionally, I have heard a person say this). If divine command theory is correct, those ordinary people who "merely" correctly discern that a particular course of action would be the only good moral course of action are not obligated to act in the way they have seen to be the only good course of action! According to divine command theory, it would be *best* for these people to act as they have discerned they should, and to act in any other way would be *bad,* but unless and until God actually *commands* them to act in this way, they are not obligated to behave this way rather than in the alternative ways.

The command-obedience model of divine-human interaction does reflect truth about how God sometimes relates to humans and how humans are obligated to behave, but the command-obedience model does not capture the whole picture of how humans are designed to function. The same Bible that depicts God commanding the Israelites to obey a system of laws that he has revealed also depicts God's relationship to Israel and later the church in the language of father or a spouse. Jesus calls his followers "friends" rather than "servants" because "the servant does not know what the master is doing; but ... I [Jesus] have made known to you everything that I have heard from my Father" (Jn 15:15 NRSV). These other metaphors suggest that, in addition to obeying any divine commands we receive, we are also designed to do the following (this list is by no means exhaustive):

1. Seek out God's will for our own lives by consulting other people and praying for guidance from the Holy Spirit. (Note that, even if all such received guidance is automatically classified as "command" rather than "counsel," it makes no sense that we should be obligated to *pray for* such commands prior to receiving them if obligations do not exist until divine commands are actually given. One tries to determine one's obligations when one is uncertain about those obligations, but one does not *ask* for new obligations to be created for the sake of having more obligations.)

2. Use our reasoning capacities to evaluate how various courses of action and even life paths available to us will likely affect other people and ensure that such considerations inform our decisions.

3. Use our moral reasoning capacities to consider how Jesus responded to specific circumstances, seek to determine what his actions might reveal about what is best for all circumstances, seek to determine what his actions might reveal about what is best for all human beings, and ensure that such considerations inform the decisions we make in the (often) rather different circumstances in which we find ourselves.

4. Use our moral reasoning capacities to consider counsels (advice) that God has given to other people in particular circumstances, seek to determine what those counsels might reveal about God's will for all human beings, and ensure that such considerations inform the decisions we make in the (often) rather different circumstances in which we find ourselves.

5. Use our moral reasoning capacities to consider commands that God has given to other people in particular circumstances, seek to determine what those commands might reveal about God's will for all human beings, and ensure that such considerations inform the decisions we make in the (often) rather different circumstances in which we find ourselves.

Note that the approach to determining right and wrong described in (5) may sound like a simple implementation of divine command theory (since attending to God's commands is so central a feature of the approach described), but (5) is not actually an application of divine command theory. If I witness my boss tell someone else to respond to a particular situation in a particular way, it makes sense for me to use this knowledge as a guide to "what my boss would want" in other circumstances. However, it does not follow that my boss has actually told *me* to act in this way (whether in the same circumstances or similar ones). Similarly, the fact that God commanded the Israelites not to charge interest when making loans to their fellow Israelites (Deut 23:19) and not to pick the corners of their fields but to instead leave the edges for "the poor and the alien" (Lev 19:9-10) informs us of God's concern for the weakest members of society. This recognition of God's heart must inform how we act and shape our societies. Nonetheless, we cannot avoid the fact that, unlike the Israelites, those who live in the present-day United States have not actually been commanded to set up their societies in any particular way to serve the needs of the weakest members. Strictly speaking, not all modern people have even been commanded to set up society in a way that ensures all people may have their basic needs met. Yet modern people do not need to be commanded by God to be aware that they are responsible for the needs of their fellow human beings. Simply seeing need should move us to inquire about appropriate action.

One could object that followers of Jesus who have access to the New Testament *have* been commanded to take responsibility for the needs of their fellow humans: Jesus has specifically commanded his followers to love one another as he loved us, and it is quite obvious that such love will involve placing a high premium on ensuring that peoples' basic needs are met. I would agree that followers of Jesus have been commanded in this way, but many of us live in secular societies, and not all secular individuals have been commanded as Jesus' followers have. This does not mean, however, that secular persons are exempt from responsibility for the livelihood of their neighbors. Similarly, the fact that neither Cain nor anyone prior to Cain was forbidden from committing murder does not mean that Cain's act of murder was *bad* but not technically *wrong*. *If* actual divine commands and prohibitions were required for actions being right (or wrong), these conclusions would follow and we would have to affirm with Cain that he need not be his brother's keeper (Gen 4:9). However, murder and neglect of one's fellow humans are wrong—and can be appreciated as such—even before divine prohibitions come along. While divine commands and prohibitions sometimes create moral obligations, more often divine commands and prohibitions do not so much create obligations as provide greater clarity about the obligations that existed all along. Humans were created as social creatures intended to respect and care for one another. Almost all of us readily appreciate this fact when we experience feelings of injustice and hurt in response to others ignoring the well-being of their fellow humans. The fact that we were designed to live in relationship with others is enough to make it wrong for us to ignore others, and the fact that we are all capable of seeing this truth is enough to make us responsible when we violate it. Divine commands often provide unambiguous reminders of these facts that were true all along, but the commands themselves are not required for the facts to be true.

# A Prophetic Ethics Response

*PETER GOODWIN HELTZEL*

The sea is calm tonight.
The tide is full, the moon lies fair
Upon the straits; on the French coast the light
Gleams and is gone; the cliffs of England stand. . . .

The Sea of Faith
Was once, too, at the full, and round earth's shore
Lay like the folds of a bright girdle furl'd.
But now I only hear
Its melancholy.[1]

With the receding light from the coast of France, "the cliffs of England stand" as an impregnable line of defense for "the empire on which the sun never sets." The British Empire was built on business. Whether it was the English East India Company in the Americas or the British South Africa Company that founded Rhodesia (now Zimbabwe and Zambia) in 1895, British colonialism made money for the Crown. Prosperity led to the *Pax Britannica*, the myth of "perpetual peace" during the royal reign of Queen Victoria.

In an age of optimism, Arnold hears the melancholy melody of the sea. Once an ocean full and free, the Sea of Faith is now at its low western tide. As Sophocles on the Aegean, Arnold's heart is awakened by the "the turbid ebb and flow" of the English Channel.

At the beginning of the end of the British Empire, Arnold finds the only thing left to cling to is love:

Ah, love, let us be true
To one another!

---

[1]Matthew Arnold, "Dover Beach," 1867.

In a world full of darkness and decline, Arnold offers a fiery call for commitment to *true* love, warmly embracing the body of his lover. While Matthew Arnold clings to love, John Hare clings to command.

Why is Anglican philosopher John Hare so invested in commands? Hare argues "the main concern of divine command theory is that we remember to love God's law and God's command." Theologies that disregard the Jewish law unveil the problem of Christian supersessionism, an interpretation of the New Testament that sees God's relationship with Christians as *replacing* God's covenant with the Jews. Christian "replacement theology"—the idea that Christianity replaces Judaism—is a heresy that must be continually resisted in Christian ethics. Hare's divine command theory is one strategy to deal with Christian supersessionism.

While affirming God's commands as the primary source of ethics, Hare relies more on Kant of Königsberg than Jesus of Nazareth. Hare mentions Kant thirty times and Jesus only once. For Hare, Kant's philosophy helps us recognize our ethical duties as God's commands, while Jesus teaches us to love our enemy. Kant provides Hare with a philosophical vehicle—*autonomous submission* to divine commands conceived as our civic duty—for a distinctively *Christian* command ethics.

"Humanity is at its greatest perfection in the race of the whites. The yellow Indians do have a meager talent. The Negroes are far below them and at the lowest points are a part of the American peoples," writes Kant, whose philosophy is based on a racial hierarchy.[2] Buried beneath Kant's doctrine of dignity is a *moral contradiction*—only white men have the capacity for rational autonomy to be full human persons and active moral agents, while Jews, blacks, and women are irrational others who are subhuman.[3] Kant argues women's propensity is "not to reason, but to sense. . . . I hardly believe that the fair sex is capable of principles."[4]

---

[2]Immanuel Kant, selections from "Physical Geography," cited in Thomas E. Hill Jr. and Bernard Boxhill in "Kant and Race," *Race and the Enlightenment: A Reader*, ed. Emmanuel Chukwudi Eze (Oxford: Blackwell, 1997), 455.

[3]Charles W. Mills argues that Kant's derogatory characterizations of women and people of color unveil his belief that they were subhuman, see his "Kant's *Untermenschen*," in *Race and Racism in Modern Philosophy*, ed. Andrew Valls (Ithaca, NY: Cornell University Press, 2005), 167-93.

[4]Immanuel Kant, "On the Distinction of the Beautiful and Sublime in the Interrelations of the Two Sexes," section 3 in *Observations on the Feeling of the Beautiful and the Sublime*, trans. John T. Goldthwait (Berkeley: University of California Press, 1960), 79-81.

There is "one shepherd" of the flock, and his name is Jesus.[5] As Jesus was an *obedient Son* to the heavenly Father, cosmopolitan citizens should be obedient "citizens of an ethical state."[6] An honest analysis of the moral topography of the "New World" unveils the *fragile* heart of Kant's rational white man in a world without "help for pain."

When considered from the subject position of the oppressed, a new objection to divine command theory is unearthed—the *objection from the underside of modernity*: How is the call to obey commandments heard by those on the margins who are poor and oppressed?[7]

Britain controlled their colonial subjects through a *command-obedience structure*, illustrated in the racial hierarchy of the slave ship—white sailors are above deck, enslaved Africans are below deck, and a white male captain is in charge. When sailors or slaves resisted the captain's command, they were brutally beaten or thrown overboard. A slave's fate could turn on a typhoon as we see evoked in the dreamlike stormy sea scene of J. M. W. Turner's painting *Slavers Throwing Overboard the Dead and Dying—Typhoon Coming On* (1840). Willie Jennings writes, "All were bound together in this ecology, captain, sailor, and slave by the *fragility* that is creation."[8]

When Hare writes "moral obedience is *fragile*," he testifies to the truth in Jennings's trope about the "fragility that is creation." We hear the sorrow songs of old women and men of the sea, hidden under coral islands. Hare continues, "Duty presents us with the need to do what we do not have an inclination to do." When we face a decision between happiness and duty, what *inclines* us to do our duty?

The Eucharistic Liturgy of the Episcopal Church (Rite I) begins with a public reading of the Ten Commandments, where the people respond after

---

[5]Immanuel Kant, *Religion and Rational Theology*, trans. and ed. Allen W. Wood and George di Giovanni (Cambridge: Cambridge University Press, 1996), 276, quoted in J. Kameron Carter, *Race: A Theological Account* (Oxford: Oxford University Press, 2008), 80.

[6]Immanuel Kant, *Religion Within the Boundaries of Mere Reason*, trans. and ed. Allen Wood and George Di Giovanni (Cambridge: Cambridge University Press, 1998), 6:143.

[7]I am drawing here on Enrique Dussel's concept of "the underside of modernity." See Enrique Dussel, *The Underside of Modernity: Apel, Ricoeur, Rorty, Taylor, and the Philosophy of Liberation*, trans. Eduardo Mendieta (Atlantic Highlands, NJ: Humanities Press, 1996).

[8]Willie James Jennings, *The Christian Imagination* (New Haven, CT: Yale University Press, 2010), 179.

**Joseph Mallord William Turner. *Slavers Throwing Overboard the Dead and the Dying—Typhoon Coming On.* 1840**

each commandment is read with the refrain "Lord, have mercy upon us, / and incline our hearts to keep this law."[9]

Historically within Anglican ethics, the Ten Commandments form one's moral *inclinations*. Christian command ethics was problematized through the catechetical instruction of Episcopalian slaves in the antebellum South:

Q. What do you mean by doing no bad things, such things as the devil tempts you to do?

A. I mean that I must not hurt any body; must not disobey my parents—[nor disobey my master] nor disobey God.

---

[9]Before the reading of "The Decalogue I: Traditional" the priest begins the eucharistic liturgy with "An Exhortation" proclaiming: "Examine your lives and conduct by *the rule of God's commandments*, that you may perceive wherein you have offended in what you have done or left undone, whether in thought, word or deed" [italics added]. In this passage, we see that Christians are to conform our conduct to the "rule of God's commandments." The Holy Eucharist: The Liturgy for the Proclamation of the Word of God and Celebration of the Holy Communion, *The Book of Common Prayer and Administration of the Sacraments and Other Rites and Ceremonies of the Church According to the use of The Episcopal Church* (New York: Church Hymnal Corporation, 1979), 317-18.

Q. But can you not disobey your parents [and your master] without their knowing it?

A. Yes; but God knows it; for God always sees me.[10]

We see in this Episcopal Catechism how the analogies between God and master are deployed to offer theological legitimation for the subjugation of slaves. Christian command ethics conceals colonial violence.

At the end of "Dover Beach," Arnold writes:

And we are here as on a darkling plain
Swept with confused alarms of struggle and flight,
Where ignorant armies clash by night.

Reclaiming the structures of obedience through a Christologically anchored ethic was integral to Britain's imperial and civilizing mission. *The blue note* of "eternal sadness" that Arnold hears in Britain's Victorian soul would become *postcolonial melancholia* "as soon as the natives and savages began to appear and make demands for recognition in the empire's metropolitan core."[11] The alien presence of the French on Dover Beach is now echoed in the alien presence of the Arab in London or the black female wearing a hijab in Wheaton, Illinois.

How does Christian ethics respond to the presence of the nonwhite "alien" in our midst? Hare's one sentence on Jesus' encounter with the Canaanite woman raises the question of neighbor love and love of the enemy that are central to prophetic ethics (Mt 15:21-28).[12] Since the Jews conquered the Canaanites as they captured the Promised Land, Jesus' call to love the Canaanite woman illustrates the importance of crossing cultural boundaries into experiences of oppression in occupied territory. As white male Christian professors, Hare and I need to ask ourselves tough questions: What is our

---

[10] *Catechism, To Be Taught Orally to Those Who Cannot Read; Designed Especially for Instruction of the Slaves. Protestant Episcopal Church in the Confederate States* (Raleigh, NC: Office of "The Church Intelligence," 1862), 24-25.

[11] Paul Gilroy, *Postcolonial Melancholia* (New York: Columbia University Press, 2005), 91.

[12] Hare has a more extensive discussion of the Canaanite woman in "Karl Barth on Divine Command," in *God's Command* (Oxford: Oxford University, 2015), 164-66. Interestingly, Karl Barth vigorously rejects the attempt to deduce "good and evil in particular instance of human conduct" from the divine command as a universal rule, arguing that it is a "casuistry" that does not do justice to the "prophetic ethos" of Christian ethics. Karl Barth, *Church Dogmatics* III/4, 9, 10, ed. and trans. G. W. Bromiley and T. F. Torrance (London: T&T Clark, 2009).

family's history of interacting with peoples of other ethnicities? In what ways are we complicit with systemic oppression? What ways does our privileged identity give us opportunities to participate in healing and solidary love? How are we encouraging and advancing students and colleagues of color, especially women of color?

With the "eclipse of the light of heaven," Martin Buber reminds us that ethics is not primarily about obedience to a "heavenly command" but rather "imitation of God by man, the 'following in His way,'...in justice and love."[13] Our call as humans is not primarily to "love God's law and love God's command," but to *love our living God* through a personal I-Thou relationship. Loving God entails "listening to the 'voice of a thin silence' (1 Kg 19:21)."[14] Like God who heard Israel "crying out because of their slave drivers" (Ex 3:7 NIV), we need to open our hearts to hear the cry of the suffering other, especially the cries of black women who Eboni Marshall Turman says are "left black and blue from enduring the injustice perpetrated against their bodies according to their flesh, which is neither white, nor male."[15]

[13]Martin Buber, "Religion and Ethics," in *Eclipse of God: Studies in the Relation Between Religion and Philosophy* (New York: Harper, 1952), 137.
[14]Martin Buber, "On the Suspension of the Ethical," in ibid., 154.
[15]Eboni Marshall Turman, "Black & Blue: Uncovering the Ecclesial Cover-Up of Black Women's Bodies Through a Womanist Reimagining of the Doctrine of the Incarnation," in *Reimagining with Christian Doctrines: Responding to Global Gender Injustices*, ed. Grace Ji-Sun Kim and Jenny Daggers (New York: Palgrave MacMillan, 2014), 82.

# Prophetic Ethics

*PETER GOODWIN HELTZEL*

*Are we human or are we dancer?*

THE KILLERS, "HUMAN"

**There is a deep wound** within Christianity because theology and ethics have been divorced from one another. In modernity, Christian faith has been circumscribed, privatized, policed, and relegated to the space of idiosyncratic private beliefs and a small range of private practices. Content to stay within these prescribed boundaries, Christian ethics has often become relegated to personal ethics focused on our individual actions instead of considering our collective responsibility for society.

The current global crisis offers faith leaders a new set of moral challenges, including global economic instability, displaced people, racial antagonism, religious conflict, and ecological vulnerabilities. Because of these combined crises, it is vital that we move from a one-sided emphasis on personal ethics to an ethic that is both personal and social. Rooted in a tradition of generously orthodox Christianity, prophetic ethics turns outward toward action, discipleship, embodiment, mission, justice, and—above all—revolutionary love.

In this chapter I present prophetic ethics as a model of Christian ethics that discerns and partners with the Holy Spirit's movement in our world, transforming lives and communities, witnessing to Christ and the kingdom, and holding out hope for the restoration of God's good creation. When we understand the structural causes of oppression, we are better equipped to work for positive social change. The fight to abolish the death penalty and transform America's system of mass incarceration are presented as a case study to illustrate the important role prophetic ethics plays today in the faith-rooted struggle to dismantle institutional racism. Shaped by a rigorous social analysis, prophetic ethics integrates Christian theology with social practices drawn from faith-rooted organizing to build a more just and sustainable world.

## HOLY SCRIPTURE: THE PRIMARY SOURCE OF PROPHETIC ETHICS

Holy Scripture is the primary source of prophetic Christian ethics. Like Glen H. Stassen and David P. Gushee's *Kingdom Ethics*, prophetic ethics seeks "to consider important issues in Christian ethics on the basis of an informed focus on the teachings and practice of Jesus, in the context of the prophetic tradition of Israel, yet in dialogue with other important approaches both historic and contemporary."[1] Improvising on the Hebrew prophets' vision of shalom justice, Jesus proclaims and embodies the kingdom of God, a Spirit-led movement fueled by the fire of revolutionary love.[2]

Prophetic ethics has a *theological* focus on our knowledge of God, discerning its relevance for the work of transformative mission in and for the world. It seeks to answer questions like, Where is God present in our current moment? Where are people suffering from injustice, and what can we do to help them? How is the Word of God speaking to the great ethical

---

I want to thank J. Kameron Carter, Christian T. Collins Winn, David P. Gushee, David Lauber, Jennifer McBride, Justin Phillips, Patrick T. Smith, Aaron Stauffer, Reggie L. Williams, and Peter J. Paris for carefully reading my chapter and providing helpful insights on how to improve it.

[1] Glen H. Stassen and David P. Gushee, *Kingdom Ethics: Following Jesus in Contemporary Context* (Downers Grove, IL: InterVarsity Press, 2003), 81.

[2] Recognizing the imperial and patriarchal overtones of "kingdom," I use this translation of *basileia tou theou* because in Jesus' context "kingdom" implied that God was the sovereign King and God's reign was greater than all earthly kingdoms, including the Roman Empire. Bruce J. Malina writes, "The proclamation of the kingdom of God meant at least that the God of Israel would be taking over the country soon." Bruce J. Malina, *The Social Gospel of Jesus: The Kingdom of God in Mediterranean Perspective* (Minneapolis: Fortress, 2001), 1; Obery M. Hendricks Jr., *The Politics of Jesus: Rediscovering the True Revolutionary Nature of the Teachings of Jesus and How They Have Been Corrupted* (New York: Doubleday, 2006), 27-28. For the etymology of *basileia tou theou*, see Gerhard Kittel, ed., *Theological Dictionary of the New Testament* (Grand Rapids: Eerdmans, 1969), 1:564-93. "Reign of God" is an alternative translation of *basileia tou theou*. Ada Maria Isasi-Diaz uses the term *kindom*, emphasizing the kinship of all creation and the promise of a just future. See Ada Maria Isasi-Diaz, *Mujerista Theology: A Theology for the Twenty-First Century* (Maryknoll, NY: Orbis, 1996), 103n8.

challenges of today? Scripture's stories awaken our prophetic imagination to feel the pain of the poor, connecting it to the pathos of God and collectively plotting a pathway toward a more just world.[3]

Challenging the disembodied epistemologies of modernity, prophetic ethics is *performative*, calling us to embody Scripture's wisdom in our fleshly existence as persons in transformational communities. Holy Scripture is a script that we creatively perform in the world. As actors study the script of a play that they are preparing to perform, we are called to rigorously and prayerfully study the Holy Scripture. God's Spirit leads us toward interdisciplinary wisdom as we study the two books of revelation: the book of Scripture and the book of nature.[4] Our moral formation always takes place in the context of the struggle for justice in our local community as we simultaneously think globally about eco-human flourishing in the "community of creation."[5] We seek to proclaim and embody God's justice in and for the world, shaped by Holy Scripture, tradition, culture, critical reasoning, and personal experiences.

## BIOGRAPHY AS ETHICS

We all come to the task of Christian ethics from a unique experience of the world based on our social location and life history.[6] How does your autobiography shape your Christian ethic and the questions you ask about Christian life and social existence? How does your race, gender, and class affect your experiences in the world? When have you experienced injustice in your life?

---

[3]For a biblical theology of the prophetic imagination see Walter Brueggemann, *Prophetic Imagination*, 2nd ed. (Minneapolis: Fortress Press, 2001).

[4]See my discussion of interpreting the book of nature through the book of Scripture: Peter Goodwin Heltzel, "Interpreting the Book of Nature in the Protestant Tradition," *Journal of Faith and Science Exchange* 1, no. 3 (2000): 223-39.

[5]On the concept of the "community of creation," a broader, ecological framing of God's good creation from a Native American perspective, see Randy Woodley, *Shalom and the Community of Creation: An Indigenous Vision* (Grand Rapids: Eerdmans, 2012). On the role of moral communities in shaping our Christian social ethic, see Larry L. Rasmussen, *Moral Fragments and Moral Community: A Proposal for Church in Society* (Minneapolis: Augsburg Fortress, 1993). Rasmussen's later work turns in an ecological direction as he broadens the category of moral community to include the earth community. Larry L. Rasmussen, "Earth Community," in *Earth Community, Earth Ethics* (Maryknoll, NY: Orbis, 1996), 322-43. For a thoughtful theology of flourishing in the context of economic globalization, national sovereignty, and civil society, see Miroslav Volf, *Flourishing: Why We Need Religion in a Globalized World* (New Haven, CT: Yale University Press, 2015).

[6]On the importance of biography for Christian theology and ethics see James William McClendon Jr., *Biography as Theology: How Life Stories Can Remake Today's Theology* (Philadelphia: Trinity Press, 1990).

When were you baptized into the movement for justice? How have your life experiences shaped your activism? Taking time to reflect on how God's Spirit has been moving in our own life and the life stories of others helps us discern our own contribution to the movement for love and justice.

My own experiences as an activist minister in New York City have shaped my particular perspective on prophetic ethics. On September 11, 2001, I was supposed to be working for Fidelity Investments in the World Financial Center in New York City. That ill-fated day when the World Trade Center Towers fell, my job was lost and my life was saved. While serving as a volunteer at Ground Zero, I felt the call to work for a better future, a more just New York City, and a more peaceful world. I marched in Manhattan with the peace movement against the war in Iraq, organized faith leaders in New Jersey to shut down Walmart Supercenters, and organized faith leaders in a living wage campaign with African American female leaders like Onleilove Alston.

Onleilove Alston, executive director of Faith in New York, is a leader of moral courage in the faith-rooted movement for justice in New York City. Growing up in Brooklyn, Alston experienced poverty, discrimination, and homelessness. As a leader at the Poverty Initiative at Union Theological Seminary, she researched the role of black women leaders of faith in social movements, including the Poor People's Campaign that Dr. Martin Luther King Jr. launched in November 1967.[7] With a heart to work for the full liberation of her people, Alston began a journey of faith-rooted organizing, from the Federation of Protestant Welfare Agencies to leading Faith in New York.

Founded in 2013, Faith in New York is a new and growing interfaith, multicultural network of congregations working together for faith justice. Its mission is to develop grassroots leaders and equip congregations to stimulate significant public policy change to fulfill a vision of a more just New York with excellent public schools, violence-free neighborhoods, access to living wage jobs, adequate and affordable health care, decent housing for all, and a place where people of all backgrounds can fully participate in economic and civic life. Growing up in poverty like Jesus, Alston is committed to making sure the gospel is heard as "good news to the poor" (Lk 4:18). As a bright star guiding the poor-led movement for justice in

---

[7]The Poverty Initiative, *A New and Unsettling Force: Reigniting Rev. Dr. Martin Luther King's Poor People's Campaign* (New York: Poverty Initiative, 2009).

New York City, Alston seeks the shalom of the city from the deepest wells of her faith (Jer 29:4-7).

Faith is indispensable to the movement for justice. Our attempts to embody God's justice take place within the travail and tragedy of human history, which is also the history of redemption.[8] God acts in human history and so do we. Following in the footsteps of the incarnate Christ, we are moral agents in a historical drama, richly contoured with "local conditions, contingent events, particular circumstances, and individual actions."[9]

## ORGANIZING, SOLIDARITY, AND PRAYER: THE PRACTICES OF PROPHETIC ETHICS

Prophetic ethics transforms people to transform the world. Prophetic ethics' primary source is Holy Scripture, placing priority on the perspective of the poor.[10] Inspired by Micah's challenge to "act justly and to love mercy and to walk humbly with your God" (Mic 6:8),[11] prophetic ethics has three primary practices: faith-rooted organizing (justice), embodied solidarity (mercy), and daily prayer (walk humbly with your God). *Faith-rooted organizing* is gathering people to create systemic change in a way that is completely shaped by our faith.[12] As Jesus compassionately entered into solidarity with humanity,

---

[8]Jonathan Edwards frames American theology around the history of redemption in his classic work "A History of the Work of Redemption," *Works of Jonathan Edwards*, ed. John F. Wilson (New Haven, CT: Yale University Press, 1989), 9:111-530. God is graciously acting in history to redeem humanity and restore the world. As Christians our own moral agency takes place in the context of God's movement in history and the community of creation.

[9]Mark Noll, *Evangelical Christianity: An Introduction* (Oxford: Blackwell, 2001), 228. My historical drama approach to Christian ethics is indebted Charles Marsh, "The Civil Rights Movement as Theological Drama: Interpretation and Application," *Modern Theology* 18, no. 2 (April 2002): 231-50; James William McClendon Jr., *Ethics: Systematic Theology*, vol. 1 (Nashville: Abingdon, 2002); and Glen Stassen, *A Thicker Jesus: Incarnational Discipleship in a Secular Age* (Louisville, KY: Westminster John Knox Press, 2012), 3-15.

[10]On the priority of the perspective of the poor see Gustavo Gutiérrez, "Preferential Option for the Poor," in *Gustavo Gutiérrez: Essential Writings*, ed. James B. Nickoloff (Maryknoll, NY: Orbis, 1996), 143-46; Walter Kasper, "God's Option for Life and the Poor," in *Mercy: The Essence of the Gospel and the Key to Christian Life* (New York: Paulist Press, 2014), 55-58; cf. Alexia Salvatierra and Peter Goodwin Heltzel, *Faith-Rooted Organizing: Mobilizing the Church in Service to the World* (Downers Grove, IL: InterVarsity Press, 2014), 42-64.

[11]Unless otherwise designated, Scripture in this chapter is taken from the NIV.

[12]The term "faith-rooted organizing" was coined at Clergy and Laity United for Economic Justice (CLUE) in Los Angeles when Rev. Alexia Salvatierra was executive director. Alexia, a Latina Lutheran activist from Los Angeles, joined forces with me to write the book *Faith-Rooted Organizing*, offering a primer that introduces the primary principles and practices of organizing and advocacy from the deepest wells of our faith. Prophetic ethics follows the "turn to community

we are called to compassionately enter into the experiences of the oppressed in *embodied solidarity*, sharing a commitment to put our bodies on the line for a more just and sustainable world. Through *daily prayer* we commune with God through contemplation, community, and holy conversation, crying out for Christ and the kingdom to be manifest "on earth as it is in heaven" (Mt 6:10). Through the energies of the Holy Spirit (Jn 16:8-13; Rom 8:26-27), we are rooted in mystical union with Jesus Christ and sanctified as we work together toward the social sanctification of the world.[13]

## LOVE AND JUSTICE: THE MORAL NORMS OF PROPHETIC ETHICS

Justice (*mišpāṭ*) and righteousness (*ṣədāqâ*) are two pillars of the prophetic imperative in Hebrew Scripture. When we see the word *righteous* in the Bible, we often think of private morality. While biblical righteousness is personal, it is also social. Tim Keller writes,

> When these two words, *tzadeqah* and *mishpat*, are tied together, as they are over three dozen times, the English expression that best conveys the meaning is "social justice." It is an illuminating exercise to find texts where the words are paired and to then translate the text using the term "social justice." Here are just two:

> *The Lord loves social justice; the earth is full of his unfailing love.*
> Psalm 33:5.

> And

> *This is what the LORD says: "Let not the wise man boast of his wisdom or the strong man boast of his strength or the rich man boast of his riches, but let him who boasts boast about this: that he understands and knows me, that I am the LORD, who exercises kindness and social justice on earth, for in these I delight," declares the LORD.*
> Jeremiah 9:23-24.[14]

---

organizing" in social ethics we see in the work of Luke Bretherton, *Resurrecting Democracy: Faith, Citizenship, and the Politics of Common Life* (Cambridge: Cambridge University Press, 2015); Melissa C. Snarr, *All You That Labor: Religion and Ethics in the Living Wage Movement* (New York: New York University Press, 2011); and Jeffrey Stout, *Blessed Are the Organized: Grassroots Democracy in America* (Princeton, NJ: Princeton University Press, 2010).

[13]John Wesley said "all holiness is social holiness." John Wesley, preface to *Sacred Hymns and Poems*, 1739.

[14]Timothy Keller, *Generous Justice: How God's Grace Makes Us Just* (New York: Dutton, 2010), 14-15. Cf. Jer 22:3-5; Is 28:17-18; Ps 89:14; 97:2.

It is one thing to cognitively understand the concept of justice; it is another thing to embody it in our personal and political life.[15]

*Ṣədāqâ ûmišpāṭ* is first used in Genesis when God chooses Abraham, not because he keeps kosher or believes in God but because he knows how to "keep in the way of the Lord by doing what is right and just" (Gen 18:19). Who are God's people? They are a people that do justice and righteousness. Justice and righteousness are the essential foundation of the covenant, revealing our true identity as image-bearers of God. In summary, justice is not just a matter of personal morality but also refers to social relations. The call to justice was the heartbeat of the Hebrew prophets.

Described by Abraham Heschel as "some of the most disturbing people who have ever lived," prophets deeply feel the pain of the people and the pathos of God, and seek to disturb the peace of the powerful to address the people's pain.[16] In *Prophetic Imagination*, Walter Brueggemann argues that prophets *criticize* royal power and *energize* people to fight for justice.[17] While in captivity under the royal regime of Pharaoh in Egypt, the people of Israel cried out to God to liberate them from their suffering in slavery, and God responded: "I have indeed seen the misery of my people in Egypt. I have heard them crying out because of their slave drivers, and I am concerned about their suffering. So I have come down to rescue them from the hand of the Egyptians"(Ex 3:7-8). In contrast to Pharaoh, who hardens his heart to the cries of the suffering, God hears the harrowing cry of the poor and responds with compassion and justice.

Responding to the people's cry, God calls Moses to prophetically confront the royal power of the Pharaoh in order to set Israel free (Ex 9:1). Chased by the chariots of the Egyptian army, Moses led the Israelites to liberty across the Red Sea. In response to God's victory over Pharaoh's army, Moses and Miriam, Aaron's sister, led the women of Israel in celebration

---

[15]See Temba L. J. Mafico, "Just, Justice," in *The Anchor Bible Dictionary*, ed. David Noel Freedman (New York: Doubleday, 1992), 3:1127-29. Cf. James L. Mays, "Justice: Perspectives from the Prophetic Tradition," in *Prophecy in Israel*, ed. David L. Peterson (Philadelphia: Fortress, 1987), 144-58.

[16]Abraham Joshua Heschel, *The Prophets* (New York: Harper & Row, 1962), 3-26.

[17]Walter Brueggemann discusses the prophet's call to criticize and energize in *Prophetic Imagination*, 2nd ed. (Minneapolis: Fortress Press, 2001), 1-19. For a good overview of the moral vision of the Hebrew Bible as a source for Christian ethics, see Bruce C. Birch, *Let Justice Roll Down: The Old Testament, Ethics, and the Christian Life* (Louisville: Westminster John Knox Press, 1991).

through singing and dancing with tambourines (Ex 15:21).[18] Through disrupting an unjust social order, prophets draw people into deeper worship of the living God. In contrast with the "royal consciousness" that seeks to fulfill imperial ambitions, "prophetic consciousness" is concerned about the establishment of God's shalom justice. While the royal powers use "bread and circus" diversion tactics to keep the citizenry numb to their deepest feelings, the prophet uses prophetic imagination to awaken a slumbering people to a large-hearted love. When Moses descends from Mount Sinai with the Ten Commandments and sees the people dancing around the golden calf, he throws the tablets down in anger, dramatically breaking them into pieces at the foot of the holy mountain (Ex 32:19).

The eighth-century BCE prophet Micah clearly sums up the prophetic imperative (Mic 6:8):

> He has told you, O man, what is good;
> And what does the LORD require of you
> But to do justice, and to love kindness,
> And to walk humbly with your God? (NASB)

Micah brings together God's call to doing justice with the practice of lovingkindness. In his teaching of the kingdom of God, Jesus brings further depth and clarity to prophetic ethics' two primary moral norms: justice and love.[19]

## JESUS THE REVOLUTIONARY PROPHET

"Jesus of Nazareth was a revolutionary prophet," writes Obery Hendricks Jr.[20] Growing up in impoverished Nazareth in a country colonized by the Romans, Jesus compassionately connected with the poor.[21] Baptized in the Jordan River by John the Baptist, Jesus was anointed by the Spirit to

---

[18]See Phyllis Trible, "Bringing Miriam Out of the Shadows," *Bible Review* 5, no.1 (February 1989): 13-25.

[19]For an insightful discussion of the moral norms of love and justice, see Nicholas Wolterstorff, *Justice in Love* (Grand Rapids: Eerdmans, 2011); and Stassen and Gushee, *Kingdom Ethics*, 327-68. I have adopted Wolterstorff's formulation "justice in love" at many points throughout the text.

[20]Hendricks, *Politics of Jesus*, 5.

[21]When Joseph and Mary took Jesus to the temple to dedicate him as a child, they could not afford a lamb for the ceremonial sacrifice, so they took two turtledoves instead (Lk 2:24), unveiling the poverty that Jesus grew up in. As Howard Thurman writes, "The economic predicament with which he was identified in birth placed him initially with the great mass of men on the earth." Howard Thurman, *Jesus and the Disinherited* (Boston: Beacon Press, 1976), 7.

empower his prophetic vocation (Lk 3:21-22).[22] Jesus launched his public ministry with a reading from the Isaiah scroll (Lk 4:16-19 NRSV):

> The Spirit of the Lord is upon me,
>> because he has anointed me
>>> to bring good news to the poor.
> He has sent me to proclaim release to the captives
>> and recovery of sight to the blind,
>>> to let the oppressed go free,
> to proclaim the year of the Lord's favor.

Invoking Isaiah's prophecy of "year of the Lord's favor" (Is 58; 61; Lev 25; Deut 15:4-11), Jesus' Nazareth manifesto declares the start of the sabbath Jubilee Year (Lk 4:21).[23] According to the Torah rules (Lev 25:23-24), during the sabbath Jubilee Year

1. slaves are to be freed,

2. debts are to be canceled,

3. the land is to lie fallow,

4. and the land (wealth) is to be returned or redistributed to its original holder.

After reading Isaiah, Jesus proclaimed that Jubilee justice was fulfilled in their midst, inaugurating a season of freedom and economic redistribution for all God's children. The coming kingdom Jesus announces is marked by the preaching of the good news to the poor, healing the hurting, comforting the mourners, releasing the prisoners, liberating the oppressed, empowering the economically excluded, and bringing hope to all people, especially those on the margins. Poor people living under

---

[22]When the Spirit descends on Jesus as John the Baptist immerses him, it is a fulfillment of Isaiah's prophetic promise: "Behold My Servant, whom I uphold, / My chosen one *in whom* My soul delights. / I have put My Spirit upon Him; / He will bring forth justice to the nations" (Is 42:1 NASB). We see in this instant that Jesus is a Spirit-bearer of justice, who "brings forth justice to the nations." John the Baptist is an important forerunner of prophetic ethics. See Walter Wink, *John the Baptist in the Gospel Tradition* (Cambridge: Cambridge University Press, 1968).

[23]In his book *Jesus and the Nonviolent Revolution*, André Trochmé argues that the "year of the Lord's favor" is a reference to this Jubilee justice tradition, revealing that Jesus' teaching of the kingdom of God is fundamentally a teaching on economic justice. André Trochmé, *Jesus and the Nonviolent Revolution*, trans. Michael H. Shank and Marlin E. Miller (Scottdale, PA: Herald Press, 1956), esp. 48-52. John Howard Yoder continues this tradition in *The Politics of Jesus*, 2nd ed. (Grand Rapids: Eerdmans, 1994), esp. 60-75.

Roman oppression found great hope when Jesus came proclaiming "good news to the poor" (Lk 4:18).[24]

"If any want to become my followers, let them deny themselves and take up their cross daily and follow me," says Jesus as he calls disciples to follow him on the path of costly discipleship (Lk 9:23 NRSV). Prophetic ethics is *transformational discipleship* in "the Way" of Jesus Christ (see Jn 13:12-20; 14:5-7; Heb 12; 1 Pet 2:21-24). As Keith Johnson argues that theology is a "form of discipleship," I see Christian ethics as a form of discipleship.[25] Transformational discipleship in the Jesus way is a Spirit-led process of forming persons and communities to be just, loving, and connected to God the Creator (Mic 6:8).

Like Moses climbing up Mount Moriah and receiving the Ten Commandments (Ex 12–20), Jesus climbs a mountain to teach about the kingdom (Mt 5:1-2).[26] Jesus' Sermon on the Mount (Mt 5–7) is a manifesto of prophetic ethics that begins with the Beatitudes (Mt 5:1-12 NRSV):[27]

Blessed are the poor in spirit . . .
Blessed are those who mourn . . .
Blessed are the meek . . .
Blessed are those who hunger and thirst for righteousness . . .
Blessed are the merciful . . .
Blessed are the pure in heart . . .
Blessed are the peacemakers . . .

---

[24]Paying Jewish temple tax as part of their tithe, Jews in Jesus' day also owed taxes to the Roman Empire. As the Roman economy expanded, taxes were raised and Jews often became displaced from their ancestral lands. Monographs that provide insight into the economic context of Jesus' movement in the context of Second Temple Judaism and the Roman Empire include Warren Carter, *Matthew and the Margins: A Sociopolitical and Religious Reading* (Maryknoll, NY: Orbis, 2000); Sean Freyne, *Galilee from Alexander the Great to Hadrian: A Study of Second Temple Judaism* (Wilmington, DE: Michael Glazier, 1980); and Richard Horsley, *Jesus and Empire: The Kingdom of God and the New World Disorder* (Minneapolis: Fortress, 2003).

[25]Keith Johnson, *Theology as Discipleship* (Downers Grove, IL: InterVarsity Press, 2015), 166.

[26]See Dale C. Allison Jr., *The New Moses: A Matthean Typology* (Minneapolis: Fortress Press, 1993). For an overview of the moral vision of Matthew's Gospel see Richard B. Hays, *The Moral Vision of the New Testament: Community, Cross, New Creation; A Contemporary Introduction to New Testament Ethics* (San Francisco: HarperCollins, 1996), 93-111.

[27]For an insightful interpretation of the Sermon on the Mount that offers practical guidelines, see Glen H. Stassen, *Living the Sermon on the Mount: A Practical Hope for Grace and Deliverance* (San Francisco: John Wiley, 2006). Dietrich Bonhoeffer has a theologically deep interpretation of the Sermon on the Mount in *Discipleship*, ed. Geoffrey B. Kelly and John D. Godsey, trans. Barbara Green and Reinhard Krauss, Dietrich Bonhoeffer Works (Minneapolis: Fortress, 2001), 4:100-82. For a solid biblical and theological introduction to the Sermon on the Mount, see John Stott, *The Message of the Sermon on the Mount* (Downers Grove, IL: InterVarsity Press, 1978).

Blessed are those who are persecuted for righteousness' sake . . .
Blessed are you when people revile you and persecute you and utter all
kinds of evil against you falsely on my account.

*In the middle is mercy,* the fifth of the nine beatitudes. Mercy is the heartbeat
of the Jesus way.

Jesus calls his disciples to "seek first the kingdom and God's *justice*"
(Mt 6:33).[28] Justice restores the poor to their rightful place amid economic inequity, confronting corrupt leaders who are concerned more with
personal purity than with helping the needy (Mt 23:25; Lk 6:37-42).
With compassion for the outsiders, Jesus taught, "in everything do to
others as you would have them do to you" (Mt 7:12). The Golden Rule
ignites the disciple's prophetic imagination as Jesus exhorts them to "treat
the people and their needs as holy."[29] When the disciples deny the
children access to Jesus, large-hearted Jesus says, "Let the little children
come to me" (Mt 19:14). Jesus continually challenges his disciples to open
up their hearts to meet the felt needs of others, embodying an ethic of
nonviolent love (Mt 7:24-27).

While on the mountain, Jesus teaches his disciples the Lord's Prayer,
unveiling the spiritual power behind prophetic ethics (Mt 6:9-13):[30] "*Our
Father in heaven*" expresses the communal constitution of our unique
identity as children of our Creator. As in the Jewish Kaddish prayer, "Hallowed be your name" magnifies and sanctifies the name of God.[31] "Your
kingdom come. Your will be done, on *earth*" is a cry for God's righteous reign
of justice to be established on *earth* in an eschatological horizon of hope.
Provisional and limited, our prayers and acts of justice are *parables of the*

---

[28]Following Obery Hendricks Jr., I think *dikaiosynē* is best translated as "justice" in Matthew 6:33,
expressing Jesus' commitment to meeting poor people's basic human needs in the context of the
oppressive economics of the Roman Empire. See Hendricks, *Politics of Jesus,* 160.
[29]Ibid., 112. Stassen writes "The Pharisees and the scribes taught that holiness means separateness
and exclusion, Jesus taught that holiness means compassion and mercy." Stassen, *Living the Sermon,* 100.
[30]The soul of Jesus' Sermon on the Mount, Jesus' prayer (Mt 6:9-13) is presented in a section on
spiritual practice, including prayer, fasting, and almsgiving to the poor (Mt 6:1-18) between the
two larger teachings of Matthew 5:1-48 and 6:19–7:27.
[31]"Hallowed be your name" hearkens back to the *Shema Yisrael:* "Hear, O Israel: The LORD our God
is one" (Deut 6:4-9; 11:13-21; Num 15:37-41). As the first commandment is to "have no other gods"
than God (Ex 20:3), we are called to be loyal to God and God alone.

*kingdom,* pointing to Christ and the coming kingdom of God.[32] Every day we pray this prayer with "*Jesus Christ, who is the fulfillment of all petitions.*"[33]

Toward the end of his public ministry, Jesus "resolutely set out for Jerusalem" (Lk 9:51) with a laser-like focus on reforming the practice of Jewish temple worship and courageously confronting Roman royal power. Collectively calling for the Year of Jubilee, the disciples placed their bodies in public places to convert them into subversive spaces of *authentic* Passover celebration (Mt 21:1-11). When Jesus witnessed the money changers in front of the temple, he was incensed because these financial transactions hurt the poor, the very people the money was supposed to help. Through turning over the temple tables, Jesus dramatically disrupted bad business in a sacred place, declaring to the ruling powers the promise of a resurrection of love. Anointed to bring good news to the poor and liberty to the captives, Jesus claimed the moral mantle of the Hebrew prophets, ushering in God's Jubilee justice in Jerusalem and throughout Israel.

In contrast to the *priestly ethic* of the temple that had become complicit in the economic corruption of the Roman regime, Jesus' *prophetic ethic* called for a "large-hearted love" of God and the neighbor, especially the "least and the last," who he announced would become the "greatest and the first" (see Mt 12:11; 18:1-4; 25:40).[34] While Jesus' intervention at the temple was disruptive, no one was killed, in contrast to the armed insurrection of the Sicarii and the Zealots.

Forsaken by his Father and abandoned by his disciples, Jesus pours out his heart in a lament over Jerusalem. While praying through the night on the Mount of Olives (Lk 22:39-46), a mob came for him, including Judas, who betrayed him with a kiss (Lk 22:47-53). Incensed with anger, Peter pulls

---

[32]My reference to "parables of the kingdom" is an allusion to the theology of Karl Barth, who writes, "The action of those who pray for the coming of God's kingdom and therefore for the taking place of his righteousness will be *kingdom-like,* and therefore on a lower level and within its impassable limits will be *righteous* action." Karl Barth, *The Christian Life: Church Dogmatics* IV/4, Lecture Fragments (Edinburgh: T&T Clark, 1981), 266.

[33]Bonhoeffer, *Discipleship,* 157-58.

[34]Dietrich Bonhoeffer writes that to be a Christian is to "have some share in Christ's largeheartedness by acting with responsibility and in freedom when the hour of danger comes, and by showing a real compassion that springs, not from fear but from the liberating and redeeming love of Christ for all who suffer." Dietrich Bonhoeffer, "After Ten Years: A Letter to the Family and Conspirators," in *A Testament of Hope: The Essential Writings of Dietrich Bonhoeffer,* ed. Geffrey Kelly and F. Burton Nelson (New York: HarperCollins, 1995), 483-84.

out his sword and chops off the right ear of the slave of a high priest, giving
Jesus the opportunity to teach Peter that the kingdom is a *nonviolent* revolution: "Put your sword back into its place; for all who take the sword will
perish by the sword" (Mt 26:52 NRSV). The Jesus Way is not a way of violence but the way of restorative justice through nonviolent love. Jesus heals
the slave's ear, restoring him in body and soul (Lk 22:51). In contrast to the
*priestly ethic* of the temple elite and violent tactics of the *zealot ethic*, Jesus
calls us to a *prophetic ethic* of nonviolent revolution through practicing restorative justice, enemy love, and praying "Your kingdom come," which is
an improvisational restatement of Micah's call to do justice, love mercy, and
walk humbly with God (Mic 6:8).

Heeding Christ's call to "Go ye therefore, and teach all nations" (Mt 28:19
KJV), we need to teach the kingdom and work for justice in the world as we
share the gospel with others. Many Christians interpret Jesus' Great Commission as only a call to personal evangelism, but Jesus's kingdom teaching
demonstrates that ministries of mercy and justice are inseparable from evangelism. Beginning with our union with Christ Jesus, transformational discipleship is embodied in evangelism *and* justice. As Jesus called his followers
to a life of transformational discipleship, God is calling us to join the improvisational movement for justice and love.

## IMPROVISING FOR LOVE AND JUSTICE: THE METHOD OF PROPHETIC ETHICS

While love and justice are the moral norms of prophetic ethics, improvisation is its method.[35] As Samuel Wells argues, improvisation is the "task
of Christian ethics."[36] The improvisation involved in jazz music offers a way
of thinking about ethical action in creative and collaborative terms as we
seek to perform biblical justice in the world. When seen through a jazz lens,
Jesus is a Jewish improviser for justice.

Improvisation is innovation through collaboration. Jazz musicians study
the tradition through practicing the "standards," so they can make new
music for a new moment. We hear this dynamic in John Coltrane's 1961

---

[35]See my discussion of improvisation in jazz music in *Resurrection City: A Theology of Improvisation*
(Grand Rapids: Eerdmans, 2012), esp. 13ff.
[36]Samuel Wells, *Improvisation: The Drama of Christian Ethics* (Grand Rapids: Brazos, 2004), 65.

rendering of "My Favorite Things," the classic show tune in *The Sound of Music*, where Maria (Julie Andrews) cheers up the von Trapp children on a cold, rainy night under Nazi occupation. In a musical conversation with Richard Rodgers, Coltrane deepens the tonality of the piece, propelled by a bebop rhythm and colored with a blues sensibility. Coltrane's interpretation of "My Favorite Things" expresses the tragedy and triumph of the black freedom struggle. Against the stubborn scourge of sinful segregation, Coltrane invokes the favorite things that keep black people whole in a fearful and fragmented America.

As a black man, Coltrane had to negotiate two identities, being black and being American. This "double consciousness" that W. E. B. Du Bois described in *The Soul of Black Folks*, Coltrane expressed musically.[37] An idiom equipped to explore the twoness of identity, Coltrane's jazz music moved beyond the black-white binary toward a more open-ended, intercultural space for grace. With themes of "religious transcendence and political opposition," Coltrane's jazz is a countercultural practice of large-hearted love, witnessed in his American anthem *A Love Supreme*.[38]

Like a jazz musician improvising on standards, Jesus improvises on Scripture when he preaches and teaches.[39] With an improvisational interpretation of the Sermon on the Mount, Jesus says, "You have heard that it was said ... *But* I say to you," riffing on the Torah with his own interpretive style (e.g., Mt 5:21-22, 27-28, 31-32, 33-34, 38-39, 43-44). Jesus qualifies these radical statements with "Do not think that I have come to abolish the Law or the Prophets; I have come not to abolish but to fulfill" (Mt 5:17). Jesus says,

> You have heard that it was said, "An eye for an eye and a tooth for a tooth." But I say to you, Do not resist an evildoer. But if anyone strikes you on the right cheek, turn the other also; and if anyone wants to sue you and take your coat, give your cloak as well; and if anyone forces you to go one mile, go also the second mile. Give to everyone who begs from you, and do not refuse anyone who wants to borrow from you. (Mt 5:38-42 NSRV)

---

[37]W. E. B. Du Bois, *The Souls of Black Folk* (New York: Dover, 1994).
[38]Cornel West, *Prophetic Fragments* (Grand Rapids: Eerdmans, 1988), 5; and Paul Gilroy, *The Black Atlantic: Modernity and Double Consciousness* (Cambridge, MA: Harvard University Press, 1993), 1-40. For my theological interpretation of John Coltrane's "A Love Supreme," see my *Resurrection City*, 144-71.
[39]See Heltzel, *Resurrection City*, 49-72.

Justice in ancient Near Eastern legal codes often followed the principle of *lex talionis*, the law of retaliation, which said that a punishment should correspond in degree and kind to the offense of the wrongdoer, as an "eye for an eye." In the Code of Hammurabi, if a man killed the daughter of another man, the courts punished the murderer by killing his daughter. Jesus categorically rejects physical retaliation as a form of justice.[40]

In contrast to retributive justice of punishment through physical mutilation, Jesus calls for *restorative justice* focused on repair of broken relationships. According to Glen Stassen, when Jesus addresses retaliatory justice, he diagnoses the vicious cycle of violence, contrasting traditional righteousness (*lex talionis*) with a *transformational* initiative (restorative justice).[41] In a society with great economic inequity, when one generously gave away their coat *and* cloak, their own vulnerable nakedness stood as a nonviolent indictment of economic injustice.

Restoring broken relationships and systems also entails an internal transformation of the heart. Jesus says, "You have heard that it was said to those of ancient times, 'You shall not murder'; and 'whoever murders shall be liable to judgment.' But I say to you that if you are angry with a brother or sister, you will be liable to judgment" (Mt 5:21-22 NSRV). Jesus condemned anger

---

[40]David Daube offers the classic articulation of the ancient legal concept in *Studies in Biblical Law* (Cambridge: Cambridge University, 1947), 102-53; See Bernard S. Jackson's response "*Lex Talionis:* Revisiting Daube's Classic," a paper presented at the Biblical Law Section of the Society of Biblical Literature, 2001. Building on David Daube's idea of compensation within the legal logic of retaliation, Bernard S. Jackson unveils more compensatory alternatives to physical retaliation in Israel's legal codes in the ancient Near East and Second Temple Period. While the principle of *lex talionis* was used in the legal codes of the Amorites, the judges of Israel sought to settle legal disputes through financial compensation. While the Hebrew Bible uses the *lex talionis* formula (e.g., Ex 21:24; Lev 24:19-21; Deut 19:21), it seems to do so as a figure of speech, intended to make sure punishments fit the crime, rather than being excessive. Financial compensation instead of physical retaliation and mimetic mutilation was seen as the wisest course toward justice among the people of Israel because it disrupted the spiral of violence and fostered more peaceful social relations. Jesus boldly rejects the *lex talionis* principle, drawing on streams in the wisdom literature that focused on compassionately meeting the needs of the enemy in a spirit of nonviolent love as a form of restorative justice: "Do not say, 'I'll do to them as they have done to me; / I'll pay them back for what they did'" (Prov 24:29); "If your enemies are hungry, give them bread to eat; / and if they are thirsty, give them water to drink; / for you will heap coals of fire on their heads, / and the LORD will reward you" (Prov 25:21-22 NSRV). Cf. Bernard S. Jackson, "Law, Wisdom and Narrative," in *Narrativity in Biblical and Related Texts*, ed. G. W. Brooke and J.-D. Kaestli (Louvain: Peeters, 2000), 31-51; and J. Weingreen, "The Concepts of Retaliation and Compensation in Biblical Law," *Proceedings of the Royal Irish Academy* 76, sec. C, no. 1 (1976): 1-11.

[41]Stassen, *Living the Sermon*, 6.

as well as murder, lust as well as adultery, calling for a conversion of the heart. When Jesus' disciples got angry, they were encouraged to reconcile rather than fight. When they married, Jesus called them to be faithful to their covenantal partners, physically and emotionally (Mt 5:27-32; 19:3-9; Heb 13:4). In the life of chastity, single disciples bear witness through single-hearted devotion to loving God and others that Jesus modeled in his own life of singleness (Mt 19:10-11; Mk 10:28-30; 1 Tim 5:9-10).

Loving the enemy is the great challenge.[42] Jesus said, "You have heard that it was said, 'You shall love your neighbor and hate your enemy.' But I say to you, Love your enemies and pray for those who persecute you" (Mt 5:43-44 NSRV). Since our enemies are included in God's community of mercy, we are to love them, respect them, and pray for them. Loving our enemy does not mean agreeing with them, but it does mean respecting them as children of God. Loving our enemy keeps alive a glimmer of hope for real restoration within the broken community.

A jazz approach to Christian ethics improvises for justice and love. Jazz never simply argues or critiques; it riffs on themes, transforms or transposes them, and subverts popular forms of culture by making new music for a new age. Like Moses and Miriam, Jesus and Coltrane, we need to listen to the cry of the poor, sing songs of hope, and heal the racial divide.

## RACISM: AMERICA'S ORIGINAL AND ONGOING SIN

"'Black Lives Matter' is a movement of mission because it demands that we face the facts and tell the truth: Black Lives Matter is a global prophetic movement. It demands that I know myself and I see you. It demands that those who have been imprisoned, incarnated, and executed at astonishing rates because of their skin color are no longer devalued, but we see them and

---

[42]The call to love the enemy is central to the moral vision of the Sermon on the Mount (Mt 5:38-48). Jesus echoes this teaching in the parable of the unmerciful servant (Mt 18:21-35). In the chiastic structure in Jesus' shorter Sermon on the Plain, the teaching on enemy love is the heart of the sermon (Lk 6:27-36). Jesus' teaching on loving the enemy was anticipated by Exodus 23:4-6 (NSRV): "When you come upon your enemy's ox or donkey going astray, you shall bring it back. When you see the donkey of one who hates you lying under its burden and you would hold back from setting it free, you must help to set it free. You shall not pervert the justice due to your poor in their lawsuits." See Glen H. Stassen, "The Politics of Jesus in the Sermon on the Plain," in *The Wisdom of the Cross*, ed. Stanley Hauerwas, Chris Huebner, and Marm T. Nation (Grand Rapids: Eerdmans, 1999), 150-67.

*free* them," said Michelle Higgins on December 28, 2015, at Urbana 15, InterVarsity's twenty-fourth Mission Conference.[43] Boldly confronting the institutional racism in our criminal justice system, Higgins awakened millennial evangelicals to follow the black woman–led Black Lives Matter movement, provoking a critical conversation on Jesus, race, and justice in the evangelical world. As a young black female, Michelle Higgins claimed her power through delivering the most prophetic word heard at Urbana since Tom Skinner's "The Liberator Has Come" speech in 1970.[44]

Racism is America's original and ongoing sin.[45] It is more than personal prejudice; it is prejudice *plus* power. In the United States, racism manifests itself in an ideology of white supremacy, the idea that whites are superior to people of other races and ethnicities and that society should be organized to maintain and protect the power and property of white people. While the Declaration of Independence states that all people have the right to "life, liberty and the pursuit of happiness," it also refers to Native Americans as "merciless Indian Savages," creating the condition for the Trail of Tears—the path walked by members of the First Nations who were forcibly removed from the southeastern United States to the lands west of the Mississippi River.[46]

---

[43]Michelle Higgins, "Black Lives Matter Address," Urbana 15, InterVarsity Student Missions Conference, December 28, 2015.

[44]In his "Christ the Liberator" address in 1970, Tim Skinner said, "Any gospel that does not talk about delivering to man a personal Savior who will free him from the personal bondage of sin and grant him eternal life and does not at the same time speak to the issue of enslavement, the issue of injustice, the issue of inequality, any gospel that does not want to go where people are hungry and poverty-stricken and set them free in the name of Jesus Christ—is not the gospel." Skinner's call for Jesus and justice was crystal clear, but it has taken evangelicals decades to catch up with his evangelical liberation theology. See my discussion of Tom Skinner's "The Liberator Has Come" in *Jesus and Justice: Evangelicals, Race and American Politics* (New Haven, CT: Yale University Press, 2009), 167.

[45]I am indebted to Crossroads Antiracism Organizing and Training for introducing me to the institutional racism as an ethical problem that American Christians must face. I gained insight into the problem of institutional racism from the book of one my trainers: Joseph Barndt, *Dismantling Racism: The Continuing Challenge to White America* (Minneapolis: Augsburg Fortress, 1991). See Jim Wallis, *America's Original Sin: Racism, White Privilege, and the Bridge to a New America* (Grand Rapids: Brazos, 2016), esp. 33-56. Ta-Nehisi Coates's book *Between the World and Me* (New York: Spiegel & Grau, 2015) and subsequent articles have sparked a deep national conversation on reparations. Michelle Alexander writes, "it may be impossible to overstate the significance of race in defining the basic structure of American society." Michelle Alexander, *The New Jim Crow: Mass Incarceration in the Age of Colorblindness* (New York: New Press, 2010), 25.

[46]See John Ehle, *Trail of Tears: The Rise and Fall of the Cherokee Nation* (New York: Anchor Books, 1988); cf. Stuart Banner, *How the Indians Lost Their Land: Law and Power on the Frontier*

From the establishment of the Jamestown, Virginia, settlement in 1607 to the adoption of the US Constitution in 1789, every settlement, document, and procedure in the United States was established to legitimate and perpetuate the power of white land-owning men. The US Constitution counted enslaved Africans as three-fifths of a person. The only people who were truly free in colonial America were white, land-owning men, excluding women and people of color from claiming their "inalienable rights." White supremacy took on systemic forms in America's social institutions, including government, banks, entertainment, education, and churches.

During the colonial conquest of the Americas, whiteness was forged through the architecture of Christian theology. In *The Christian Imagination*, Willie James Jennings argues that Christian theology was misused to sanctify the political power and colonial ambitions of European nations as they enslaved Africans and killed indigenous people.[47] When Jesuit missionary José de Acosta Porres arrived in Peru in 1572, he adapted Thomas Aquinas's theology to stabilize Christian identity in the new colonial circumstance.[48] Based on an Aristotelian hierarchy, Thomism pressed Acosta to appeal to a natural order to account for difference in the New World. Acosta theorized white supremacy through a racial typology structured around three levels of barbarism as a way of discerning the work of "the demonic" in the indigenous population on the bottom of the racial hierarchy, while watched by the white gaze of the European men on the top.[49]

---

(Cambridge, MA: Harvard University Press, 2005); Robert Warrior, "Canaanites, Cowboys and Indians," *Natives and Christians*, ed. James Treat (New York: Routledge, 1996), 93-100; On the doctrine of discovery see Steven T. Newcomb, *Pagans in the Promised Land: Decoding the Doctrine of Christian Discovery* (Golden, CO: Fulcrum, 2008).

[47]Willie James Jennings, *The Christian Imagination: Theology and the Origins of Race* (New Haven, CT: Yale University Press, 2010). Jennings's work is part of constellation of postcolonial accounts of the theological origins of race, including Brian Bantum and J. Kameron Carter, *Race: A Theological Account* (Oxford: Oxford University Press, 2008); Peter Goodwin Heltzel, "Revival, Race and Reform: The Roots of Modern Evangelical Politics," in *Jesus and Justice*, esp. 13-44; Reggie L. Williams, *Bonhoeffer's Black Jesus: Harlem Renaissance Theology and an Ethic of Resistance* (Waco, TX: Baylor University Press, 2014); and Jessica Wai-Fong Wong, "The Anti-Iconicity of Blackness: A Theological Reading of the Modern Racial Optic," PhD diss., Duke University, 2015.

[48]For Jennings's full discussion of José de Acosta Porres, see *Christian Imagination*, 65-118.

[49]A chart of the José de Acosta Porres's typology of the barbarians is provided in ibid., 103. Through analyzing the cultural practices of different people groups in the Peru, Acosta categorizes barbarian identity through the white gaze of Western theology that became "the trigger for the classificatory subjugation of all nonwhite, non-western peoples." Ibid., 87.

Acosta's colonial categorization system relied on a Christian logic; that is, Christian theology provided the social imaginary for colonial conquest. Salvation was refracted through a racial optic where enslaved Africans and indigenous people were measured by their likeness to the white male body.[50] This process of racialization worked together with a European imperial worldview where Israel was replaced by the colonial church as the community of God's chosen people, and Christ became a white European man.[51]

Jennings connects Acosta's colonial Catholicism with contemporary neo-traditionalist defenses of Aquinas's theology like that of Alasdair MacIntyre, who advocates virtue ethics, encouraging Christians to cultivate positive character traits. Jennings critiques theologians who have followed MacIntyre's thinking on tradition "for not seeing the effects on the Christian tradition triggered by the modernist elements at the beginning of the age of Iberian conquest,"[52] while perpetuating theology as a project that seeks the moral redemption of Western civilization, a form of theologizing that has moral resonances with Acosta's basic theological moves.

Virtue ethicist Stanley Hauerwas argues that the first task of the church is "to be the church."[53] Rejecting justice as "a *bad idea* for Christians," Hauerwas argues that Christians should develop their ethical analysis through being "uninvolved in the politics of our society and involved in the polity of the church."[54] Hauerwas ontologizes the church, focusing on its *being* in community rather than its *doing* the work of love and justice in and for the

---

[50]Ibid., 58-59. For an analysis of racism that foregrounds the aesthetics of whiteness see Cornel West, *Prophesy Deliverance: An Afro-American Revolutionary Christianity* (Philadelphia: Westminster, 1982), 47-68.

[51]See J. Kameron Carter, *Race: A Theological Account* (Oxford: Oxford University Press, 2008). With the advent of European colonialism and the trans-Atlantic slave trade, Western Christianity's supersessionism (Christianity replacing Judaism) creates the conditions for whiteness to replace Judaism as a new center of Christian identity. Prophetic ethics stands against these anti-Jewish, anti-black tendencies within Western Christianity through reclaiming Jesus' Jewish heritage, especially the Torah and the Hebrew prophets, and connecting Jesus' teaching of the kingdom to the experiences of the poor and oppressed, especially black and brown people, in the Americas.

[52]Jennings, *Christian Imagination*, 70-71. Alasdair MacIntyre, *After Virtue: A Study in Moral Theory* (Notre Dame, IN: University of Notre Dame Press, 1981); and Alasdair MacIntyre, *Whose Justice? Which Rationality?* (Notre Dame, IN: University of Notre Dame Press, 1988).

[53]Stanley Hauerwas, *Peaceable Kingdom* (Notre Dame, IN: University of Notre Dame Press, 1991), 100.

[54]Stanley Hauerwas, *After Christendom: How the Church Is to Behave If Freedom, Justice and a Christian Nation Are Bad Ideas* (Nashville: Abingdon, 1991), 45-69, italics added; and Stanley Hauerwas, *A Community of Character: Toward a Constructive Christian Social Ethics* (Notre Dame, IN: University of Notre Dame Press, 1981), 74.

community. This is problematic in several ways: The mere existence of the church as an alternative community of virtue does not necessarily inspire and equip its members to engage in the work of social transformation. The church as "contrast community" of virtue does not give an account of how structural sins like racism are part of the structures of congregational and community life. In fact, its silence may make it complicit with them.[55]

## MARTIN LUTHER KING JR. AND THE BELOVED COMMUNITY

Rev. Dr. Martin Luther King Jr. writes,

> The church . . . is the greatest preserver of the status quo. So it was very easy for slavery to receive a religious sanction. The church is one of the chief exponents of racial bigotry. . . . Since this is the case, we must admit that the church is far from Christ. What has happened is this: the church, while flowing through the stream of history has picked up the evils of little tributaries, and these tributaries have been so powerful that they have been able to overwhelm the main stream. In other words, the church has picked up a lot of historical vices.[56]

Calling for the church to confess the sin of racism, King publicly repents of racism through his faith-rooted organizing for racial justice from the deepest wells of Christian faith. In contrast to the tributaries of vices, King calls for justice to "roll on like a river" (Amos 5:24).[57]

Living in captivity on plantations, enslaved Africans fought for freedom, improvising to survive. In contrast to the slave-holding religion of their masters, out in the clearing "slaves redeemed the religion that the master had profaned in their midst."[58] In her haunting novel *Beloved*, Toni Morrison

---

[55]For a contrast between the ethical vision of Stanley Hauerwas and that of Martin Luther King Jr., see Bruce Ellis Benson, Malinda Elizabeth Berry, and Peter Goodwin Heltzel, "Stanley Hauerwas, Martin Luther King, Jr., and the Quest for Justice," *Prophetic Evangelicals* (Grand Rapids: Eerdmans, 2012), 20-30.

[56]Martin Luther King Jr., "Is the Church the Hope of the World?," in *Martin Luther King, Jr.: Advocate of Social Gospel, September 1948-1963*, ed. Clayton Carson et al. (Berkeley: University of California Press, 2007), 105-6.

[57]Following Dietrich Bonhoeffer, Jennifer M. McBride argues that confession unto repentance offers a concrete form of public witness. See Jennifer M. McBride, *The Church for the World: A Theology of Public Witness* (Oxford: Oxford University Press, 2012).

[58]Howard Thurman, *The Negro Spiritual Speaks of Life and Death* (Richmond, VA: Friends Press, 1975), 40.

describes "the Clearing" as "a wide-open place cut deep in the woods," where Baby Suggs, "an unchurched preacher," would deliver sonorous sermons:

> "Let the children come!" and they ran from the trees toward her.
>
> "Let your mothers hear your laughter," she told them, and the woods rang. The adults looked on and could not help smiling.
>
> Then "Let the grown men come," she shouted. They stepped out one by one from among the ringing trees.
>
> "Let your wives and your children see you dance," she told them, and groundlife shuddered under their feet.
>
> Finally she called the women to her. "Cry," she told them. "For the living and the dead. Just cry." And without covering their eyes the women let loose.
>
> It started that way: laughing children, dancing men, crying women and then it got mixed up. Women stopped crying and danced; men sat down and cried; children danced, women laughed, children cried until, exhausted and riven, all and each lay about the Clearing damp and gasping for breath. In the silence that followed, Baby Suggs, holy, offered up to them her great big heart.[59]

Like Jesus, Baby Suggs was a healer with a "big heart." Given the ghosts of the Middle Passage and slavery, the Clearing was a space of healing, hope, and large-hearted love.

Large-hearted love was both the means and the end of the civil rights movement: "The end is reconciliation, the end is redemption, the end is the creation of the beloved community."[60] Shaped by evangelical revivalism and slave religion, King's prophetic Baptist ethic was rooted in the freedom and dignity of all people.[61] King expanded Roger Williams's conception of "soul freedom" to include "social freedom."[62] Combining a commitment to the

---

[59]Toni Morrison, *Beloved* (New York: Vintage, 2004), 103-4.

[60]Martin Luther King Jr., "Facing the Challenge of a New Age," in *The Papers of Martin Luther King, Jr.*, vol. 3, *Birth of A New Age, December 1955-December 1956*, ed. Stewart Burns, Susan Carson, Peter Holloran, and Dana L. H. Powell (Berkeley: University of California Press, 1997), 458.

[61]Heltzel, *Jesus and Justice*, 87-93.

[62]In "A Plea for Religious Liberty," in *The Bloudy Tenent of Persecution* (1644), Roger Williams advocated "Soul liberty," the right and responsibility of individuals to decide for themselves what they believe and how to live. Roger Williams, *The Bloudy Tenent of Persecution, for Cause of Conscience*, ed. Richard Groves (Macon, GA: Mercer University Press, 2001). In the shadows of the great wars of religion in Europe, Williams believed people should be free to express their religious convictions without coercion or constraint. Robert Bellah argues that Roger Williams, not Jonathan Winthrop, is the "founding" political theorist in the United States. Robert N. Bellah, "Is There a Common American Culture?," *Journal of the American Academy of Religion* 66 (1998): 613-26. Cornel West writes, "For prophetic Christianity, the two inseparable notions of freedom

freedom of the individual with responsibility for others, King advanced a unique vision of beloved community, inspiring everyday people to march shoulder to shoulder in the struggle for justice.

The young Dr. King reluctantly decided to step up as the clergy leader of the Montgomery Bus Boycott.[63] After studying nonviolent civil disobedience at the Highlander Folk School, Rosa Parks bravely kept her seat on a segregated bus and was arrested on December 1, 1955. A few days later, King delivered a speech, saying, "standing beside love is always justice, and we are only using the tools of justice." An economic boycott was the "tool of justice" that King deployed to integrate the Montgomery bus system. During the speech, King says that Mrs. Rosa Parks was a person of "character," demonstrating the importance of personal righteousness, as King and the movement pressed for social righteousness through the establishment of new laws, policies, and institutions.[64]

The problem of racism was more than a problem of personal prejudice; it was a problem of sinful social systems. King illustrated the problem of social sin through his interpretation of Jesus' parable of the compassionate Samaritan (Lk 10:25-37).[65] In the story a man was robbed, wounded, and left in a ditch on a road from Jerusalem to Jericho, a notoriously dangerous road. "But a Samaritan while traveling came near him; and when he saw him, he was moved with pity" (Lk 10:33 NSRV). King writes:

---

are existential freedom and social freedom." Cornel West, *Prophecy Deliverance! An Afro-American Revolutionary Christianity* (Philadelphia: Westminster Press, 1982), 18.

[63]When he arrived in Montgomery, Dr. King learned of a bus boycott being planned by Jo Ann Robinson, Rosa Parks, and the Women's Political Council. When his elders in his Baptist clergy group asked Dr. King to lead the movement, he was initially reluctant, but prompted by the Spirit, he stepped up to lead the Montgomery Bus Boycott. Charles Marsh describes Dr. King's transformation into a faith-rooted activist pastor in *The Beloved Community: How Faith Shapes Social Justice, from the Civil Rights Movement to Today* (New York: Basic, 2005), 11-50.

[64]King, "Montgomery Improvement Association Mass Meeting at Holt Street Baptist Church," *Papers of Martin Luther King, Jr.*, 3:71-79.

[65]Popularly known as the parable of the good Samaritan (Lk 10:25-37), I name it the parable of the compassionate Samaritan following Glen Stassen and David Gushee, foregrounding the centrality of compassion in action in Jesus' story. Stassen and Gushee, *Kingdom Ethics*, 229, 327-54. For an insightful and inspiring introduction to the practice of compassion in the walk of Christian discipleship see Donald McNeill, Douglas A. Morrison, and Henri Nouwen, *Compassion: A Reflection on the Christian Life* (New York: Image Books, 1982). See also Robert C. Roberts's discussion of compassion as a spiritual emotion in *Spiritual Emotions: A Psychology of Christian Virtues* (Grand Rapids: Eerdmans, 2007), 179-98.

On the one hand we are called to play the Good Samaritan on life's roadside; but that will be only an initial act. One day we must come to see that the whole Jericho road must be transformed so that men and women will not be constantly beaten and robbed as they make their journey on life's highway. True compassion is more than flinging a coin to a beggar; it is not haphazard and superficial. It comes to see that an edifice which produces beggars needs restructuring.[66]

While saving the life of the man in the ditch is an important step in embodying neighbor love, King argues we also need to transform the whole Jericho road.[67]

When you challenge the system, expect resistance. On January 27, 1956, Dr. King received a death threat: "Leave Montgomery immediately if you have no wish to die." Dr. King brewed a pot of coffee, sat down at his kitchen table, and said a prayer:

I am here taking a stand for what I believe is right. But now I am afraid. . . . I've come to the point where I can't face it alone. At that moment, I experienced the presence of the Divine as I had never experienced God before. It seemed as though I could hear the quiet assurance of an inner voice saying: "Stand up for justice, stand up for truth; and God will be at your side forever." Almost at once my fears began to go. My uncertainty disappeared. . . . I was ready to face anything.[68]

Personally experiencing the divine presence, King had a vibrant relationship with God and a clear calling from God to "stand up for justice." Three days later his house was bombed; Coretta and their little daughter were inside, but their lives were spared. When an angry crowd of friends arrived, King met them with a quiet confidence and proclaimed, "We must meet the force of hate with the power of love; we must meet physical force with soul force."[69] At his kitchen table, King *prayed for the kingdom*, in the

---

[66]Martin Luther King Jr., "A Time to Break Silence," in *A Testament of Hope: The Essential Writings and Speeches of Martin Luther King, Jr.*, ed. James M. Washington (New York: HarperOne, 1986), 241.

[67]King writes, "On the one hand I must attempt to change the souls of individuals so that their societies may be changed. On the other hand I must attempt to change the society so that the individual soul will have a change. Therefore, I must be concerned about unemployment, slums and economic insecurity." Martin Luther King Jr., "Preaching Ministry," in Carson et al., *Martin Luther King, Jr.*, 72.

[68]Martin Luther King Jr., *Stride Toward Freedom: The Montgomery Story* (New York: Harper, 1958), 134.

[69]Martin Luther King Jr., "Experiment in Love," in Washington, *Testament of Hope*, 17. Hereafter I

streets he engaged in *faith-rooted organizing* for justice, expressing *embodied solidarity* in the liberation struggle of African Americans.

## BONHOEFFER'S BLACK JESUS

"It was the Sermon on the Mount, rather than a doctrine of passive resistance, that initially inspired the Negroes to dignified social action. It was Jesus of Nazareth that stirred the Negroes to protest with the creative weapon of love," said King.[70] Jesus' Sermon on the Mount was central to prophetic black Christianity, with echoes heard in the sermons of Rev. Adam Clayton Powell Sr. at Abyssinian Baptist Church. Dietrich Bonhoeffer was enraptured by Powell's preaching while attending Abyssinian during a Sloane Fellowship at Union Theological Seminary in 1930–1931.[71] According to Reggie Williams, Powell's sermons "A Hungry God" and "A Naked God" offered an innovative interpretation of Matthew 25:31-46,

---

will refer to this work as *Testament of Hope*. The nonviolent struggle for justice in the transportation system lasted a year and nineteen days, seeing the desegregation of Montgomery's public transportation system on December 20, 1956.

[70]Ibid., 16. While Jesus' Sermon on the Mount gave Dr. King the motivation for his love ethic, it was Mohandas Gandhi who presented him a method for nonviolent direct action giving love a political form. John Lawson taught Dr. King in this tradition of Gandhian nonviolence. Following in the footsteps of many African American ministers, including Mordecai Wyatt Johnson, Benjamin Mays, and Howard Thurman, who traveled to India to meet with Gandhi and his circle, Dr. King, Coretta Scott King, and Lawrence Reddick embarked on a five-week tour of India on February 3, 1959, an experience that made him realize the breadth and depth of embodied solidarity in the freedom movement globally. See Martin Luther King Jr., "My Trip to the Land of Gandhi" (Washington, *A Testament of Hope*, 32-30). Cf. *Gandhi on Nonviolence*, ed. Thomas Merton (New York: New Directions, 1964); Robert Ellsberg, ed., *Gandhi on Christianity* (Maryknoll, NY: Orbis, 1991); Ignatius Jesudasan, *A Gandhian Theology of Liberation* (Maryknoll, NY: Orbis, 1984); Terrence J. Rynne, *Gandhi and Jesus: The Saving Power of Nonviolence* (Maryknoll, NY: Orbis, 2008); and John Thatamanil, "The Hospitality of Receiving: Mahatma Gandhi, Martin Luther King, Jr. and Interreligious Learning," in *An Inescapable Network of Mutuality: Martin Luther King, Jr. and the Globalization of an Ethical Ideal*, ed. Lewis V. Baldwin and Paul R. Dekar (Eugene, OR: Cascade, 2013), 131-51.

[71]On a Sunday in November 1930, Albert Franklin Fisher, a black student at Union Theological Seminary from Birmingham, Alabama, invited Bonhoeffer to join him for morning worship at Abyssinian Baptist Church in Harlem. This Sunday was Bonhoeffer's baptism into the black social gospel in America. Rev. Powell was part of a national movement of black social gospel preachers who "taught that God favors the oppressed and excluded. They preached about equality, democracy, peacemaking, and Jesus loving all the children. They puzzled that white Christians ignored the central gospel teachings. And they kept alive the hope of breaking white supremacy." Gary Dorrien, *The New Abolition: W. E. B. Du Bois and the Black Social Gospel* (New Haven, CT: Yale University Press, 2015). For a thoughtful discussion of Rev. Adam Clayton Powell and Abyssinian Baptist Church, see ibid., 425-58.

having a lasting impact on Bonhoeffer's theology and ministry.[72] Powell helped Bonhoeffer to see the "Black Jesus" who is present in our fellow humans who are hungry, thirsty, naked, and imprisoned.[73] The insight that Jesus is a cosufferer hidden in black suffering helped Bonhoeffer experience Christ in the suffering other. Through his experiences in the black church in Harlem, Bonhoeffer returned to Germany prepared to empathetically enter the experience of Jews who were being oppressed by the Nazis, placing his own body on the line in solidarity with the Jews.

The living Christ is met in the encounter with others. "Because Jesus is life, through him all life is determined as the incarnational (or empathetic) responsibility," writes Bonhoeffer.[74] Empathetic responsibility means opening our heart to feel others' pain, so we are better positioned to act ethically in the world with attunement to others' emotions, struggles, and dreams. While we are able to cultivate empathy in our relationships with friends and family, Jesus challenges us to empathize with poor people and victims of violence, crossing boundaries of race and religion that keep us divided. Claude McKay explores empathy and its absence in his poem "The Lynching":

> His spirit is smoke, ascended to the high heaven.
> His father, by the cruelest way of pain,
> Had bidden him to his bosom once again.
> The awful sin remained still unforgiven.
> All night a bright and solitary star

---

[72]Reggie Williams, *Bonhoeffer's Black Jesus: Harlem Renaissance Theology and an Ethic of Resistance* (Waco, TX: Baylor University Press, 2014), 101-15.

[73]Arriving shortly after the Great Depression (1929–1939), Bonhoeffer saw abject poverty in the black community in Harlem in the context of brutal racial violence in Jim Crow America. Since Jesus suffered for all people who suffered, the black social gospel offered hope of a this-worldly liberation for the oppressed. See ibid. Cf. Peter Goodwin Heltzel, "Jesus the Revolutionary: Christology After Bonhoeffer," *Politik und Ökonomie der Befreiung. Politics and Economics of Liberation*, ed. Ulrich Duchrow and Martin Hoffman (Berlin: LIT Verlag, 2015), 215-39; and Soong-Chan Rah, "Ferguson," in *Prophetic Lament: A Call for Justice in Troubled Times* (Downers Grove, IL: InterVarsity Press, 2015), 198-203.

[74]Dietrich Bonhoeffer, "The Structure of Responsible Life," in *Ethics*, Dietrich Bonhoeffer Works (Minneapolis: Fortress, 2008), 6:268, quoted in Stassen, *Thicker Jesus*, 233n7. Stassen's *Thicker Jesus* is an attempt to synthesize the best insights from Bonhoeffer's *Discipleship* and his *Ethics*. In *Ethics* Bonhoeffer does not deeply engage the discipleship motif. I agree with Stassen that discipleship is a helpful way to frame Christian ethics. While he speaks of incarnational ethics, I prefer the term *transformational ethics*. See my brief discussion of transformation in *Resurrection City*, 128-30.

Perchance the one that ever guided him,
Ye gave him up at last to Fate's wild whim
Hung pitifully o'er the swinging char,
Day dawned, and soon the mixed crowds came to view
The ghastly body swaying in the sun.
The women thronged to look, but never a one
Showed sorrow in her eyes of steely blue;
And little lads, lynchers that were to be,
Danced around the dreadful thing in glee.[75]

With the rising of the sun, everyone sees the aftermath of the lynching. With a dead black body smoldering, wives see what their husbands had done, and children play, oblivious. This disturbing image unveils the depth of racism in the very fabric of America. We see this same incapacity for empathy among some whites who are resistant to the Black Lives Matter movement, empathizing more with George Zimmerman, the Latino self-appointed neighborhood watchman who is an embodiment of white anxiety, than with Trayvon Martin, a young black man with a bag of Skittles, brutally gunned down while trying to make his way home. With the moral courage of Moses and Miriam, Jeremiah and Jesus, we are called to empathetically enter the experience of our fellow humans, especially the marginalized who are victims of violence.

## CHRIST AND THE POWERS

As whites empathetically enter into the experience of the oppressed, we deepen our understanding of the social sources of oppression. Experiencing discrimination within white-dominated social systems, most black evangelicals acknowledge social sin, while white evangelicals with a commitment to individualism, relationalism, and antistructuralism are often blinded from seeing racism as a structural reality.[76] Throughout the Holy Scripture, we see that sin is both individual and institutional (Is 1:10-26; Amos 2:6-8; Mic 2:1-10; Rom 1:28-32). Sin and the demonic are not abstract, invisible forces

---

[75]Claude McKay, "Lynching," in *Harlem Shadows: The Poems of Claude McKay* (New York: Hardcourt, Brace, 1922), 51. I'm indebted to Reggie Williams for introducing me to this poem, which he explicates in *Bonhoeffer's Black Jesus*, 63.
[76]Michael Emerson and Christian Smith, *Divided by Faith: Evangelical Religion and the Problem of Race in America* (Oxford: Oxford University Press, 2000), 76-81.

but embodied realities in concrete structures and institutions. These social forces that Paul calls "principalities and powers" (Eph 6:12) shape our subjectivities and communities. They define who is human and who is not, whose lives are grievable and whose are not.

Dying for the forgiveness of our sins on a Roman cross, Jesus Christ "disarmed the powers and authorities, [and] he made a public spectacle of them, triumphing over them" (Col 2:15).[77] Jesus Christ's courageous confrontation of "the powers" in the religious and political institutions of his day provides an inspiring example for our courageous confrontation of social sin today. Kristin Heyer writes, "In its broadest sense social sin encompasses the unjust structures, distorted consciousness, and collective actions and inaction that facilitate injustice and dehumanization."[78] In our faith-rooted activism it is vital that we address the presence of harm caused by the workings of social sin instead of furthering the suffering of those wounded by its working.

## THE NEW JIM CROW AND RESTORATIVE JUSTICE

As Michelle Alexander argues in *The New Jim Crow*, the US prison system is broken. African American males are 6 percent of the US population and 40 percent of those who are incarcerated. One in three young African American males are under the jurisdiction of the criminal justice system. African American men have been imprisoned at rates more than thirteen times higher than that of white men, sustaining a racial caste system in our

---

[77]In developing the theme of Christ as victor over the principalities and powers of this world, I am working the prophetic tradition of Johann Christoph and Christoph Friedrich Blumhardt, Karl Barth, and more recent theologians like Walter Wink. See Johann Christoph Blumhardt, *Blumhardt's Battle: A Conflict with Satan*, trans. Frank S. Boshold (New York: Thomas E. Lowe, 1970); Karl Barth, *The Christian Life: Church Dogmatics* IV/4, Lecture Fragments (Grand Rapids: Eerdmans, 1981), 213-33; Hendrikus Berkhof, *Christ and the Powers*, trans. John Howard Yoder (Scottdale, PA: Herald Press, 1962); John Howard Yoder, *The Politics of Jesus* (Grand Rapids: Eerdmans, 1972); William Stringfellow, *An Ethic for Christians and Other Aliens in a Strange Land* (Waco, TX: Word, 1973); Walter Wink, *Naming the Powers: The Language of Power in the New Testament* (Philadelphia: Fortress, 1984); Walter Wink, *Unmasking the Powers: The Invisible Forces that Determine Human Existence* (Philadelphia: Fortress, 1986); and Walter Wink, *Engaging the Powers: Discernment and Resistance in a World of Domination* (Minneapolis: Fortress, 1992).

[78]Kristin E. Heyer, *Kinship Across Borders: A Christian Ethic of Immigration* (Washington, DC: Georgetown University Press, 2012), 37. For a thoughtful theological introduction to social sin see Stephen Ray, *Do No Harm: Social Sin and Christian Responsibility* (Minneapolis: Augsburg, 2002). Sociologist Lowell Nobel offers an insightful analysis of systemic oppression in *From Oppression to Jubilee Justice* (Jackson, MS: Urban Verses, 2007).

criminal justice system.[79] On their reentry into society, former "felons" are still criminalized and face discrimination in employment, housing, and education, creating a moral crisis that must be addressed.

Rev. Michael McBride is an African American pastor and organizer who is director of the LIVE FREE Campaign, a national project of PICO, a network of faith-based organizations and congregations committed to addressing the causes of pervasive violence and crime in American cities. With roots in Alinsky-style organizing, PICO's founder Father John Bauman brought a deep Catholic spirituality to broad-based community organizing. Through the prophetic leadership of Michael McBride, Onleilove Alston, Alvin Herring, and Michael-Ray Mathews, PICO has worked hard to engage racial justice and reconciliation from the deepest wells of our faith. PICO leadership played an important role in organizing faith leaders in Ferguson and are currently advancing the faith-rooted fight to reduce gun violence, dismantle mass incarceration, and end the criminalization of race.

As a response to problems such as gun violence, mass incarceration, and other issues within the criminal justice system, white evangelical activists like Jennifer M. McBride have joined the fight to abolish the death penalty. The execution of Kelly Renee Gissendaner became a wake-up call for the evangelical community. After having a Christian conversion, Kelly was executed by lethal injection on September 30, 2015. She had been convicted of orchestrating the murder of her husband, Douglas Gissendaner, in 1997. While Kelly was in Metro State Prison for Women near Atlanta, McBride became her professor in 2010 through a theology certificate program sponsored by four Atlanta seminaries. Kelly read German theologian Jürgen Moltmann's *Theology of Hope*, which quickly became her favorite book.[80] Through an active correspondence, a friendship developed that resulted in Prof. Moltmann delivering the commencement address at the theology graduation inside the prison in October 2011.[81]

---

[79]Michelle Alexander, *The New Jim Crow: Mass Incarceration in the Age of Colorblindness* (New York: New Press, 2010), 59, 98. Alexander argues that a racialized caste system has taken four different forms in US history: slavery, Jim Crow, segregation, and the mass incarceration of African American men.

[80]Jürgen Moltmann, *Theology of Hope*, trans. James W. Leitch (Minneapolis: Fortress Press, 1993).

[81]On the day that Prof. Moltmann delivered his commencement address in the prison, he was able to join Jennifer McBride in a two-hour pastoral visit with Kelly Gissendaner.

Even though she was on death row, Kelly was inspired to trust in the "God of hope" (Rom 15:13). In September 2015, when Kelly's execution was rescheduled for five days later, Moltmann joined members of the Atlanta theological community in launching a major social media campaign to set her free. Using the hashtag #kellyonmymind, within five days they were able to reach over four million people, gather letters in solidarity with Kelly from theologians, and start Faith Leader and Groundswell petitions, delivering over eighty thousand signatures to the governor's office. This innovative digital organizing campaign for Kelly happened quickly, improvisationally, and was planned *by* women *for* a woman, unveiling new trends in faith-rooted organizing. The Black Lives Matter Movement demands that our antiracism activism work in synergy with a sharp critique of patriarchy in order to deconstruct and dismantle the white masculine ideal of the Western civilization project. Rooted in an interactionalist analysis of injustice, the #kellyonmymind campaign inspired many new activists across the lines of race and religion to join the faith-rooted fight to abolish the death penalty.[82]

"So I should just get this out in the open: I have an agenda. It is about grace. I want to build a movement of grace-driven abolitionists—people of faith and conscience who want to put an end to death forever," writes Shane Claiborne.[83] Through living with the poor in the abandoned places of empire, new urban monastics like Claiborne are committed to faith-rooted organizing and advocacy for justice. Jonathan Wilson-Hartgrove, founder of the Rutba House community in Durham, North Carolina, has joined Rev. Dr. William Barber II in the growing Moral Monday Movement for a Third Reconstruction.[84] As Rev. Dr. Barber mentors Wilson-Hartgrove, John Perkins mentors Shane Claiborne, demonstrating the importance of white Christians having mentors of color as we seek to abolish racism in every heart and social institution.[85]

---

[82]Jennifer M. McBride, *Reducing Distance* (Minneapolis: Fortress, forthcoming). The *New York Times*, the *Washington Post, Huffington Post,* CNN, Fox News, and the Christian Broadcasting Network were just some of the prominent media outlets that covered the campaign.

[83]Shane Claiborne, *Executing Grace: How the Death Penalty Killed Jesus and Is Still Killing Us* (New York: HarperOne, 2016), 3.

[84]William J. Barber II and Jonathan Wilson-Hartgrove, *The Third Reconstruction: Moral Mondays, Fusion Politics, and the Rise of a New Justice Movement* (Boston: Beacon Press, 2016).

[85]Jonathan Wilson-Hartgrove tells the story of meeting Dr. Perkins and learning from him twenty years ago in his book *Free to Be Bound: Church Beyond the Color Line* (Colorado Springs: NavPress,

Every cultural shift begins with a small group of people acting together in creative and collaborative ways. Communities of new urban monastics start each day with a prayer and talking circle, providing a regular rhythm for spirituality and a space for God's Spirit to expand the number of those who are being saved from the principalities and powers.[86] Daily prayer with friends, family, and fellow disciples of Christ is a vital spiritual practice for a new generation of grace-driven abolitionists.

## A CALL TO COMMITMENT

"What, could ye not watch with me one hour?" Jesus asked his disciples who all fell asleep during their all-night prayer vigil (Mt 26:40 KJV). The regular prayers of monks and nuns are a calling to do what the disciples could not do: to stay awake and pray with the Lord. It is time for us to join them and "pray without ceasing" (1 Thess 5:17).

In the history of the church, Christians led by God's Spirit to join monastic communities took vows, committing their lives to total surrender to God. The three standard vows taken in most religious orders are poverty, chastity, and obedience. Through these vows, monks and nuns show us what sanctity and union with Christ looks like.[87] The new monastic movement demonstrates that lay people too can follow the Holy Spirit's leading to a consecrated life of prayer seeking personal and social sanctity.

Vows offer us a unique opportunity to practice what we preach on a daily basis. Vows provide a pathway for our deepest longings to make a better world a concrete reality in our community. Like one who becomes a monk or nun, practicing our vows takes different shapes for different seasons of

---

2008). See also Shane Claiborne and John Perkins, *Follow Me to Freedom: Leading and Following as an Ordinary Radical* (Ventura: Regal, 2009).

[86] *Common Prayer,* the prayer book of the new monastic movement, provides a daily office that individuals and communities can use to structure their daily devotions. Shane Claiborne, Enuma Okoro, and Jonathan Wilson-Hartgrove, *Common Prayer: A Liturgy for Ordinary Radicals* (Grand Rapids: Zondervan, 2012). Cf. Shane Claiborne and Jonathan Wilson-Hartgrove, *Becoming the Answer to Our Prayers* (Downers Grove, IL: InterVarsity Press, 2008).

[87] Thomas Merton writes, "Every Christian is therefore called to sanctity and union with Christ, by keeping the commandments of God. Some, however, with special vocations have contracted a more solemn obligation by religious vows, and have bound themselves to take the basic Christian vocation to holiness especially seriously. . . . For them, sanctity is not simply something that is sought as an ultimate end: sanctity is their 'profession'—they have no other job in life than to be saints, and everything is subordinated to this end, which is primary and immediate for them." Thomas Merton, *Life and Holiness* (Garden City, NY: Image Books, 1965), 13.

our life. But we have to start somewhere. If God's Spirit is calling you to embody a prophetic ethic, I would ask you to consider praying and writing a rule of life to follow.

Here is my rule of life:

1. I vow to pray daily.

2. I vow to live in embodied solidarity with all God's children, loving the least and the lost.

3. I vow to organize people for justice from the deepest wells of my faith.

With Moses and Mariam, Jeremiah and Jesus, Rosa Parks and Dr. King, be the change we long to see. Embody prophetic ethics. Will you join us?

# A Virtue Ethics Response

*BRAD J. KALLENBERG*

**My initial response** to Peter Goodwin Heltzel's chapter on prophetic ethics was "Preach it, brother! Preach it!" I completely agree with his assessment that the church has so long suffered the ills of individualism that perhaps it can barely recognize social evils, much less respond to them in strategic, redemptive ways. And certainly no abstract theory will fill a gap left by years and years of inaction. So I also commend Heltzel's emphasis on ethics as active and performative. Of course, by my lights the call to action is entirely in keeping with the virtue ethics perspective that there is no character (whether of the group or individual) without practical reasoning, and there is no practical reasoning until it culminates in concrete action. I also concur with Heltzel's assessment that the "disembodied epistemologies of modernity" have further delayed action by endless abstract, skeptical nagging, "Yes, but how do I *know*?"

Nevertheless, there are more questions pertinent to the discipline of theological ethics than epistemological questions. Theological ethics also asks,

- What is going on here?
- What is broken?
- How might we faithfully respond?
- Why?
- What ought to be done?
- Why?
- What ought to be done first?

- Why?

- And by whom?

- Why?

The *why* questions are those that predominate ethics: *Why* is X wrong? or, *Why* is Y obligatory? In answering the *why* questions, theological ethicists inevitably adopt distinct styles or, to change the metaphor, thematic tunes in order to harmonize all the data.

A short musical detour may help account for the variety among, yet compatibility between, styles in theological ethics.[1] In the winter of 1898–1899, Sir Edward Elgar composed "Variations on an Original Theme for Orchestra" (the so-called Enigma Variations), Op. 36. Like Mozart's variations on "Twinkle, Twinkle Little Star," each variation is a beautiful piece in its own right. But unlike Mozart, Elgar took a mystery with him to his grave. Each variation was composed to delight (or to infuriate!) by capturing in music each of his friends' particular idiosyncrasies (thus each variation is labeled with the friend's initials). Musical scholars know the identity of each friend. As these particularities have become widely known, the identities of the friends are *not* the enigma. Rather, the enigma is that the *main* musical theme has never been identified! Each variation is a harmonizable tune meant to be played *on top* of the common theme. If ever identified, the missing theme would complete and unify the entire work. Without the theme each variation is uniquely beautiful (as is each friend), but beautiful in isolation. Many musical themes have been proposed, but the answer will never be certain since the secret died with Elgar.

So it is with theological ethics. One ethicist proposes a theme that holds all the pieces together in harmony. Another ethicist offers another theme that also holds all the pieces in harmony. But as each theme is constructed rather than divinely revealed, we'll never know for sure which theme, if any, God intended.

*Must* we be governed by a theme? No; I suppose not. And I suspect that Heltzel isn't troubled by the fact that I also can't quite manage to pigeonhole

---

[1] This paragraph is taken from another essay that makes quite a different use of it. See Brad J. Kallenberg, "Then Sings My Soul," in *Practicing to Aim at Truth: Theological Engagements in Honor of Nancey Murphy*, ed. Ryan Andrew Newson and Brad J. Kallenberg (Eugene, OR: Cascade Books, 2015), 102-24.

his prophetic ethics. However, if I cannot recognize the theme, then I can't predict the next move. And if I can't, how will anyone else do it? How will a disciple ever learn to think according to prophetic ethics if there is no identifiable pattern? Newcomers are first taught simplified types and then later inducted into increasingly complex and nuanced models. But it is precisely here that I'm having difficulty: What exactly is the thematic tune prophetic ethics offers as an answer to the question why?

Note: I quite easily understand the *what* being proposed: we are to understand "structural causes of oppression" so as to be "better equipped to work for positive social change." The moral obligation, the *what*, seems clear enough. But how does prophetic ethics explain *why* we are obligated to work for social change? Is it because we are thus commanded, as the divine command model would have it? Is it because just relations are part of the ideal definition of human beings, as natural law would have it? Is it because the human *telos* is a particular kind of friendship in community as virtue ethics would have it? In short, I'm having difficulty picking out the theme as sung by prophetic ethicists. To reply that the *why* is self-evident is, I suppose, to give one kind of answer—but that answer does not live within the field of ethics. Ethics always asks, "Why?" For example, *why* is the non-violent character of Jesus' revolutionary love required of us? We are to live in imitation of Jesus. Fine; all four authors agree on this point. But let's get specific: what aspects of Jesus' embodied form of life are *we* to emulate? Are *we* to retrace his itinerant travels throughout Palestine? Are *we* to copy his open-toed sandals? I'm obviously being facetious, but where do we draw the line? There are many devoted Christians, from Augustine to Zwingli, who claim violence is an option for Christians precisely because sinful structures of the fallen world require fighting fire with fire. Does violence comport with Jesus? If not, why not?

Let me be clear: I am a pacifist. But the pacifism I share with Heltzel is not the majority position in the long history of Christian theology. Since pacifism is the minority view, he and I cannot rely on disciples to pick up nonviolence as self-evident. Nor ought Christ-followers simply take his or my word for it. Without a careful, thoughtful, transparent method of ethical reasoning, prophetic ethics will become ensnared in a viper's nest of hermeneutical problems.

My first question for prophetic ethics is simply to inquire after the distinctive manner by which ethical *why* questions get answered. I might go further and inquire about the specific *warrants* that prophetic ethics proposes. But this would be to press on in an already too pedantic and esoteric direction. So, let me shift gears and ask practical questions of prophetic ethics.

I am sympathetic with Heltzel's implied position toward academic ethics—namely, that if we were to start with theories about virtue, natural law, or divine commands, we may never get around to fixing structural problems. After all, ethical theories have been around for a very long time, and not much has changed with structural evil! And I'm greatly in favor of Heltzel's call for us to discern where God is moving and get involved there. This is surely as clear an application of Galatians 5:25 as there ever was ("keep in step with the Spirit" [NIV]). But I'm puzzled about how all this works in real life. Since Heltzel gives Micah 6:8 as a paradigmatic verse, let me focus my thoughts there.

Micah 6:8 is putatively a *universal* ethical obligation. Although the book is addressed primarily to seventh-century BCE Jews under Hezekiah's reign, the use of the generic "O mortal" seems to give us permission to apply the verse widely:

> He has told you, O mortal, what is good;
>> and what does the LORD require of you
> but to do justice, and to love kindness,
>> and to walk humbly with your God? (NRSV)

Heltzel has given some direction as to what *justice* means. But I find that the second phrase needs some clarification. What does it mean to "love kindness"? Does it mean we are to show kindness (*ḥesed*; lovingkindness and mercy) to others? If so, which others? By chapter six, Micah has already threatened God's imminent vengeance in anger and wrath on nations who have not obeyed, even to the destruction of their cities (Mic 5:14-15). Do these verses in the immediate context mean that we are required to display kindness and mercy only toward those who are like us, *insiders* to the covenant of YHWH's *ḥesed*? *That* doesn't sound right! But neither is the meaning of Micah 6:8 self-evident when read in the context of Micah 5:14-15. Apparently prophetic ethics needs there to be in place skilled (aka virtuous) scholars who have devoted their lives to the study of ancient languages and texts (rather than "organizing people for justice"—or does the scholar have a role in prophetic ethics' vision? It isn't clear) in order to guide those who today would put ancient texts into practice. Consequently, prophetic ethics is parasitic on at least some virtue-inculcating practices.

But there is a deeper issue at stake. We are told to *do* justice but to *love* kindness. A judge rendering a just verdict in a court of law does not have to possess or feel love toward the defendant. But *we* are so required. This second clause touches not just what we do, but the depths of us—namely, our passions and desires. What does prophetic ethics suggest for the trans-formation of our deepest passions? So often, if we are honest, our attempts at doing justice are tainted by the lack of genuine love. Dorothy Day re-counts the story of missionary activist Peter Claver,

> who gave a stricken Negro his bed and slept on the floor at his side. . . . Peter Claver never saw anything with his bodily eyes except the exhausted black faces of the Negroes; He had only faith in Christ's own words that these people were Christ. And when the Negroes he had induced to help him once ran from the room, panicstricken before the disgusting sight of some sickness, he was astonished. "You mustn't go," he said, and you can still hear his surprise that anyone could forget such a truth; "You mustn't leave him—it is Christ."[2]

Claver saw Christ in the face of the victim, but his compatriot had an eyesight problem: he saw only a disgusting, stinking sickness. And while the coworker had intended to do justice, his lack in the matter of "love kindness" caused him to flee in terror.

On the one hand, this lack might be likened to a problem of moral eye-sight. "I can only choose within the world I can *see*," wrote Iris Murdoch.[3] The trouble with moral eyesight is that a lone individual cannot make self-corrections (the log-in-thine-own-eye problem). We need others to guide us into knowledge. And the journey from initial faith to full-blown love travels by way of virtue cultivation as step 2 of 7.

---

[2]Dorothy Day, "Room for Christ," *The Catholic Worker*, 1945, www.catholicworker.org/dorothyday /articles/416.html.
[3]Iris Murdoch, *The Sovereignty of Good* (London: Routledge & Kegan Paul, 1970), 35-36.

Now for this very reason also, applying all diligence,

   in your faith supply virtue [*aretē*],

     and in *your* virtue [*aretē*], knowledge,

       and in *your* knowledge, self-control,

         and in *your* self-control, perseverance,

           and in *your* perseverance, godliness,

             and in *your* godliness, brotherly kindness,

               and in *your* brotherly kindness, love.

For if these *qualities* are yours and are increasing, they render you neither useless nor unfruitful in the true knowledge of our Lord Jesus Christ. . . . As long as you practice these things, you will never stumble. (2 Pet 1:5-8, 10 NASB, modified)

Alternatively, the lack might be described as "incontinence," a weakness, powerlessness, or inability to follow through. Follow through on what? To follow through on the act of doing justice? No! What we are to follow through on is the *preparation* that readies us to act. We are to follow through on *the training* for the doing of justice. (If a burglar is breaking into the house it is too late to *start* lifting weights.) Doing a single act of justice is the culmination of many previous, smaller acts. The one who is faithful in much began by being faithful in little. The need for guided preparation is the ironic backdrop to the image of jazz improvisation to which Heltzel draws attention. Only very skilled musicians are able to play jazz improvisationally. Years and years of daily, grinding practice makes stable the skilled reflexes, muscle memory, ear, and know-how that improvisational music depends on. Improv does not reduce to these skills, but neither can improvisational jazz be done without skills honed by years of daily practice.

The significance of the small stuff, the daily practice, is also captured in the third clause of Micah 6:8, "walk humbly." If the first clause emphasizes the deed of justice, and the second clause calls to mind the preparation that precedes the deed, the third clause emphasizes the time-intensive nature of the just life. What do I mean? Well, we would not describe someone who moves from the fridge to the table as "walking." Nor is someone who "walks in place" really walking. Walking implies ongoing movement through space and time. Walking with God is a 24/7 process that encompasses the most boring, menial, mundane (dare we say "humble") activities of the everyday, and not only those moments when we are speaking truth to power or correcting unjust systems. It is the little things that make for the journey of walking with God. And it is faithfulness in the little things that prepare us for faithfulness in bigger ones (Lk 16:10). We can walk well or poorly, but the manner in which we walk today will become the habitual way we walk tomorrow.

# A Natural Law Response

*CLAIRE BROWN PETERSON*

**Peter Goodwin Heltzel's prophetic ethics** urges Christians to bring about justice in society through the practices of faith-rooted organizing, embodied solidarity, and daily prayer. For Heltzel, we must set our eyes on ambitious goals for the transformation of society, and we must work toward these goals through loving, nonviolent means. Prophetic ethics thus looks to peaceful struggles such as the American civil rights movement as inspiration for how God's people are intended to engage a larger world. I am in full agreement with Heltzel in holding that seeking God's kingdom "on earth as it is in heaven" (Mt 6:10) means seeking a society that is structured in just ways and that prayerful, coordinated, open, nonviolent campaigns are some of the most inspiring and effective ways for bringing the sort of lasting social change that allows for genuine reconciliation. My concerns with prophetic ethics are the following:

1. Prophetic ethics presupposes a notion of "social justice" toward which we are to strive, but an adequate discussion of the requirements of justice must reference human nature and human flourishing.

2. Prophetic ethics neglects the more local and private dimensions of ethics.

3. Prophetic ethics' practices of collective organizing and embodied solidarity are not the only appropriate responses to social injustices.

I will examine each of these issues in turn.

## SOCIAL JUSTICE MUST BE DEFINED BY REFERENCE
## TO THE HUMAN GOOD

Prophetic ethics is clearly focused on bringing about a more just society, but one does not need to look far to see fundamental disagreements about what makes for a just society. Thus, in the present-day United States, one finds people speaking in terms of what is "just" and "fair" while defending divergent positions regarding tax policy, public education, family law, and the criminal justice system. Clearly, we need a way to begin to discuss what justice really is and what a just society would look like. But the requirements of a just society often cannot be discussed apart from questions about the essential natures of specific human activities and, more broadly, human nature and human flourishing.[1]

To understand how discussions of human nature and human flourishing are unavoidable when talking about how a just society would function, consider decisions about child-custody contracts and payment for surrogacy and egg donation. Suppose that a couple enters into an agreement with a woman for her assistance in providing them with a child: the couple will provide the sperm (whether the man's own sperm or sperm selected from a sperm bank based on the donor's possession of desired characteristics), and the surrogate will either provide her own egg or use an egg the couple has purchased and carry any resulting child to term. After the birth, according to the terms of the contract, the surrogate will surrender the child to the couple, and the couple will pay the surrogate for her participation.

Michael Sandel points out that there are two primary reasons one might object to an agreement of this sort. In the first place, one might be concerned about whether or not an agreement like this is truly consensual.[2] Contracts of this sort are signed before the birth mother has had the experience of carrying and giving birth to the child, a child that in some cases is her own genetic offspring. Perhaps she would not enter into such an agreement if she knew what it would feel like to later surrender a child she has carried. (Indeed, there have been multiple cases in which surrogates have

[1]Michael Sandel discusses this point, attributing it to Aristotle, in *Justice: What's the Right Thing to Do?* (New York: Farrar, Straus & Giroux, 2009), 186-87.
[2]Michael Sandel, "What Money Can't Buy: The Moral Limits of Markets," *The Tanner Lectures on Human Values*, ed. Grethe Petersen (Salt Lake City: University of Utah Press, 2000), 21:94, 99-100.

changed their minds and wanted to maintain parental rights after birth.[3]) Or perhaps the woman would have never entered into an agreement to birth a child to be given over to strangers if she were not herself in a financially vulnerable position. When one party is desperate, we question whether genuine consent has occurred or is even possible.[4] But, as Sandel notes, there is another reason for wondering whether or not society should allow and enforce surrogacy contracts of the kind described, a reason distinct from worries about coercion and genuine free agency, and a reason instead rooted in our notions of parenthood and the value of children.[5]

Suppose that the surrogate has entered into similar (albeit noncontractual) arrangements before, so that upon signing this contract she feels reasonably confident that she will not later want to keep the child at birth. Suppose further that she is not financially disadvantaged, that she is as financially secure as the couple but sees surrogacy as an all-things-considered worthwhile way to supplement her already adequate income. In a situation of this sort, although concerns about coercion have been assuaged, we might still recoil at the thought of a legal system that facilitates and enforces these contracts. The practices of selecting sperm and egg on the basis of desired donor characteristics and paying a person for the use of her womb treat the procreative process as a consumer activity and children as consumer products.[6] But children should not be treated as consumer products (not even highly valued consumer products, like custom cars). Note, though, that to state that children should not be treated as highly valued consumer products is to make a fundamental claim about human nature. We thus cannot avoid discussions of human nature in arguing about how a just society should be organized and whether, for instance, it should allow and enforce surrogacy contracts the way it enforces more mundane contracts.

The debate over paid surrogacy may at first seem to be an isolated case in which a judgment about justice happens to be intimately tied up with debates about human nature, yet once one appreciates examples like the surrogacy case, it is easy to see how beliefs about human nature impinge on

---

[3]Ibid., 99-100.
[4]Ibid., 94.
[5]Ibid., 100-102.
[6]Ibid., 100-103.

more commonplace discussions of justice. Debates about paid maternity and paternity leave turn on questions of (1) the shape the employer-employee relationship ought to take and (2) whether having children is to be viewed as a personal choice, a natural part of life, a social good, or a public burden. Turning to controversies in education, in my own hometown (and in many others across the United States), there is currently a heated debate about the role that standardized testing ought to play in the public school system. All parties are united in wanting good schools, but while some hold that standardized testing serves this end, others insist that frequent testing stunts childhood curiosity and incorrectly treats only a narrow range of (always academic) skills as worthy of cultivation. Fundamental to the debate over school testing is thus a debate over what we think about childhood and who we want our children to become. Similar fundamental disagreements about human life can be found in questions of fault, custody arrangements, child support, and alimony when it comes to divorce; debates about work requirements for social welfare programs; arguments about health care reform; and almost every specific controversy over religious liberty. Work, food, housing, family, childrearing, and religion are basic elements of human life, and we have to discuss the importance and proper shape of these things if we are to understand how a just society is to be structured. Thus, a robust account of human flourishing must inform the notion of social justice that prophetic ethics urges us to pursue.

## THE PURSUIT OF SOCIAL JUSTICE IS ONLY ONE PART OF THE HUMAN GOOD

Not only does prophetic ethics need natural law to inform its notion of social justice, it also needs a broader conception of the goods of human life. More specifically, prophetic ethics needs to open itself to the more private and local aspects of the good life that a single-minded pursuit of a just society will ignore. While prophetic ethics is certainly right that the church should be working toward the realization of a more just society, each of us also needs to attend to how we relate to those in our immediate circles and whatever individual projects we may be pursuing. Significantly, the reason for such attention is not simply that loving those around us or becoming an avid gardener, say, is likely to play a positive role in the movement for more just social structures. The character of our relationships with our families, colleagues, friends, jobs, and personal projects may well serve the interests of social transformation, but caring for those around us is valuable even if it is not part of a larger social movement. Indeed, to value such activities as friendship, music, and athletics only as means to social change is to miss the full value of a number of dimensions of a good human life. Some individuals may even find themselves in situations in which it is simply not possible for them to join nonviolent movements for social change, but any ethical theory should still have much to say about how such individuals ought to conduct their lives. Prophetic ethics, if it is to offer a full theory of ethics, must provide a framework for recognizing that living with compassion, mercy, faith, and fortitude is always highly valuable even if few outside one's immediate circle see the fruits of one's life and actions. In other words, it must look to more than a collective quest for social justice to find the elements of a life well-lived.

## THE PRACTICES OF PROPHETIC ETHICS ARE NOT THE ONLY APPROPRIATE RESPONSES TO INJUSTICE

My final worry about prophetic ethics concerns what may at first blush appear to be the least objectionable and even most inspiring aspect of prophetic ethics: its emphasis on faith-rooted organizing, embodied solidarity, and daily prayer as the practices for social change. While Heltzel makes clear that the particular methods one adopts in implementing these practices in the pursuit of social justice allow for improvisation, the practices themselves nonetheless turn out to provide quite specific guidance on how social change should be sought. Even with allowed variation in methods, any nonviolent campaign of faith-rooted organizing, embodied solidarity, and daily prayer will stand in contrast to the vast majority of campaigns for social change that one finds historically. Of course, the mere fact that the practices of prophetic ethics are unusual is hardly a mark against those practices. The American civil rights movement of the 1960s was nothing short of remarkable, and the loving, nonviolent approach that prophetic ethics trumpets was crucial to that movement's success and its ability to inspire decades later. Consider how participants in that movement were so utterly insistent on peacefully bringing about an end to racial segregation that they put themselves in positions in which they knew they would suffer abuse while refusing to return violence with violence. Such collective, open, nonviolent action forced the racial majority to see the injustice of Jim Crow laws writ large in a way that showed complete respect for the humanity of the oppressor. Embodied solidarity can be awe-inspiring!

Despite the success of the civil rights movement, one cannot help but wonder if the approach to social change there modeled is the only proper response to all social injustices. Consider the divergent responses that concerned individuals and groups may take to humanitarian crises. One approach might be called that of "neutral humanitarianism," which is the approach that has largely characterized such organizations as Doctors Without Borders (*Medicins Sans Frontieres*) and the International Committee of the Red Cross (ICRC). Both organizations routinely provide aid to victims of violence, but reaching such victims can mean refraining from criticizing—and even cooperating with—local regimes that may be perpetrators of violence. Neutral humanitarian organizations may be willing to pay this moral price in order to perform their desperately needed aid work.[7] On the opposite end of the spectrum from neutral humanitarianism is what is sometimes called the "name and shame" approach to human rights violators, an approach often associated with watchdog organizations, journalists, and some think tanks. Those who practice the name-and-shame approach document and publicize human rights violations, hoping to stir up international pressure against the perpetrators of the abuses.

While no single individual (or organization) can fully engage in both neutral humanitarianism and name-and-shame tactics, *both* approaches may nonetheless be necessary and helpful responses to a number of moral crises: one approach (name and shame) addresses an important cause of the problem; the other (neutral humanitarianism) addresses the present needs of the victims. Yet note that *neither* approach amounts to the faith-rooted organizing and embodied solidarity of prophetic ethics. Many name-and-shame practitioners will never put their own bodies on the line with victims in calling out and bringing pressure to bear on corrupt regimes. Effective

---

[7]Jakob Kellenberger, a former president of the International Committee of the Red Cross, addresses this challenge and the Red Cross's emphasis on access to victims in "Speaking Out or Remaining Silent in Humanitarian Work," *International Review of the Red Cross* 86, no. 855 (2004): 600-601.

criticism can come from a distance. Those practicing neutral humanitarianism do often put themselves at risk, but they also do little to challenge unjust structures, and they may even resort to accommodating oppressors for the sake of assisting victims. Doctors Without Borders, for instance, previously paid an al-Qaeda affiliate thousands of dollars in order to maintain its humanitarian operations in Somalia.[8] No organization or set of practices can do everything, and the practices of prophetic ethics may well be but one set of practices among several that is necessary for addressing injustices in the world.

---

[8]Guy Gugliotta, "The Big Dilemma Facing Doctors Without Borders," *Smithsonian*, April 2013, www .smithsonianmag.com/innovation/the-big-dilemma-facing-doctors-without-borders-4946758.

# A Divine Command
# Theory Response

*JOHN HARE*

**I have very little to disagree with** in Peter Heltzel's eloquent
account of prophetic ethics. This is not surprising, because the basic structure
of his account is generated by the three *divine commands* reported in Micah
6:8, "And what does the LORD require of you but to do justice, and to love
kindness, and to walk humbly with your God." This is supplemented with
sections of his argument that rely on the divine command to love the enemy
and the various "You have heard it said, but I say to you" commands in the
Sermon on the Mount. Moreover, Heltzel is repeatedly concerned to point
out that we cannot simply rely on our vision of what we and the world are
like, because social sin has distorted our vision so that we do not clearly see
without special revelation what God is requiring of us. Throughout our
history, including especially our ecclesiastical history, we have been blinded
by racial and sexual and class prejudice.

I am therefore going to mention just a few quibbles I have with his account, and then I am going to take the opportunity to say some things about
what a divine command theorist is likely to hold about social justice. This was
not the topic of my own account of divine command theory in this volume
because I was concerned with areas in which I thought I was likely to have
disagreement. As I see it there is no serious disagreement between prophetic
ethics and divine command ethics, and they are entirely complementary.

I do, however, have a few quibbles with the chapter, and I will mention
three. First, I think Heltzel makes an unnecessary dichotomy between a

concern with personal purity and a concern with helping the needy. He says that Jesus "resolutely set out for Jerusalem" (Lk 9:51), and his exegesis of this is that Jesus had "a laser-like focus on reforming the practice of Jewish temple worship and courageously confronting Roman royal power." It is true that Jesus had these concerns, but he had other concerns also. He was concerned with our salvation and our standing with God. This salvation and this standing certainly involve our social sin, but this is not the whole story. There is also personal sin. Heltzel acknowledges this later, when he says sin is "both personal and social." The same is true with the powers that oppose Jesus. These certainly encompass unjust social structures. But the passage from Luke 9 is preceded by the story of the unclean spirit, which the disciples could not cast out of the boy when Jesus and Peter, John, and James were on the mountain of transfiguration. There is no substantial disagreement here between Heltzel and me. It is just that he is so eager not to leave out the social dimension that sometimes his rhetoric discounts the personal.

My second remark is closely linked to the first. Heltzel distinguishes a prophetic ethic from a priestly ethic and a zealot ethic. But it might be better to say that Jesus has roles as prophet, priest, and king, and he gives us a share in all three of these roles. Heltzel has emphasized the prophetic, and that is quite appropriate. But we do have some responsibilities as Christians that derive from being stewards of the creation. And we also have responsibilities as Christians that involve holiness and sacrifice in a way foreshadowed in the teaching of the Hebrew Scriptures about priests. This is true even if we think that there is a special anointing of human kings (and queens) and human priests, even though only Jesus perfectly fulfills the three roles. Again, there is no substantial disagreement here between Heltzel and me. He is criticizing not priestly ethics in general but "the priestly ethic of the *temple elite*," and in particular their complicity with economic corruption.

A final quibble is about improvisation. The comparison of Jesus' teaching and the Christian life to playing jazz is brilliant and illuminating. But like all such comparisons it has limits, and in this case the limits are important. Did Jesus improvise on Scripture when he preached and taught? In the Sermon on the Mount he says, "You have heard that it was said, but I say to you." But we are also told in the same Sermon that he comes not to abolish the law but to fulfill it. Holding these two texts together is difficult, and the comparison with what a jazz musician does to a well-known song is helpful. But we should also say that what Jesus does with the law is normative for us in a way that the jazz musician's riff is not normative for future improvisations on the same song. There would indeed be something wrong if someone who admired the master tried to "improvise" with just the same notes. This is a subtle matter, and more work is required to analyze just what it means to ask in some situation, what would Jesus do? We do not live, for example, in the first century in Palestine. My point is simply that there is more to Jesus' authority than that of the master musician whose example we want to emulate. Again, I am not disagreeing here with Heltzel. I am just pointing to the need for more philosophical work.

The main point of this reply is to say more about the position of a divine command theorist about social justice. I am using the term *divine command theorist* here as though it were a term with a definite meaning. But in fact there are many different divine command theories. I have said in my chapter more about the kind of divine command theory I think we should accept. The basic point of the theory is that it is God's command that makes something morally obligatory or morally forbidden. So if we want to know what our moral obligations are with regard to social justice, we should ask, what does God command? And the answer is relatively clear. God commands caring especially for those who are oppressed, and condemns those who oppress them. In the Hebrew Scriptures, the main examples of those who need this care are the poor, orphans, widows, and resident aliens (strangers in the land). Lists with these items occur repeatedly, though not usually all together. For example, in Deuteronomy 24:17-18 God commands the people, "You shall not deprive a resident alien or an orphan of justice; you shall not take a widow's garment in pledge. Remember that you were a slave in Egypt and the LORD your God redeemed you from there; therefore I command you to do this."

There are many such divine commands, and the motivation that comes from remembering the people's own previous oppression in Egypt is also repeated. The justice that should not be taken away includes juridical process but is probably not confined to this. It is plausible to say that there are some basic goods (e.g., enough food to live on) that God cares that the people have, and the poor, the orphans, the widows, and the resident aliens are those most in danger of being deprived of these goods (so the people are told, for example, to leave enough grain and grapes for gleaning). There is frequent condemnation of those who seek to deprive those who are vulnerable—for example, those

> who make iniquitous decrees,
> > who write oppressive statutes,
> to turn aside the needy from justice
> > and to rob the poor of my people of their right,
> that widows may be your spoil,
> > and that you may make the orphans your prey! (Is 10:1-2)

Is this a "preferential option for the poor?" Yes and no. In Leviticus 19:15, for example, the people are told, "You shall not render an unjust judgment; you shall not be partial to the poor or defer to the great; with justice you shall judge your neighbor." This sort of text requires impartiality in dealing with both poor and rich. But inasmuch as the needy are most at risk, God commands special attention to them.

In the New Testament, Jesus turns the usual rankings upside down. He is deliberately subverting or (in Nietzsche's term) *transvaluing* our conception of the good. It is instructive to compare his views as recorded in the New Testament with the views of Aristotle as recorded in the *Nicomachean Ethics* and *Eudemian Ethics*. The chief contrast has to do with what we might call "competitive goods." A competitive good is one where, in order for one person to have it, another person has not to have it, or to have less of it. Wealth and power are good examples, and so is honor in the sense of being well thought of by other people. In the *Gondoliers* by Gilbert and Sullivan, the Grand Inquisitor sings, "When everyone is somebody, then no one's anybody." Most of the time, when Aristotle considers the best life for human beings, he says that it requires wealth, power, and honor. For example, in the *Eudemian Ethics* (III, 4, 1231b28) he says that to have the virtue he calls "generosity" (in Greek *eleutheriotēs*, which really means the virtue of a free man, in Greek *eleutheros*, rather than a slave), we have to behave in a way appropriate to high status.[1] If we behave appropriately to our low status, or

---

[1] Aristotle, *Eudemian Ethics* 3, 4, 1231b28.

behave inappropriately to our high status, we fail to hit the "mean" that the virtue requires. To have the virtue of magnanimity requires being worthy of great honor and deeming ourselves worthy of it. The best life is that of the ruler since the life of action is aimed at the highest good, and the life of the statesman realizes this good most completely.[2] As Meno says, when Socrates asks what human excellence is in Plato's dialogue named after him, "it is simply the capacity to govern human beings, if you are looking for one quality to cover all the instances."[3] There is a large secondary literature about how to fit the beginning and the end of the *Nicomachean Ethics* together, and I will not go into this here. But my point is that Aristotle is right about what we naturally desire, in the sense of the desires we are born with and tend to develop as we get older. We do desire a large share of the competitive goods, and we admire those who have attained this. The Gospels record Jesus as reversing this ordering of goods, and the rest of the New Testament follows suit. Aristotle says that humility (*tapeinotēs*) is the state in which persons are so low they should not even aspire to virtue.[4] In the New Testament (Phil 2:3) we are told in humility (*tapeinophrosunē*) to consider others better than ourselves. For a second example, Jesus commends the widow who put two small coins, all she had in the world, into the temple treasury (Mk 12:42), and says she gave more than the rich people who gave out of their abundance. Aristotle would deem such an act wasteful; she simply could not afford it. For a third example, Jesus describes the prevailing opinion that we should hate our enemies, and says, "But I say to you, Love your enemies" (Mt 5:43-44). There is valuing that the world does, and our perception is skewed here and often deeply wrong. Jesus tells us, "This is the verdict: Light has come into the world, but people loved darkness instead of light because their deeds were evil" (Jn 3:19 NIV). Christian divine command theory says that we need the commands and life of Jesus to give us a sense of what justice requires.

---

[2] Aristotle, *Nicomachean Ethics* 1, 2, 1094b9-10.
[3] Plato, *Meno* 72d1-2.
[4] Aristotle, *Nicomachean Ethics* 4, 3, 1124b20-23.

# Contributors

**John Hare** (PhD, Princeton University) has taught at Lehigh University, Calvin College, and Yale University. He has published seven books, including *The Moral Gap* (Oxford University Press, 1996) and *God's Command* (Oxford University Press, 2015), and about one hundred articles. His interests lie in moral theology, philosophy of religion, ancient philosophy, Franciscan philosophy, Kant, Kierkegaard, contemporary moral theory, theological aesthetics, and applied ethics (international affairs and medical ethics). He is also a published composer of church music.

**Peter Goodwin Heltzel** (PhD, Boston University) is associate professor of systematic theology at New York Theological Seminary. An ordained minister in the Christian Church (Disciples of Christ), he serves on the Anti-Racism Team and Commission of Ministry in the Northeastern Region. Heltzel's research explores the relationships between Christian theology, racism, and American politics. He is an Auburn Senior Fellow and the author of *Jesus and Justice: Evangelicals, Race and American Politics* (Yale University Press, 2009), *Resurrection City: A Theology of Improvisation* (Eerdmans, 2012), and *Faith-Rooted Organizing* with Alexia Salvatierra (InterVarsity Press, 2014). With Bruce Ellis Benson and Malinda Berry he edits Eerdman's *Prophetic Christianity*.

**Brad J. Kallenberg** (PhD, Fuller Theological Seminary) is professor of theology and ethics at the University of Dayton (Ohio). He is the author of *Ethics as Grammar: Changing the Postmodern Subject* (University of Notre Dame Press, 2001), *God and Gadgets: Following Jesus in a Technological World* (Cascade Books, 2011), and *By Design: Theology, Ethics and the Practice of Engineering*

(Cascade Books, 2013), and coauthor of *Virtues and Practices in the Christian Tradition: Christian Ethics After MacIntyre* (University of Notre Dame Press, 2003). His essays have appeared in such journals as the *International Journal for Philosophy of Religion*, *Journal of Religious Ethics*, *The Scottish Journal of Theology*, and *Modern Theology*, and in multiple books, including *The Oxford Handbook of the Epistemology of Theology* (Oxford University Press, forthcoming), *Vital Christianity: Justice, Spirituality, and Christian Practice* (T&T Clark, 2005), and, with Nancey Murphy, *The Cambridge Companion to Postmodern Theology* (Cambridge University Press, 2003). His research interests include biblical ethics, theological ethics, virtue ethics, engineering ethics, and Wittgenstein's philosophy of language.

**Claire Brown Peterson** (PhD, University of Notre Dame) is associate professor of philosophy at Asbury University in Wilmore, Kentucky. Her work has appeared in books by Ashgate Press and Lexington Books. She has research interests in the areas of ethics and the philosophy of religion. She is especially interested in how Christian notions of human beings as ultimately mutually dependent, weak creatures ought to properly inform specific accounts of the virtues and high moral achievement.

**Steve Wilkens** (PhD, Fuller Theological Seminary) is professor of philosophy and ethics at Azusa Pacific University in Azusa, California. He has authored numerous books, including *Beyond Bumper Sticker Ethics* (IVP Academic, 2011) and *Good Ideas from Questionable Christians and Outright Pagans* (IVP Academic, 2004), and coauthored *Hidden Worldviews* (IVP Academic, 2009) with Mark Sanford and *Christianity and Western Thought*, volumes 2–3 (IVP Academic, 2000, 2009) with Alan Padgett.

# Index

# Finding the Textbook You Need

**The IVP Academic Textbook Selector**
is an online tool for instantly finding the IVP books
suitable for over 250 courses across 24 disciplines.

**ivpacademic.com**